LETTERS HOME DURING WWII
Sergeant Martin A. Paulson
South Pacific
1943-1946

LETTERS HOME WWII
SERGEANT MARTIN A. PAULSON
South Pacific
1943 - 1946

GAIL FURFORD

June 7, 2014

ISBN: 978-0-9910654-0-0   Hard Cover

ISBN: 978-0-9910654-1-7   Soft Cover

Printed in the U.S.A. by:
THOMSON-SHORE
Dexter, MI

COVER PICTURE: The 105th Regiment adopted Okinawan orphan "JUNIOR," pictured with Sergeant Martin Paulson, who was with the 105th several months

FURFORD PUBLISHING
www.furfordpublishing.com

This book is dedicated to:
Sergeant Martin A. Paulson,
all Veterans,
all men and women who currently serve,
and
(*Martin's special request*)

ALL WHO GAVE THEIR LIVES
TO PROTECT OUR COUNTRY AND ITS FREEDOMS

CONTENTS

MESSAGE FROM THE AUTHOR

ACKNOWLEDGEMENTS

PART ONE: Basic Training   Page

Letter 1...1
Letter 2...10
Letter 3...15
Letter 4...21
Letter 5...26
Letter 6...32
Letter 7...38
Letter 8, 9..46
Letter 10...47
Letter 11...52
Letter 12...59
Letter 13, 14..64
Letter 15...69
Letter 16...72
Letter 17...74
Letter 18...78
Letter 19...79
Letter 20...81
Letter 21...83
Letter 22...87
Letter 23...94
Letter 24...98

PART TWO: Shipping Out To South Pacific & New Caledonia

Letter 25...101
Letter 26...105
Letter 27...110
Letter 28, 29...114
Letter 30...121
Letter 31...123
Letter 32...131
Letter 33...135
Letter 34...141
Letter 35...146
Letter 36...148
Letter 37...151
Letter 38, 39...153
Letter 40...156
Letter 41...163

CONTENTS... Cont.

Letter 42...165
Letter 43...169
Letter 44...174
Letter 45...177

PART THREE: **Espiritu Santo Island**
Letter 46...185
Letter 47...194
Letter 48, 49..197
Letter 50...201
Letter 51, 52..205
Letter 53...209
Letter 54...212
Letter 55...217
Letter 56...221
Letter 57...225
Letter 58...231
Letter 59...234
Letter 60...238

PART FOUR: **Okinawa – Battle of Okinawa & Mopping Up**
Letter 61...241
Letter 62...245
Letter 63...254
Letter 64...265
Letter 65, 66, 67...267
Letter 68...272
Letter 69, 70, 71...277
Letter 72, 73, 74...284
Letter 75, 76..290

PART FIVE: **Japan**
Letter 77, 78, 79...295
Letter 80, 81..303
Letter 82, 83..310
Letter 84, 85..318
Letter 86...326
Letter 87, 88..330

Epilogue
LIFE AFTER WAR
AWARDING OF THE *'BRONZE STAR'* & *'OCCUPATION OF JAPAN'* MEDALS

MESSAGE FROM THE AUTHOR
"How the journey of the letters began"

Shoe Box of Martin's Letters

This journey started with a box of letters Ruth 'Paulson' Furford handed to me in the 1970's with a request that I keep them to pass on to her grandson (my son, David Arvid Furford) when I felt he was old enough to appreciate them. At the time, I was doing genealogy research on both my family and my husband's family who were of Norwegian decent, and she felt these letters were part of the family history. I set the box aside and before I could get to them my husband's job moved us across the United States. Due to raising a family, work, etc., they remained stored with the genealogy materials until after I retired.

When I again came across the box of letters in 2012, I read them to see if they were something my son would be interested in having. He was now retired after serving 23 years in the Navy and working as a civilian on a Navy base in Pensacola, FL. To my surprise and delight the letters were from Ruth's brother, Martin A. Paulson, from the time he entered military life during WWII to the time

he got out shortly after the war had ended. After reading a few, I knew the letters needed to be preserved for future generations and asked my husband, George Furford, if he would like to scan them into the computer for me.

Figure 1 - George Arvid (Curly) & Ruth Paulson Furford 1944

George was 6 years old when his Uncle Martin was drafted into the Army. I had heard many times over the years that Martin had served during WWII, but my husband said his Uncle Martin did not talk about those years. George had said Martin was his favorite uncle and was delighted to see that the beginning letters started: *Dear Ruth, Curly, and George.*

I read the letters a second time researching weapons, places, etc. which he mentioned and found myself thinking of ideas upon ideas of how to make the letters come alive. You must understand, soldiers were censured on what they could say and not say in their letters so there was not much information in them. However, in the twenty-first century an abundance of information has been published, filmed, and documented so that with research you can fill in the blanks. The blood in my veins began to flow with excitement at the possibilities.

We had not seen Uncle Martin in many years and I wondered where he and his family were and what they were doing now. I typed Martin Paulson into my computer and MARTIN PAULSON FARMS (a cranberry farm) popped up. To my surprise Martin's son, Martin Paulson Jr (Marty), now worked the farm. Marty was 10 years old when my husband and I married and was now a grown man himself with adult children. I called the number listed for the business and left a message. Marty called shortly after very excited about what I was doing and encouraged me to call his dad who was still living. I will never forget how he spoke of his Dad with so much love, respect, honor and joy, and that at 94 plus years his dad was still sharp as a tack.

I called Martin the next morning and had a delightful chat with him. He had no idea his sister had saved the letters and said he didn't know what he could tell me, but that he would be willing to talk with me. I asked if I could visit and he said I would need to come soon as he was getting on in years! I asked if next week was soon enough. He was excited saying come right on out! His son Marty said his dad came alive! So, I scrambled to make flights, lodging, and car rental arrangements which went smother than ever before...even getting big discounts! Never had that happen before. Especially on such short notice. I flew out the next week. What a delightful visit! I returned home with 8 hrs. of video interview and great memories! And the journey with the letters began.

Gail A. Furford

Martin Albert Paulson
1941

NOTE: MARTIN'S LETTERS ARE TRANSCRIBED AS HE WROTE THEM ... MISSPELLINGS AND ALL!

ACKNOWLEDGEMENTS

IT IS REWARDING to have family support in a project of this magnitude. Not just from my family, but from Martin's family as well. My husband, George, and adult children, Barbie, David & Sharon kept me smiling with encouragement! My husband also helped with scanning some pictures and giving information on family history. And what a wonder to have "Uncle" Martin available to clarify and answer my many questions. His son, Marty, was encouraging from the moment he found out I would be writing about his Dad, and welcomed us into his home when we flew from the East coast to West coast for visits.

THANK YOU to The Bernice Pauahi Bishop Museum, designated the Hawaii State Museum of Natural and Cultural History in Hawaii, and their employees who took time to research and direct me to valuable information. The only information I had to submit to them was that a man from their museum was on Espiritu Santo in 1944! They took that information and ran with it which resulting in amazing WWII information.

THANK YOU to The Martin & Osa Johnson Safari Museum for allowing me to use photos and information from the book "I Married Adventure – The Life of Martin & Osa Johnson" by Osa Johnson, which was a valuable resource for understanding native life in the South Pacific Islands.

INVALUABLE THANKS to the National Archives in College Park, MD., who took time to consult with me and made my military research seamless and rewarding. Their employees were wonderful! They took time to understand what I was researching and pulled specifically related material down to the detail of Martin's Infantry Division.

A SPECIAL THANK YOU to Fort Lewis-McCord in Washington State for sending a Full Honor Guard and Media Group (the 5th Mobile Public Affairs Detachment) for the ceremony of presenting the Bronze Star and Occupation of Japan medal to 95 year old Martin A. Paulson for his service during the Battle of Okinawa and the Occupation of Japan. What an Honor! Martin tried very hard to stand TALL to have his medals pinned.

A BIG THANK YOU to Donna Shubel of Thomson-Shore Printing who took time to answer my many questions and was of invaluable help in finalizing this book. Thank you, Donna!

BASIC TRAINING

Pvt Martin A. Paulson

LETTER 1

  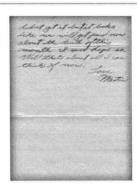

Pvt Martin Paulson
Co A Reception Center
Fort Lewis, Wash
Posted: Tacoma, Washington
Oct 11, 1943 1:30 PM

Note "FREE" (above)

BUY
WAR SAVINGS
BOND and STAMP

Dear Ruth,   September 30, 1943

There isn't a heck of a lot that I can tell you about where I am and what I am doing that I haven't already wrote. If I could write everything I wanted to there still wouldn't have been much.

There aren't any towns at all on this island I am on now. I have heard that there are a few white people here but I haven't seen any yet. I am going to take a trip around the island tomorrow so maybe I will have something more to write about next time.

Yesterday all of us got issued a case of beer. It cost one sixty two, but that is pretty cheap isn't it. Well they didn't give it to us all at one time. We got ten bottles last night and will get some more tonight. Do you know what brand I got. It is Sicks Select. That is the first beer I have got from near home so far.

You remember or I think I mentioned to you that I signed the pay roll for fifty bucks. Well I didn't get it but it looks like we will get paid now about the tenth of this month. I sure hope so. Well that about all I can think of now.

Love   Martin

Martin was single without dependents when drafted. At that time his family consisted of his father, *Adolf Manuel Paulson*, his sister *Karen Paulson* (3 years younger), his sister *Myrtle 'Paulson' Rae* (5 years older), and his sister *Ruth 'Paulson' Furford* (3 years older). Martin was living with his sister, Ruth, at the time he was drafted. Ruth was married to Arvid (Curly) Furford and had one child, 6 year old George who idealized his Uncle Martin. Ruth is the person to whom the letters were addressed, and to whom Martin chose to handle his finances while serving in the Army.

Martin was inducted into the Army as *Private Martin A Paulson* at Fort Lewis and spent a short time on an island associated with Fort Lewis. He was older than most of the young men who were drafted. He was excused from being drafted earlier due to his importance at Seattle-Tacoma Shipbuilding and the death of his mother, Rakel 'Titland' Paulson, in 1941 from cancer. In 1943 the war effort was needing more man power, so on June 15, 1943 at age 25, Martin was drafted.

The War Department's definition of *'term of enlistment'* (draft) in WWII: *Enlistment for the duration of the War or other emergency, plus six months, subject to the discretion of the President or otherwise according to law*[1] [This policy comes into play during the last months of Martin's service].

Fort Lewis, Washington 1930

Fort Lewis received its name from Meriwether Lewis, who was part of the original Lewis and Clark expedition across the United States. Covering over 80,000 acres of land, it is one of the largest and most active US military installations in the world. The army base began life as Camp Lewis in 1917 when the citizens purchased the land and donated it to the US government for military use. They maintained that it had to be a permanent army post, which was accepted as a stipulation. Nearly 60,000 men used the army installation for training for WW1. During the WPA (see definition below) projects in the 1930s, an army air field which later became McChord Air Force Base was constructed.

The base also served as a training and staging area for troops in WWII. During the two years prior to Pearl Harbor, the number of men at Fort Lewis and McChord rapidly increased from 7,000 to more than 26,000. After Pearl Harbor, more than 50,000 soldiers at a time trained at Fort Lewis.

WPA commonly refers to the many agencies established by the Federal Government in the 1930s during Franklin D. Roosevelt's administration. Brought into being on May 6, 1935, as an independent agency funded directly by Congress, the Works Progress Administration was the Federal Government's most ambitious undertaking yet to provide employment for the jobless.

---

[1]Http://aad.archivesgov/aad/record-detail

The purpose of the Works Progress Administration was to provide jobs for the unemployed who were able to work. It was not a program for the aged, handicapped or other unemployables, all of whom would be helped by state and local governments, but rather it provided assistance to people who simply could not find a job. Sometimes called a "make work" program, the WPA eventually employed approximately one-third of the nation's 10,000,000 unemployed, paying them about $50.00 a month.

In the early 1930s, most of the work provided was in the construction industries.

Prior to being drafted into the Army, Martin was a skilled Welder and Flame Cutter working at the Seattle-Tacoma Shipbuilding yards in Washington State which produced a significant number of ships during the war, from *escort carriers* and *destroyers* to *merchant vessels*. On Liberty Fleet Day 27 September 1941 one of the first Liberty ships the *SS Fredrick Funston* was launched by Seattle-Tacoma. Martin spoke of working on Liberty ships.

USS Frederick Function APA-89

The shipyard had existed since the 1920s as part of the Todd Dry Dock & Construction Company, but had shut down some time after the First World War. In 1939, the old shipyard in Commencement Bay, Tacoma, was revived by Todd and Kaiser Shipbuilding together with the aid of some $15 million in capital provided by the US Navy, for the production of vessels in anticipation of possible US entry into World War II. [2]

There was another shipyard in the Seattle area, the Bremerton Ship Yards. After the attack on Pearl Harbor (December 7, 1941) five of the six surviving battleships were sent to the Bremerton shipyards for modifications and repairs. These battleships were dubbed the "Pearl Harbor Ghosts" because the Japanese had declared them sunk. During the war, Bremerton Ship Yards repaired 26 battleships (some more than once), 18 aircraft carriers, 13 cruisers, and 79 destroyers. In addition, the 30,000-plus workers built 53 new vessels including five aircraft carriers, 13 destroyers, eight destroyer escorts, and they overhauled, repaired, or fitted out another 400 warships. Bremerton Ship Yards was operating 24 hours a day.

With the scarcity of housing in Bremerton and Kitsap County plus gasoline rationing, many of the shipyard workers lived in Seattle, commuting to Bremerton by ferry. An important part of WWII history in Washington State centers around the

---

[2]http://en.wikipedia.org/wiki/Seattle-Tacoma_Shipbuilding_Corporation

ferry system. The Black Ball Line had six ferryboats on the Seattle-Bremerton route making more than 35 trips a day, the most famous being the ferry *Kalakala,* carrying thousands of workers and naval personnel. Martin mentioned riding on this ferry 2-3 times and said it really rattled when picking up speed and slowing down.

KALAKALA

An early promotional postcard of the KALAKALA

As the new flagship of the Black Ball Line (a.k.a. Puget Sound Navigation--PSN), the *Kalakala* was a workhorse and also a social boat. PSN had envisioned the ferry to be used as an excursion vessel as well as a ferry. Shortly after starting her career during the Depression, the *Kalakala* embarked on "*Moonlight Cruises*" on Puget Sound. She had her own band, "*The Flying Bird Orchestra*" which made live broadcasts from the ferry (the first of their kind). Passengers danced to the swing music of the Flying Bird Orchestra from 8:30pm-12:30am for only $1.00. People met their future spouses on these festive cruises, and life-long memories were made dancing to the sounds of Benny Goodman and Glen Miller as the *Kalakala* cruised aimlessly around Puget Sound under star-filled skies. For those few hours, life aboard the *Kalakala* relegated the Depression years to the background, and gave people a break from the stress of those hard times.

KALAKALA on a 'Moon Light' sailing - Seattle Harbor

The 'Work Horse of Puget Sound' during WWII, George Bayless Collection

The *Kalakala* was, however, first and foremost, a ferry. She quickly became a workhorse on the Sound, completing thousands of trips from Seattle to Bremerton. After the outbreak of World War II, the ferry's role became critical by carrying workers to the Puget Sound Naval Shipyard (*PSNS*). PSNS shipbuilding was in full swing after the navy lost most of its fleet at Pearl Harbor. Because of the ship yards tremendous expansion due to WWII needs, the *Kalakala* carried as many as 5,000 shipyard workers and sailors per trip and increased from 14 round trips daily to 23 by adding two more ferries, the *Willipa* and the *Enetai*.

In 1942 passengers had to check in all cameras and binoculars when boarding because of the close proximity of the Bremerton ferry dock to the naval shipyard. The *Malta* ferry joins the Bremerton run and 29 trips are run daily with the *Kalakala*, being the leading carrier.

The *Kalakala* was noted for her design, certainly, but also for her general reliability and seaworthiness. She was also noted, however, for her teeth-rattling vibration. Apparently her engines had not been properly aligned and the ferry shook like a 6.0 earthquake the entire way across the Sound. Running at full speed, it became necessary to fill coffee cups only half full in the galley to prevent spillage. The situation was remedied a bit in 1955 when a 5-blade propeller replaced her original 4-blade prop. Vibration was reduced by about 40%, but the *Kalakala* shook her entire life.

The KALAKALA & WILLIPA 1947

Martin said, *"She would shake like the thunder when pulling out and coming into dock!"*

Ferry Chippewa after collision with Kalakala 1936

She also took a liking to running into things. Her first accident took place in November of 1936 when she rammed the Chippewa. Most of the blame could be placed on human error (and, some would say the Captain of the Chippewa) over confusion from the ferries' whistle signals. Proving the strength of her construction, the Kalakala punched a 40- foot hole in the Chippewa's wooden superstructure, demolishing 5 cars in the process. The Kalakala was hardly damaged, suffering from a few broken windows and dents.

In **1938**, her engines refused to back down as she approached Colman dock. With timbers flying, she smashed into the dock. A six foot hole was punched into the ferry and ten people were slightly injured. In **1943** while cruising through fog, she rammed into a barge and knocked two railroad cars into the Sound. In all fairness, it should be noted that this was in the days before radar and the method of navigation in fog was to sound the whistle, listen for the reply, then alter course according to where the echo bounced back from. In **1949** her engines didn't back down again and she again rammed Colman Dock. This time at full speed. According to witnesses, the ferry looked as if she had no intention of stopping. There was only slight damage sustained to the *Kalakala,* and she missed only one day of service.

Toward the end of her career with Puget Sound Navigation the *Kalakala* became noted for another milestone. In addition to her historic status as the first (and only) streamlined ferry in the world, she was chosen to be the first commercial vessel to receive radar after the technology was declassified.

KALAKALA receiving radar

After WWII, Puget Sound Navigation found itself experiencing a myriad of problems. Traffic from the money-making navy yard route to Bremerton had been cut in half, and the cost of union labor was rising. In July 1951, Puget Sound Navigation (the Black Ball line) ceased to exist on the waters of Puget Sound, but the *Kalakala's* story did not end there. Though she was no longer needed as *"The Workhorse of Puget Sound,"* she continued to sail running various ferry routes throughout her remaining years. [3]

In 2004 the *Kalakala* found a new home with the help of Craig Mar Chun and Karl Anderson, and berthed her at Tacoma's Hylebos Waterway for $1 month.

Washington, a comparatively small and undeveloped state, played a disproportionately important role in the country's efforts to gear up for war. During WWII, Washington State produced more war materiel per capita than anywhere else in the country. Warships, bombers, tanks, transport, plutonium for the atom bomb, wood products, and minerals were produced in Seattle's air fields, shipyards, and laboratories and from new mills in Spokane, Vancouver, and Tacoma. Geographically strategic in a war against Japan, Seattle was transformed by the war effort. In addition to industry, the University of Washington hosted military personnel and a Navy unit, while academic departments from home economics (training students to can food for shipment overseas) to chemistry (which developed a laboratory for chemical warfare) were induced by the Department of Defense to provide for the war. Yet the civilian-military consensus was also strained by the war: on August 6, 1945, the day the atomic bomb exploded on Hiroshima, residents near Hanford, in south central Washington, were told for the first time what had been produced on the 400,000-acre lot near their homes. [4]

In January 1943, Washington Secretary of State Belle Reeves issued a report titled *War Production in Washington*. A year and a month after Pearl Harbor, she wrote:

"No state has been more profoundly affected economically by the expansion of war industries than Washington. By the middle of 1941, migration of war workers was already at full tide and the relation of prime military contracts in the Puget Sound

---

[3] http://www.kalakala.org/history/history_timeline.html

[4] http://depts.washington.edu/antiwar/pnwhistory_wwii.shtml

area to the value of manufacturing products in 1939 was relatively five times greater than for the country as a whole. The relationship of war work to normal activity has been about twice as great as for Los Angeles and four times greater than for San Francisco." [5]

Martin mentions they were issued a case of Sicks Select beer. It was a normal practice of the military to issue beer for the purpose of helping soldiers to relax, especially those who were homesick and under strenuous training. Here is historical information to help you understand Martin's comment about it being the first beer he has had from near his home in Kent, Washington, just outside of Seattle.

"Sick's Select" beer was introduced to Seattle in August of 1939 and was produced in the main plant on Airport Way. In 1940, Brewmaster, John A. Weiss was still producing "Rheinlander," and had added "Boss' Ale" to the line-up. Then in Sept. of '41, they transferred production of "Sick's Select" to the Century plant where it rapidly became Century's leading brand, eclipsing "Rheinlander."

By 1942, co-managers L. R. McCash & F. W. Shepard had increased annual production to 80,000 barrels and continued to increase production with the purchase of the Salem Brewery Assn. (Oregon) in October '43. In January 1944, the name Sick was added to all the company's breweries and the Century Brewery now became Sicks' Century Brewery - and "Sick's Select" was

Chevy Delivery Van

changed to "Sicks' Select." By now the "Rheinlander" brand had been discontinued due to poor sales, and "Sicks' Select" was Century's primary focus. [6]

Martin says he signed a payroll of $50 which equals $600/yr, and in our interview said he received 20% more for serving overseas which would be $60/mo. and $720/yr.

---

[5] _historylink.org/index.cfm?DisplayPage=output.cfm&file_id=1664

[6] www.brewerygems.com/horluck.htm#Sicks_Century_Brewery

BELOW IS AN EXCERPT FROM:
Barron's National Business and Financial Weekly
April 24, 1944
by Malvern Hall Tillitt
This excerpt gives an illustration of a month's pay
for a soldier with the rank of Buck Private.

UNMARRIED BUCK PRIVATE MAY "NET" $420

The lowest pay in the Army is the $50 a month; or $600 a year, received by the buck private, while in service within the bounds of the United States. The man may have given up a $3,600-a-year civilian job on entering military service. And, from the figures alone, he may apparently be taking a loss of $3,000 a year.

Army pay is not entirely velvet. Personnel below the commissioned ratings must take care of a number of minor needs and wants out of earnings. On the basis of itemized statements obtained in interviews with selectees in training and old timers in service, and with privates, corporals, and sergeants, expenditures out of pocket run at about the same level for men and non-commissioned officers.

Passing by the spendthrift and the tight-wad, and figuring by the month for ordinary spenders, these expenditures include:
two 50-cent haircuts by barber,

> $1.50 for laundry,
> $1.50 for tailor service (pressing and dry-cleaning),
> $1.40 for movies,
> $3 for tobacco,
> 60 cents for soap, tooth paste, and razor blades,
> and $4 for other incidentals ...

purchased at commissary or Post Exchange or outside camp limits. Miscellaneous outlays through the year -- for civilian shoes and repairs, garrison cap, shoe polish, metal polish, and other articles -- may run to $24, or an average of $2 a month.

The enumerated expenditures out of pay, including miscellaneous expenses, add up to $15 a month, or $180 a year -- which leaves the buck private in service within the bounds of the United States *with an annual remainder of $420.* And this is the measure of his "net" annual income, if he has no other revenues, for Federal income taxes do not apply to Incomes of men in military service below $1,500 -- and above that the serviceman also has his personal exemptions. These expenditures do not include the cost of sprees during excursions out of camp on leave, if any, or lavish entertainment of girl friends or losses at

"Georgia dominoes." The buck private's net income, as here worked out, simply represents the yearly remainder of earnings during normal training camp life.[7]

What Was your World War II Pay?

Rank	Insignia	Yearly Pay	Rent Allowance (Mo.) with dependents	single
General	★★★★	$8,000	$120	$105
Lt. General	★★★	8,000	120	105
Maj. General	★★	8,000	120	105
Brig. General	★	6,000	120	105
Colonel	(eagle)	4,000	120	105
Lt. Colonel	(Silver)	3,500	120	105
Major	(Gold)	3,000	105	90
Captain	(bars)	2,400	90	75
1st Lieutenant	(Silver)	2,000	75	60
2nd Lieutenant	(Gold)	1,800	60	45
Warrant Officer (chief)	(Brown)	2,100	75	60
Warrant Officer (j.g.)	(Brown)	1,800	60	45
Flight Officer	(Blue)	1,800	60	45

Rank	Sleeve Insignia	Monthly Base Pay
Private (7th grade)	no chevrons	$50
Private first class (6th grade)	∧	54
Corporal (5th grade)	∧	66
Sergeant (4th grade)	∧	78
Staff Sergeant (3rd grade)	⩘	96
Technical Sergeant (2nd grade)	⩙	114
Master Sergeant, First Sergeant (1st grade)	⩙ ⩙	138

In the above, all officers with dependents receive $42 per month (30 day period) subsistence allowance; single officers, $21. (Exception: Lt. Col. and Maj., married, receive $63.)

FLYING PAY—Flying officers and enlisted men receive an increase of 50% of their base pay when by orders of competent authority they are required to participate regularly and frequently in aerial flights and when as a result of orders they do participate in such flights. Non-flying officers receive flying pay at the rate of $60 per month when they participate in regular and frequent aerial flights ordered by competent authority.

Pay scale noted above shows base pay amounts. This is the lowest amount paid to each grade. To this may be added other amounts for flying pay, longevity, etc., descriptions of which follow.

LONGEVITY—Every enlisted man receives an increase of 5% of his base pay for each 3 years of service up to 30 years.

FOREIGN SERVICE—The base pay of officers is increased by 10% (enlisted men 20%) for any service while on sea duty or duty in any place beyond the continental limits of the U. S. or in Alaska.

ALLOWANCE FOR DEPENDENTS (Class F Allotment)—Under the Oct. 26, 1943 amendment to the Servicemen's Dependent Allowance Act of 1942, dependents of enlisted men receive increased benefits. Several classes of benefits are allowed—for wife and children, for parents, brothers and sisters whose chief support is the serviceman, and for combinations of these family relationships. Men with dependents allow the government to deduct $22 per month from pay, the remainder of the amount received by the family is contributed by the government. A wife will receive $50 per month; with one child, $80, and $20 for each additional child. A mother as a dependent will receive $37, in cases of total dependency, $50.

---

[7] www.cbi-history.com/part_xii_wwii_pay

LETTER 2

Postage: Free
Posted: October18, 1943 6 PM
Camp Roberts, Calif

From: Pvt Martin A. Paulson
Co C 77th Tng Bn *(training battalion)*
Camp Robert, CA

To:
Ruth Furford
Rt 1 Box 352
Kent, Washington

(Post Card)

"I am just writing a card to let you know that I am in Camp Roberts now. We left Wednesday and got down here this morning. Write and let me know how things are."

OCTOBER 1943

Sunday	Monday	Tuesday	Wednesday	Thursday	Friday	Saturday
					1	2
3	4	5	6	7	8 Yom Kippur begins at sunset	9
10	11	12 Columbus Day (trad)	13	14	15	16
17	18	19	20	21	22	23
24	25	26	27	28	29	30
31 Halloween						

According to the 1943 calendar, they left on Wednesday the 13th and it took them till Monday the 18th to travel from Fort Lewis, Washington to Camp Roberts, in northern California. Five days!

WWII Camp Roberts Postcard

Camp Roberts, located on the Salinas River approximately halfway between San Francisco and Los Angeles, is named after Corporal Harold W. Roberts, a California born enlisted man who gave his life for a comrade in WW1. It officially began its mission as a replacement training center March 1941. Both the Infantry and Field Artillery Replacement Training Centers at Camp Roberts achieved enviable proficiency records where it counted, in the combat zones and around the world in WWII to which their graduates were sent. Some 436,000 Infantry and Field Artillery troops passed through the intensive seventeen week training cycle. [8]

One of the largest Infantry and Artillery Replacement Training Centers in the world, Camp Roberts covers 47,000 acres. More than 9,000 workmen spent 6,000,000 man hours building this huge camp. During WWII, Camp Roberts consisted of an ULTRA-MODERN HOSPITAL, with a capacity of approximately 1,300 beds it maintained for the soldiers; NINE CHAPELS in which services for each of the three great faiths were held; THE AMERICAN RED CROSS which was housed in its own building with a large staff in attendance; THE SOLDIER BOWL, a natural amphitheater large enough to hold the entire personnel of the camp – an ideal setting for the many outdoor shows – and on its stage world famous stars of stage, screen and radio appeared; THE SPORTS ARENA, a huge gymnasium where soldiers could take any of various forms of exercise, and the scene of theatricals and sports shows during the winter months; A SERVICE CLUB which was maintained for the exclusive use of the enlisted men and their guests. It contains a lounge, cafeteria and a well-stocked library; A GUEST HOUSE, centrally located where

Bob Hope being escorted off stage by MP's 1942

relatives and guests of soldiers could secure emergency accommodations not to exceed three days; FOUR THEATERS which offered the latest in film entertainment;

---

[8] www.militarymuseum.org/campbob.html comments from *Historic California Posts CAMP ROBERTS by Master Sergeant (Retired) Al Davis*

THREE BOWLING ALLEYS, each with eight alleys; RECREATION HALLS were located in each of the battalion areas; CAMP EXCHANGES in each of the regimental areas sold toilet articles, magazines, candy, writing materials, soft drinks, beer and other items; TAILOR and BARBER SHOPS were located in each Camp Exchange; and THE CAMP ROBERTS DISPATCH, written by soldiers, for soldiers, distributed more than 15,000 copies free of charge each week.[9]

Camp Roberts in Postcards during WWII:[10]

At left....Infantry Training Center -- At right...full view of Camp Roberts

At left....Theater and Camp Headquarters Bldgs. – At right...Sleeping Quarters

---

[9] www.wartimepress.com/archives
[10] www.militarymuseum.org/CpRoberttsPostcards.html

At left…Mess Hall – At right…Station Hospital

When asked what he remembered about Camp Roberts Martin said: *"Confining, they told you when you could breath and when not to breath. We were shipped to Camp Roberts by train, lined up along the train depot upon arrival and they announced ...'this is an infantry training center and not to worry about it because there was nothing we could do about it and that we were in the infantry now'!"*

In our interviews, he said: *"There was one time we were in our barracks and our Sergeant told us that we would be cleaning up the barrack and to get started. No one moved. I decided it best to get it over with so started picking up. The Sergeant stuck his head around the door and told me to step aside. He made all the other scrub and clean. All I had to do was empty the ashtrays! They couldn't make you do anything, but they can make you wish you had!!*

It was said that President Franklin D. Roosevelt did not want the same mistake to happen in this War that happened in WWI where so many men were lost due to lack of training and, therefore, wanted his military to have extensive training. As we continue with the letters, you will see how Camp Roberts prepared their soldiers for war.

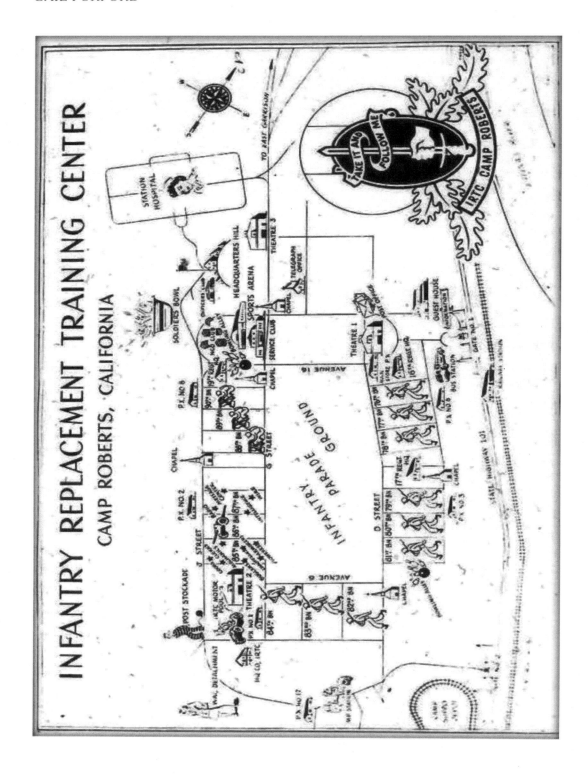

LETTER 3

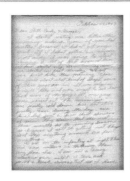   

Pvt Martin A Paulson
Co A 88 Inf Tng Bt
Camp Roberts, California

To: Mrs. A. Furford
Rt. 1 Box 352
Kent, Washington

Postage: Free
Posted: October 30, 1943
Camp Roberts, Calif

Dear Ruth Curly & George,   *October 28, 1943*

I started writing one letter this morning asking you if you had written because I didn't get any mail. If I hadn't gotten an answer right away I was going to start raising a lot of hell around here. I have started my Basic Training now, we started in last Monday. We got our first hike this morning. You can guess about what kind of shape some of these guys are in. It was only a 4 mile and you ought to see how tired some of the guys got, one guy even passed out. The mornings are pretty cold down here, but it is pretty nice during the day. We have had just a few short showers of rain. They claim that the next three months is the raining season so I guess I will be getting wet. They dont stop anything around here for anything.

I am in the infantry all right. There are more welders in the Army than any place else. I am in a heavy machine gun outfit. I took and passed a truck drivers test so I have a small chance of being one. About half of the guys in this company are from Washington and the other half is from Texas. I am going to try and get my picture taken pretty soon and if they flatter me enough I will send you one. I have been going around with a couple of guys since I got in here. One is from Oregon and the other has lived up at Lake Maridian all his life. His father still lives up there. His name is Bower maybe you know him.

They passed out a lot of leaves the other day and then they canceled them. I haven't had a chance to get out of here yet. The only thing we can do is drink beer for 10 cents a bottle and go to the show.

They claim that this is the toughest training center in the U.S.A. (at least it has the highest rating) and I sure believe it. They can even grow grass around here. It got up to 140 last summer so I am glad it is winter time.

I bet there are a lot of guys that would like to get a hold of my gun. They

15

gave me a brand new M1. They sure are a swell gun and I bet there are a lot of hunters that would like to get ahold of one of them.

One good thing about the Army is the grub. We usually get all the meat we want and boy I have sure been making up for lost time eating meat.

Thats all I have time to write now, we are going to have a practice air raid and all of us have to run out in the hills and lay around for about an hour. After that I have to make up some time that I missed by going to the dentist the other day. I went at 7 o'clock in the morning and waited until two in the afternoon to get a couple of small fillings. It took them about 10 minutes.

Martin

New Infantry Arrivals, Camp Roberts

Martin sounds a little home sick! Basic Training consisted of 17 weeks of intensive training. As one ex-infantry soldier stated, he didn't know when Boot Camp ended and advanced training started/ended. As the US forces got more feedback from the fighting fronts, combined basic/advanced infantry training gradually increased from 8 to 12 to 13 to 15 to 17 weeks. Camp Roberts consisted of 17 weeks. A big part of the problem was the War Department's total underestimation of infantry casualties and replacements that would be needed. At the outbreak of war, the War Department thought 75% infantry replacement rate would be OK, it turned out to be 92%! [11]

The United States has traditionally fought its wars with a citizen army mobilized and trained after the emergency arises. Its members on their induction into the Army face an abrupt transition to a life and pattern of behavior altogether foreign to their previous experience. For their assistance the Army has provided an initial period of basic military training, a course of instruction intended to transform the raw recruit into a soldier. This basic training includes instruction in military

---

[11]http://wiki.answers.com

discipline and courtesy, close order drill, first aid and protection against disease, physical conditioning, defense against enemy attack, and the care and use of weapons. Only after completion of basic training are recruits, in theory, advanced to instruction in the technical specialties of the particular Army arm or service to which they are assigned. In practice, however, it has not always been possible to follow the theory. Both in World War I and during the first year and a half of World War II, certain phases of basic training were sometimes slighted in order to speed the training in specialties for which a critical need existed. [12]

Martin said there were more welders in the Army than any place else. Bremerton Shipyard, where Martin was a welder, was one of the largest ship builders during WWII. As men were pulled from their jobs to fight in the war, women were trained to take their place. Women stepped up in the factories to produce the heavy machinery needed for the war and at home to keep the country running. Women quickly picked up and excelled at historically male-dominated trades such as welding, riveting and engine repair, and were essential for the production and supply of goods to our troops fighting abroad.

WWII Poster

Martin talks of different individuals he served with or knew throughout his letters. In this letter he mentions *"Bower"* from Lake Meridian, Washington. Lake Meridian is a fresh water lake in Kent, Washington. In our interview there were a lot of names Martin could not remember saying…*"that was such a long time ago."* Even though Martin could not remember some of the men, each will be noted and honored throughout this book.

Martin took and passed a truck drivers test, mentions being in a heavy machine gun outfit, and seems very proud of the M1 rifle. In 1943 in

Camp Roberts Truck 1943

Washington State most families owned guns and hunted to provide meat for their families and is the reason he says:

"I bet there are a lot of hunters that would like to get ahold of one of them."

The M1 Garand was the first semi-automatic rifle to be generally issued to the

---

[12]This paragraph of basic military training has been based on AHS-49, Basic Military Training in the AAF, 1939-1944.

infantry in any nation's army. It was called '*the greatest battle implement ever devised*' by General George S. Patton. In the field, the M1 gave American infantry a tremendous

M1 Rifle

firepower advantage over Axis troops (a coalition headed by Germany, Italy, and Japan that opposed the Allied Powers in World War II) who still carried bolt-action rifles such as the Karabiner 98k. With its semi-automatic operation, the M1 allowed US forces to maintain substantially higher rates of fire. In addition, the M1's heavy .30-06 cartridge offered superior penetrating power. Following the war, M1s in the US arsenal were refurbished and later saw action in the Korean War.[13]

When Martin was drafted, the United States was just coming out of *The Great Depression,* and with the onset of *World War II* numerous challenges confronted the American people. The government found it necessary to ration food, gas, and even clothing during that time. Americans were asked to conserve on everything. With not a single person unaffected by the war, rationing meant sacrifices for all.

WWII Poster from US Library of Congress

In the spring of 1942, the *Food Rationing Program* was set into motion. Rationing would deeply affect the American way of life for most. The federal government needed to control supply and demand. Rationing was introduced to avoid public anger with shortages and not to allow only the wealthy to purchase commodities. While industry and commerce were affected, individuals felt the effects more intensely. People were often required to give up many material goods, but there also was an *increase* in employment.

Individual efforts evolved into clubs and organizations coming to terms with the immediate circumstances. Joining together to support and maintain supply levels for the troops abroad meant making daily adjustments. Their efforts also included scrap drives, taking factory jobs, goods donations and other similar projects to assist those on the front. Government-sponsored ads, radio shows, posters and pamphlet campaigns urged the American people to comply. With a sense of urgency, the campaigns appealed to America to contribute by whatever means they had, without complaint. It was a highly effective tool in reaching the masses.

Rationing regulated the amount of commodities that consumers could obtain. Sugar rationing took effect in May 1943 with the distribution of *Sugar*

---

[13]http://militaryhistory.about.com/od/smallarms/p/m1garand.htm

Buying Cards. Registration usually took place in local schools. Each family was asked to send only one member for registration and be prepared to describe all other family members. Coupons were distributed based on family size, and the coupon book allowed the holder to buy a specified amount. Possession of a coupon book did not guarantee that sugar would be available. Americans learned to utilize what they had during rationing time. While some food items were scarce, others did not require rationing, and Americans adjusted accordingly.

"*Red Stamp*" rationing covered all meats, butter, fat, and oils, and with some exceptions, cheese. Each person was allowed a certain amount of points weekly with expiration dates to consider. "*Blue Stamp*" rationing covered canned, bottled, frozen fruits and vegetables, plus juices and dry beans, and such processed foods as soups, baby food and ketchup. Ration stamps became a kind of currency with each family being issued a "War Ration Book." Each stamp authorized a purchase of rationed goods in the quantity and time designated, and the book guaranteed each family its fair share of goods made scarce due to the war.

In addition to food, rationing encompassed clothing, shoes, coffee, gasoline, tires, and fuel oil. With each coupon book came specifications and deadlines. Rationing locations were posted in public view. Rationing of gas and tires strongly depended on the distance to one's job. If one was fortunate enough to own an automobile and drive at the then specified speed of 35 mph, one might have a small amount of gas remaining at the end of the month to visit nearby relatives.

Rationing resulted in one serious side effect: the black market, where people could buy rationed items on the sly, but at higher prices. The practice provoked mixed reactions from those who banded together to conserve as instructed, as opposed to those who fed the black market's subversion and profiteering. For the most part, black marketeers dealt in clothing and liquor in Britain, and meat, sugar and gasoline in the United States.

While life during the war meant daily sacrifice, few complained because they knew it was the men and women in uniform who were making the greater sacrifice. A poster released by the OFFICE OF WAR INFORMATION stated simply, "*Do with less so they'll have enough.*" And yet another pleaded, "*Be patriotic, sign your country's pledge to save the food.*" On the whole, the American people were united in their efforts.

Recycling was born with the government's encouragement. Saving aluminum cans meant more ammunition for the soldiers. Economizing initiatives seemed endless as Americans were urged to conserve and recycle metal, paper and rubber. War Bonds and stamps were sold to provide war funds, and the American people also united through volunteerism. Communities joined together to hold scrap-iron drives, and school children pasted saving stamps into bond books.

Others planted "Victory Gardens" to conserve food. For a small investment in soil, seed, and time, families could enjoy fresh vegetables for months.

By 1945, an estimated 20 million victory gardens produced approximately 40 percent of America's vegetables.

Then there were the food manufacturers who took advantage of the wartime shortages to flaunt their patriotism for profit. The familiar blue box of *Kraft Macaroni and Cheese Dinner* gained great popularity as a substitute for meat and dairy products. Two boxes required only one rationing coupon, which resulted in 80 million boxes sold in 1943. Food substitutions became evident with real butter being replaced with Oleo margarine. Cottage cheese took on a new significance as a substitute for meat, with sales exploding from 110 million pounds in 1930 to 500 million pounds in 1944.

After three years of rationing, World War II came to a welcome end in 1945. Rationing, however, did not end until 1946. Life resumed as normal and the consumption of meat, butter, and sugar inevitably rose. While Americans still live with some of the results of World War II, rationing has not returned.[14]

Food Prices and Rationing Points
March 1943

FOOD	PRICE	RATION POINTS
Apples	$.33 two pounds	20 points
Bread	$.10 loaf	0 points
Butter	$.22 pound	20 points
Cheerios	$.14 box	7 points
Cheese	$.35 pound	42 points
Coffee	$.24 pound	10 points
Ground Beef	$.27 pound	0 points
Eggs	$.35 dozen	0 points
Flour	$.66 ten pounds	18 points
Sugar	$.31 five pounds	80 points!
Steak	$.40 pound	13 points

---

[14] http://www.u-s-history.com/pages/h1674.html

LETTER 4

Pvt Martin Paulson
Co A. 88 Inf Tng Bn
Camp Roberts, Calif.

To: Mrs. A. Furford
Rt 1 Box 352
Kent, Washington

Postage: Free
Posted: Nov 15, 1943
Camp Roberts, Calif

Dear Ruth Curly & George,   *November 14, 1943*

Well I guess you think it is about time I wrote and let you know that I am still here. I tell you that we start out before daylight and by the time I get my rifle cleaned and everything it is time to go to bed. The other night I went down in the latreen after the lights went out to write to you. There was another guy down there that couldn't write and asked me to write for him. By the time I finished I was too tired.

Last week we were on the rifle range shooting the M1 rifle and carbine. I bet there a lot of guys that would sure rave if they knew how many rounds of amunition I shot at targets and if I ever get in combat I wont use a rifle. I did get a metal even if it wasnt the highest it is a metal.

I sure wish I had known that Gladys was in Paso Robals. I have been in there three times since I have been down here. There isnt much there, so the next pass I get I am going to go to Los Angles. By the way the drinks they make down here are a little short on wiskey, in fact you cant taste the wiskey, and they charge 45 cents a drink.

We got payed the other day, but would you draw $25 out of the bank for me and send it down by money order. It is hard to cash a check.

Rich sent a letter to me the other day offering $500 for my car. I decided if that is all I can get for it I will save it until after the war. I might get sent someplace after I leave here where I can use it so I will sure be sorry if I sell it then.

The other night we had a short bivwock. I dont suppose that is the correct way to spell it, but that is the way it sounds. What it means is we stayed out all night in pup tents. I wouldnt have minded it but I must have found the hardest spot in California to sleep. Believe it or not it was harder than my bunk.

Martin told of a soldier who could not write. The following information on the scale of illiteracy in World War II is very interesting. It is taken from *"The Uneducated"* by Ginzber and Bray 1953, and is part of a series of books on the use of labor sponsored by Columbia University. It was started by General Eisenhower because he was struck by the evidence of the wastage in manpower he saw in WWII.

Between 1940 and 1945 Selective Service held 6 registrations. Prior to V-J Day they had registered more than 22 million persons between 18 and 37 years of age. But more got in because the third registration round of Feb 1942 required men through the age of 42 to register. The fourth registration required all men between 45 and 65 to register. The 5600 registration boards had threefold responsibilities: register, classify and meet specific quotas set by the Armed Services.

The U.S. was sparsely settled compared to other industrial countries of the world at the time of WWII, but did not experience serious manpower shortages. Of the almost 5 million men examined for service during WW I, approximately 40,000 were rejected for "mental deficiency." Defined as "in general, mental deficiency of the grade of imbecility or below."

In June, 1943, the Armed Forces agreed to disregard literacy completely as a formal qualification for induction. In place of the fourth-grade standard which had been more or less in effect for the preceding two years a new set of standards was introduced. After failing the literacy test candidates were given a test of mental ability. This weeded out the mentally unstable and provided new aims for the remaining previously "mental unstable" candidates.

1. To teach the men to read at least at a fourth-grade level so that they would be able to comprehend bulletins, written order and directives, and basic Army publications.
2. To give the men sufficient language skills so that they would be able to use and understand the everyday oral and written language necessary for getting along with officers and men.
3. To teach the men to do numbers work at a fourth-grade level, so that they could understand their pay accounts and laundry bills, conduct their business in PX, and perform in other situations requiring arithmetic skills.
4. To facilitate the adjustment of the men to military training and Army life.
5. To enable the men to understand in a general way why it was necessary for this country to fight a war against Germany, Japan, and Italy.

The course ran for 120 days, approximately 40 percent of the men graduated in less than 30 days. Approximately 40 percent graduated in less than 60 days. In total about 435,000 illiterates were taken in during WWII.

Now we will look at the military performance of the uneducated. They used a sample of 400 men (200 white, 200 black) ½ from the Deep South and ½ from northern states. More than four out of every five gave satisfactory performance and more than one out of three were good or very good soldiers. For those in the sample who entered a claim for further education after they left the Army, they found that there were practically no differences between the percentages of the whites and the blacks who claimed educational benefits. The majority of the blacks undertook institutional education, whereas most of the whites entered farm training. As one might expect, there was no tremendous change in the general occupational and income circumstances of these men as a result of their military service, even with full allowance for their special training. For the most part, when men left the military service they went back to the same types of jobs and same part of country prior to their induction into the Army. [15]

The fact that Martin took time to help this fellow write a letter along with other acts in future letters strikes deeply to the core of his character. He says:

"A soldier was a soldier. There was no difference of where you were from or what you did for a living or the education you had previously – they fought the same War."

It is hard for us to imagine today the impossible battle situations these young men were in.

The picture at right is not from WWII, but shows military men at Camp Roberts today and the amount of bullets used while training. The cost of bullets must have been astounding. As Martin said:

Spent cartridges!

"A lot of guys would sure rave if they knew how many rounds of ammunition I shot at targets."

RAVE: *"to rage"* or *"talk wildly or incoherently, as if one were delirious or insane."*

Gladys (mentioned in this letter) is the sister of Ruth's husband. Travel back then was nowhere near as good as it is today so a journey from Washington State to California was a big undertaking. It is not known why she was in Paso Robles, California, but I am sure Martin would have loved to have seen a member of the family.

Martin had his sister, Ruth, manage his money while serving in the War and reason he is always asking her to draw out money.

---

[15] http://www.culturism.us/booksummaries/TheUneducatedbyGinzberg.htm   Excerpts taken from the writings

The cost of whiskey at 45 cents seemed a lot to Martin, especially when they "*didn't have much whiskey*" in the drinks. Distilleries during WWII were required to produce industrial alcohol for bombs and other armaments so no new whiskey was made in order to help the war effort. By 1944, whiskey had disappeared from liquor store shelves as distilleries converted to the production of industrial alcohol.

PRICES AND EVENTS IN 1943

Average cost of a new house	$3,600
Average wages per year	$2,000
Cost of a gallon of Gas	15 cents
Average Price for a new car	$ 900

U.S.
- U.S. The Pentagon, considered to be the world's largest office building is completed
- In the United States it is announced that shoe **rationing,** canned food, meat, cheese, butter and cooking oils will go into effect
- America takes control of **Guadalcanal**
- Future President Lt. John F. Kennedy's **PT-109** is sunk by a Japanese destroyer
- US General Dwight D. Eisenhower becomes the **supreme Allied commander**

Poland
- German forces liquidate the **Jewish ghetto** in Krakow
- Warsaw Jewish **Ghetto Uprising** against the Nazi's

Germany
- German Afrika Korps and Italian troops in **North Africa surrender** to Allied forces
- The British and Americans **bomb Hamburg** on July 24th causing a firestorm that kills 42,000 German civilians

UK
- British deception plan **"*The Man Who Never Was*"** or 'Operation Mincemeat' executed
- The **Dambuster Raids** by RAF 617 Sqdn May 17th on German dams

Italy
- **Mussolini resigns** in Italy and surrender of Italy is announced on September 8th

Hungary
- Budapest - more than 2,000 citizens sent to **Concentration Camps**
- **Allied leaders** of Britain, the United States, and the Soviet Union meet for

the first time in Iran[16]

      Martin mentions going on an overnight Bivouac and staying in a pup tent. He said in the interview: *"We went out on Bivouac several times. We were issued items to take like a half tent (another soldier had the other half). We called it a 'half rack'. We worked in teams. If we returned from Bivouac with any items missing that were issued to us, it was taken out of our pay. "*

Bivouac Definition:

  Biv-ou-ac

  bivoo ak

Noun: A temporary camp with or without tents or cover

Verb: Stay in such a camp.. "the battalion was now bivouacked in a field"

Synonyms: Camp - encampment

Fellow soldier at
Camp Roberts Bivouac
From Martin's album

---

[16] http://www.thepeoplehistory.com/1943.html

LETTER 5

Pvt Martin Paulson	Mrs. A. Furford	Postage: Free
Co A 88 Inf Tng Bn	Rt. 1, Box (note: no box #,	Posted: Nov 22, 1943 6 pm
Camp Roberts, Calif	but the letter was delivered!)	Camp Roberts, Calif
	Kent, Wash	

Dear Ruth, Curly & George   *November 18*

I am on guard tonight and I have a half a hour before I go out to my post so I guess I will write an answer to the letter I got from you today. If you write in this place you have to take advantage of every minute to get time to write. I never seen a place that they could think of so many things for you to do all the time. Last night we went on a hike so I didn't get much sleep last night and tonight if I don't go to sleep on my post I will be lucky.

We finished learning how to use the rifles last week and now they have started teaching us how to use a machine gun. Boy they are sure complicated. There are more pieces and names to remember and we have to remember them. If you dont remember them right off they sure raise cane.

Eaven if they get us up in the middle of the night and keep us going until after dark I am gaining weight. I weigh 175 now. I gained it before we really started our training and I was sure surprised that I didn't lose it afterwards.

Thats about all I can think to write about. Nothing really ever happens around here except the same old grind every day. Does George still like school? I suppose he has started to gain weight now since he got his tonsils taken out.

Martin

I wrote this letter the other day and I never got around to mail it. Right after I wrote it I went out and one guy stabed and almost killed another guy so we had a little excitement. It happened on my post too.

M1 Carbine and M1 Garand

In Martin's last letter he mentioned the Carbine which is different than the M1 Garand rifle in that the Garand is a semi-automatic rifle. The first M1 carbines were delivered in mid-1942. The carbine's exclusive use of non-corrosive primered ammunition was found to be a godsend by troops and ordnance personnel serving in the Pacific where barrel corrosion was a significant issue with the corrosive primers used in .30-06 caliber weapons.

The M1 carbine (formally the United States Carbine, Caliber .30, M1) became a standard firearm for the U.S. military during WWII and the Korean War, and was produced in several variants. It was widely used by U.S. and foreign military, paramilitary and police forces, and has also been a popular civilian firearm. In selective fire versions capable of fully-automatic fire, the carbine is designated the M2 carbine. The M3 carbine was an M2 with an active infrared scope system.

The M3 with the M1 sight had an effective range of about 70 yards (limited by the visual capabilities of the sight). Fog and rain further reduced the weapon's effective range. It

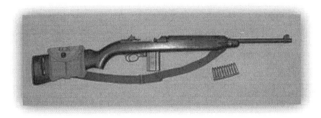

M1 Carbine

is estimated that fully 30% of Japanese casualties inflicted by rifle and carbine fire during the Okinawan campaign were caused by the M3 carbine and its M1 sniper scope (Martin served in Okinawa). The M1 Carbine has only one minor part in common with the M1 rifle (a short butt plate screw) and fires a different cartridge.[17]

Martin sounded very tired in this letter! The comment he made at the bottom of his letter strongly verifies how the stress of training affected many of the soldiers. There are many 'memoirs' from those who were trained at Camp Roberts which confirmed the stress of the training they received: strenuous hikes, drills upon drills, inspection after inspection which covered so many areas of their training, KP, guard duty, bivouacs, and so much more. When it came to weapons, there were comments on putting them together, taking them apart, putting them back together again, over and over and over until they could assemble and care for them without thinking...while under fire!

---

[17]http://www.gunsandammo.org/index.php?title=M1_carbine

WWII Poster

Martin's comment, *"They started teaching us how to use a machine gun. Boy they are sure complicated. There are more pieces and names to remember. If you don't remember them right off they sure raise a cane,"* deserves a good portion of space to include excerpts from an actual WWII manual on the Browning machine gun that was prominently used during WWII. These few pages will enlighten you as to how much these young men, who were thrust into war, had to learn...and under tremendously frightening training conditions. Martin once reminisced on the training at Camp Roberts,

"Believe me, I competed with the moles underground when crawling in the dirt while live bullets and artillery were flying overhead and around me."

Can you imagine what they faced in actual battle?

BROWNING MACHINE GUN MANUAL

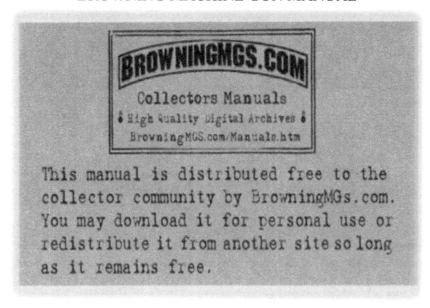

THE BROWNING HEAVY MACHINE GUN
300 calibre model 1917 (water cooled)
MECHANISM
Made Easy

FULLY ILLUSTRATED

GALE & POLDEN LTD
LONDON ALDERSHOT
AND PORTSMOUTH

Price **1/6** Nett
Per Post 1/8

http://www.liberatorcrew.com/Manuals.htm

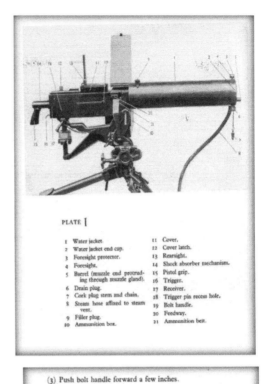

PLATE 1

1	Water jacket.	11	Cover.
2	Water jacket end cap.	12	Cover latch.
3	Foresight protector.	13	Rearsight.
4	Foresight.	14	Shock absorber mechanism.
5	Barrel (muzzle end protruding through muzzle gland).	15	Pistol grip.
6	Drain plug.	16	Trigger.
7	Cork plug stem and chain.	17	Receiver.
8	Steam hose affixed to steam vent.	18	Trigger pin recess hole.
		19	Bolt handle.
9	Filler plug.	20	Feedway.
10	Ammunition box.	21	Ammunition belt.

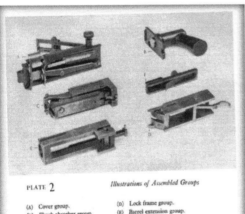

PLATE 2   *Illustrations of Assembled Groups*

(A) Cover group.
(B) Shock absorber group.
(C) Bolt group.

(D) Lock frame group.
(E) Barrel extension group.
(F) Cover latch.

FIELD STRIPPING

This should be done in the following sequence :

(1) Draw back cover latch, raise cover.
(2) Pull back bolt handle to the rearmost position, hold in this position by placing left wrist firmly on top of receiver and holding bolt handle with fingers of the left hand. Insert rim of cartridge or screw-driver into the slit of the driving spring rod, which will be found protruding from rear of back plate. Push driving rod in as far as it will go, rotate in clockwise direction until slit is vertical ; this locks the driving rod and retains driving spring fully compressed in bolt.

(3) Push bolt handle forward a few inches.
(4) Push cover latch forward with left hand. Back plate of pistol grip may now be lifted up and out of receiver with right hand.
(5) Pull bolt handle to rearmost position and withdraw bolt handle from bolt.
(6) Grasp driving spring rod with right hand, withdraw bolt and support same with left hand. Turn extractor upwards and remove.
(7) With nose of bullet, push in trigger pin (located in hole on the right side of receiver). Grasp lock frame spacer with left thumb and pull rearwards until lower projection of barrel extension drops down behind bottom plate of receiver.
(8) Grasp lock frame and push forward on tips of accelerator ; this will separate lock frame from barrel extension.
(9) Draw barrel extension and barrel to rear out of receiver.
(10) Unscrew barrel extension from barrel.

NOTE : *The above stripping 1-10 is what is normally needed under field conditions for a temporary stoppage necessitating a change of parts, etc. (see pp. 29-30, Stoppages).*

DETAIL STRIPPING OF GROUPS
(PLATES 3, 4, 5, 6, 7)

COVER

(1) With point of bullet turn cover pin spring upwards, withdraw pin, remove cover.
(2) With point of bullet turn feed lever pivot pin spring outwards, remove pivot pin, remove feed lever, remove belt feed slide.
(3) Push out feed pawl pin. Remove feed pawl and feed pawl spring.
(4) With point of bullet inserted between extractor cam and extractor spring, prise extractor spring away from extractor cam, remove extractor spring.

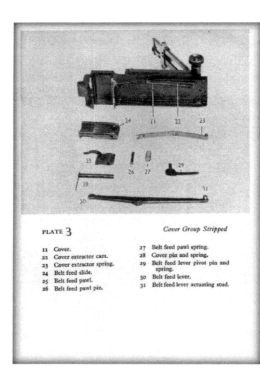

PLATE 3   *Cover Group Stripped*

11	Cover.	27	Belt feed pawl spring.
22	Cover extractor cam.	28	Cover pin and spring.
23	Cover extractor spring.	29	Belt feed lever pivot pin and spring.
24	Belt feed slide.	30	Belt feed lever.
25	Belt feed pawl.	31	Belt feed lever actuating stud.
26	Belt feed pawl pin.		

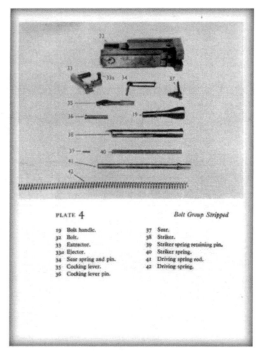

PLATE 4   *Bolt Group Stripped*

19	Bolt handle.	37	Sear.
32	Bolt.	38	Striker.
33	Extractor.	39	Striker spring retaining pin.
33a	Ejector.	40	Striker spring.
34	Sear spring and pin.	41	Driving spring rod.
35	Cocking lever.	42	Driving spring.
36	Cocking lever pin.		

SHOCK ABSORBER GROUP

(Stripping of this group is rarely needed except in case of repair)
(1) Unscrew adjusting screw.
(2) Remove adjusting screw plunger and the adjusting screw plunger spring.
(3) Remove buffer discs (there are 16 of these), buffer plug, buffer ring and buffer plate.

BOLT

(1) Remove extractor.
(2) With cocking lever in rearmost position insert point of bullet into trigger notch of sear. Press sear downwards, releasing striker.
(3) Push out cocking lever pin.
(4) Remove cocking lever.
(5) With point of bullet push sear spring to left side of bolt.
(6) Remove sear downwards. Replace sear spring in original position, sear spring and sear spring pin can now be removed upwards.
(7) Tilt bolt upwards and striker and spring assembly will fall out.
(8) To remove striker spring, push out striker spring retaining pin, taking care not to allow spring to fly out.
(9) Remove driving rod and driving spring by turning driving rod notch to horizontal position and withdrawing spring and rod under control. (The driving spring is long, and care should be taken not to kink it. A quick withdrawal of driving rod will prevent this.)

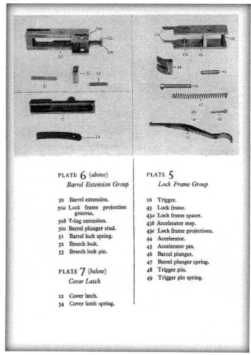

PLATE 6 (above)
Barrel Extension Group

50	Barrel extension.
50a	Lock frame projection grooves.
50b	T-lug extension.
50c	Barrel plunger stud.
51	Barrel lock spring.
52	Breech lock.
53	Breech lock pin.

PLATE 7 (below)
Cover Latch

12	Cover latch.
54	Cover latch spring.

PLATE 5
Lock Frame Group

16	Trigger.
43	Lock frame.
43a	Lock frame spacer.
43b	Accelerator stop.
43c	Lock frame projections.
44	Accelerator.
45	Accelerator pin.
46	Barrel plunger.
47	Barrel plunger spring.
48	Trigger pin.
49	Trigger pin spring.

LOCK FRAME

(1) Push out trigger pin and remove trigger pin spring.
(2) Remove trigger.
(3) Push out accelerator pin, remove accelerator.
(4) Push out barrel plunger head pin from slit in left side plate of lock frame. (Take care to keep spring under control whilst doing this.) Barrel plunger and barrel plunger spring may now be withdrawn.

BARREL EXTENSION

(1) Push out breech lock pin and remove breech lock.
(2) Insert nose of bullet under forward shoulder of barrel lock spring and prise it forwards and remove it.

COVER LATCH

Pull latch smartly to rear, removing it from its seat, remove cover latch spring.

TO REASSEMBLE GROUPS

Each group should be reassembled in detail in the reverse order in which it has been stripped.

HEAD SPACE ADJUSTMENT

This must be done before reassembly. By the term " head space " is meant the distance between the face of the bolt and the base of the barrel. When correctly adjusted the face of the bolt should firmly support the base of the cartridge in position in the chamber when the gun is fired.

TOO MUCH HEAD SPACE (*i.e., adjustment is too loose*)

The base of the cartridge will not be firmly supported by the bolt face and when cartridge is discharged a separated case or a bulged case may result, causing difficult extraction.

TOO LITTLE HEAD SPACE (*i.e., adjustment is too tight*)

(This can sometimes be detected by ear when the gun is being fired, as the bolt on its return to its forward position will give a dead sound effect.)

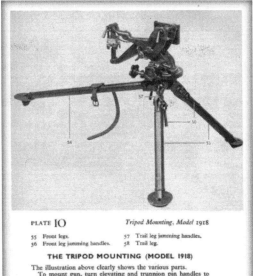

PLATE 10   *Tripod Mounting, Model 1918*

55 Front legs.
56 Front leg jamming handles.
57 Trail leg jamming handles.
58 Trail leg.

THE TRIPOD MOUNTING (MODEL 1918)

The illustration above clearly shows the various parts.
To mount gun, turn elevating and trunnion pin handles to vertical position and withdraw. Place gun on tripod so that its mounting holes coincide with the trunnion bracket holes and elevating bracket holes. Push in trunnion pin, and turn trunnion pin to lock ; reinsert elevating pin and turn to lock.
Loosen pintle lock handle, and adjust traversing dial to a horizontal position. Tighten pintle lock handle, making certain the teeth on the locking plunger are in firm engagement with the toothed sector. Place ammunition box in bracket situated on left side of tripod.

21

PLATE 13   *The Firing Position (Gun mounted on 1918 Tripod)*

BEFORE FIRING

PREREQUISITES

(1) Ammunition loaded into belts.
(2) Ammunition boxes.
(3) Water condenser filled with water.
(4) Combination tool.
(5) Cleaning rod.
(6) Separated case extractor.
(7) Spare parts.
NOTE: 4, 5, 6 and 7 are essential for possible stoppages.

(A) All mechanism must be clean, free from dust, dirt and fluff, and thoroughly oiled.
(B) When assembled, rear barrel packing should provide a smooth watertight fit in trunnion block ; copious oiling or greasing remedies slight water leak here.

26

These pages are just a few of the 35 page manual. As stated previously, men were put through intense battle situation training due to so many men losing their lives in WWI by not being trained sufficiently before being sent into battle. Martin mentioned that though he hated doing things over and over and over again, he was very glad they had as they did not have time to think things through during battle, and he was ever so grateful for what he called:

"TEDIOUS, MONOTONIOUS TRAINING!"

LETTER 6

Pvt Martin Paulson
Co A 88 Inf Tng Bn
Camp Roberts, Calif

Mrs. A. Furford
Rt.1 Box 352
Kent, Wash

Postage: Free
Nov 30, 1943 3:30 PM
Camp Roberts, California

Dear Ruth Curly & George   November 30, 1943

I meant to write sooner but I got the same old excuse. We didn't eaven get Sunday off this week and we also worked Thanksgiving. They sure gave us a good meal on Thanksgiving though. We got all the turkey and dressing we wanted and we eaven got pumpkin pie with ice cream on it. We get ice cream about 3 times a week and I am telling you it is sure good. It tastes like the kind we used to get.

We started shooting the Machine gun today. We have been practicing for a week without amunition and today they gave us amunition. I got a good enough score to make sharp shooter today so I should be able to make it when I fire for record. They have been having the guys shoot 22 shells in the machine gun, but we get the regular amunition. It sure is a lot of fun shooting it. By the way there is a lot of difference between the way we shoot them and they shoot them in shows. You shoot them in short burst and you change the position with dials. They shoot about half as fast so I thought they would.

Everything and everyone is talking about the War with Germany being over pretty soon and everything around here points to it. They have been begging everyone around her to join the air force and now no one can transfer in to it. They used to have only 13 weeks of basic training and now we get 17 weeks. They used to give guys in the machine gun outfits just enough practise with a rifle to walk guard. Now we get as much as a rifle man. There are all kinds of things like that they are changing. Maybe they aren't good signs but it means that they arn't in any hurry for us and they have more supplies to give us and everything. Eaven the officers say that the guys that know whats going on say Germany is just about out of the War. Another thing is we have a gas called, well I forgot, but anyway the Germans and Japs cant make it and it is the only kind of gas that gas masks wont protect you from. That is why they wont use gas unless they cant see any other way out.

Tell George I will bring a machine gun home with me for him. I bet he would sure get a kick out of one of them.   *Martin*

PS. Olson is in the same regiment as I am but he is in Radio now. They picked a few guys out of our outfit for Radio, and he was one of them.
I won $16 playing poker last Sunday so I went down & got my picture taken. I will send one as soon as I get them.

1942 Ad for
Safe-T Cones Ice Cream
Uniform Men Military World

Ice Cream! Who doesn't love Ice Cream? Ice cream became an American symbol during World War II (Mussolini banned it in Italy for that same reason). Each branch of the military tried to outdo the others in serving ice cream to its troops. Ice cream, was still available to civilians, but it was limited by stringent rules and conditions. The government was forced to reduce the milk and sugar available for making ice cream. Sugar was rationed at 80 points! Shortages were common and many neighborhood soda parlors could only get ice cream intermittently.

Ice cream was great for troop morale and in 1943 the U.S. Armed Forces were the world's largest ice cream manufacturers![18] During World War II, for every pilot rescued from the water by an escort destroyer, aircraft carriers would give the smaller ship a twenty-gallon reward of ice cream. The United Press reported that the Army procurement priorities rated ice cream, candy, soft drinks, chewing gum, and tobacco products as essential for maintaining troop morale.[19]

In 1945, the Navy commissioned the world's first

WWII Roadside Billboard

"floating ice cream parlor" for service in the Western Pacific. The parlor was a refrigerated concrete barge built at a cost of over one million dollars that was capable of producing ten gallons of ice cream every seven seconds. The barge had no engine of its own, but was towed around by tugs and other ships. Its sole

---

[18]   http://www.almanac.com/content/history-ice-cream-who-invented-it
[19]   http://whatscookingamerica.net/History/IceCream/IceCreamHistory.htm

responsibility was to produce ice cream for US sailors in the Pacific region.

Navy's floating ice cream parlor

America also celebrated its war victory with ice cream. Dairy product rationing was lifted in 1946 and Americans consumed over 20 quarts of ice cream per person that year![20]

As a teen, Irv Robbins (partner of current Baskin Robbins Ice Cream) worked in his father's ice cream store. And during World War II, Burt (Burton "Burt" Baskin) was a Lieutenant in the U.S. Navy and produced ice cream for his fellow troops. When the war was over, the two entrepreneurs were eager to capitalize on America's love of ice cream. [21]

Commander Joseph C. Clifton returning from a mission, 1944 eating ice cream from a huge container

As you can see from his letter, Martin mastered the many parts of the machine gun to score well enough to make him feel confident that he would make

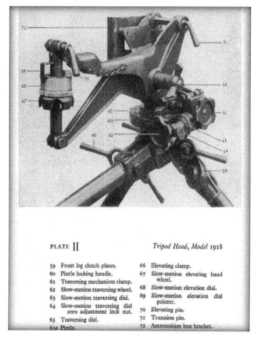

sharp shooter when he fired for record. *The beginnings of the making of a remarkable man!* But then again, there are those that would say *it was the remarkable young man that conquered the challenge!* He comments about the difference between the way they would shoot machine guns in movies and the way they are trained by shooting the machine gun in short bursts and the change of the position with dials (shown in picture). Note the number definitions, especially #62-69 of the actual Army Training Manual. Imagine trying to concentrate on this in battle with artillery shells falling all around you.

Martin sounds excited about all the talk of *"the war with Germany being over pretty soon and everything around here points to it."* One must remember that

PLATE II   *Tripod Head, Model 1918*

59 Front leg clutch plates.
60 Pintle locking handle.
61 Traversing mechanism clamp.
62 Slow-motion traversing wheel.
63 Slow-motion traversing dial.
64 Slow-motion traversing dial zero adjustment lock nut.
65 Traversing dial.
66a Pintle.
66 Elevating clamp.
67 Slow-motion elevating hand wheel.
68 Slow-motion elevation dial.
69 Slow-motion elevation dial pointer.
70 Elevating pin.
71 Trunnion pin.
72 Ammunition box bracket.

[20]http://www.idfa.org/news--views/media-kits/ice-cream/the-history-of-ice-cream/
[21] http://www.baskinrobbins.com/content/baskinrobbins/en/aboutus/history.html

communication was not at all like it is today. No immediate news of world events, or even national events was available back then. As we know now, the war with Germany didn't end until 1945. Below is a time line of U.S. involvement in military events in the war effort from *around the globe* in 1943.[22]

Russia had been at war with Germany since 1941 and was the largest offensive against Germany in 1943. The resources and equipment Canada, the US, and Britain sent to the USSR was invaluable, but at the end of the day, it was Soviet refusal to be defeated and their sacrifice in blood to hold out against the Germans that turned the tide. Below you will see the U.S. decides in December 1943 to join the offensive against Germany. One thing is for sure, it required nearly the entire globe to combine and defeat the Axis Powers (Germany, Italy & Japan). Note below that Italy turned and declared war on Germany in October.

January 2, 1943 – Australian and U.S. Army forces under MacArthur fight back the Japanese at Buna in New Guinea.

January 14, 1943 – The Casablanca Conference between the U.S. and Britain begins. Roosevelt and Churchill agree that Germany must surrender unconditionally, and plan the Allied Invasion of Sicily.

January 31, 1943 – Over 90,000 German troops at Stalingrad surrender to the Soviets. It is a significant turning point in the war against Germany.

February 8, 1943 – U.S. troops complete the capture of Guadalcanal from the Japanese.

April 19, 1943 – The Warsaw Ghetto Uprising begins after German troops attempt to deport the ghetto's last surviving Jews. About 750 Jews fought back the Germans for almost a month.

May 11, 1943 – The Trident Conference between the U.S. And Britain begins. Roosevelt and Churchill decide to delay the Allied invasion of France and in its place plan the Allied invasion of Italy. In Alaska, U.S. troops land on Attu in the Aleutian Islands to retake it from the Japanese.

May 12, 1943 – Axis forces in North Africa surrender.

This photo is one of the best-known pictures of World War II. The original German caption reads: "Forcibly pulled out of dug-outs." The boy in the picture might be Tsvi Nussbaum who survived the Holocaust.

Photo from Jürgen Stroop's report to Heinrich Himmler - May 1943

---

[22]http://en.wikipedia.org/wiki/Timeline_of_World_War_II_%281943%29

July 1, 1943 – The U.S. government begins directly withholding income tax from wages.

July 10, 1943 – Over 160,000 Allied troops land in Sicily, beginning Operation Husky.

July 24, 1943 – The Allies begin bombing Hamburg.

July 25, 1943 – Benito Mussolini's fascist government is overthrown in Italy. The new Italian government begins peace talks.

August 1, 1943 – The Allies bomb the Ploesti oil fields in Romania.

August 11, 1943 – The Quebec Conference between the U.S. and Britain begins.

August 15, 1943 – U.S. troops retake Kiska Island in the Aleutians.

August 17, 1943 – Operation Husky, the Allied invasion of Sicily, is successfully concluded when American troops take Messina.

September 3, 1943 – British troops land on mainland Italy, beginning the Allied campaign in Italy. American troops land six days later. The new Italian government formally surrenders.

September 10, 1943 – German troops occupy Rome. Mussolini soon declares himself the head of a new fascist Italian government in German-occupied northern Italy.

October 13, 1943 – Italy declares war on Germany.

November 1, 1943 – U.S. Marines land on Bougainville Island in the Solomon's.

November 20, 1943 – U.S. Army troops land on Makin Island in the Gilberts. The next day, U.S. Marines land on Tarawa. Within four days, both islands were secured, but at the cost of thousands of casualties.

November 8, 1943 – The Teheran Conference between the U.S., Britain, and the USSR begins. Roosevelt, Churchill, and Stalin meet together for the first me.

December 1, 1943 – The Teheran Conference between the U.S., Britain, and the USSR is successfully concluded. Roosevelt, Churchill, and Stalin agree that the Western Allies would invade France in June 1944 and that when it began the USSR would launch a new offensive from the east.

The Tehran conference (28 Nov 1943): Left to right: General Secretary of the Communist Party Joseph Stalin, President Franklin D. Roosevelt of the United States, and Prime Minister Winston Churchill of the United Kingdom.

December 24, 1943 – Dwight Eisenhower is named supreme commander of Allied Expeditionary Forces.

Martin mentions "Olson" in this letter. Olson was from the same hometown neighborhood. Also, Martin mentions winning $16 playing poker and with the money *"went down and got my picture taken."* He doesn't remember that particular picture. The picture below is of him as Private.

Did young George get his machine gun? George is 75 years old now and he does not recollect getting a machine gun.... and he doesn't think his Mom would have let him have one! He says Uncle Martin was right, he sure would have gotten a kick out of getting one! Kids are kids and like those that loved playing cowboys and Indians, kids in war time played "war."

General Dwight D. Eisenhower

Private Martin A. Paulson

LETTER 7

Mr. A. Furford
Rt 1 Box 352
Kent, Wash

Pvt Martin Paulson
Co A 88 Inf Tng. Bn.
Camp Roberts, Calif

Postage: Free
Posted: Dec 7, 1943 3:30 PM
Camp Roberts, California

Dear Ruth & Curly,

Here I am on guard again. I was all set to go to Los Angles, I had my pass and everything and then they gave me guard duty. This time I rated a 24 hour post too. There hasnt been much excitement. All we got is one AWL that the MP picked up in Los Angles. You were asking about the stabbing that happened the last time I was on guard. One fellow came in drunk and started making a lot of noise after the lights were out. All the fellows started telling him to shut up. He got mad and pulled a knife and started working on one guy. He cut him in the stomach and back 3 or 4 times pretty bad. They had to give him a transfusion to save his life. I got there in time to march the prisoner to the edge of my post and holler for the Corpral of the guard to come and get him. After they got him in the guard house he made so much noise no one could sleep all night.

Next week we start learning how to shoot the mortar. I dont think I am going to like them very much because they are heavier to carry then the machine gun. The trypod on a machine gun weighs 51 pounds and you get it with a full field pack.

I met that Gestine or something like that, anyway Mrs. Matsons boy down here the other day. I seen him in a Px and I thought it looked like him so I asked him. He sure has gotten big since I saw him. He is getting a discharge on account of his knee he said.

I was on guard during dinner today so I had to go over after they had finished. All I could get was all the chicken and sweet spud I wanted, a quart of milk and a quart of ice cream (I mean good ice cream).

Well thats all I can think of.

Martin

Martin describes an incident mentioned in a previous letter of a soldier who stabbed another while he was on guard duty. Research into AWOL and Desertion during WWII produced some interesting information, and provides an answer to the necessity and importance of doing GUARD DUTY during basic training. Moral, discipline and war life begins in Basic Training.

What is desertion and how does it differ from being AWOL (Absence without Leave)? A military member who is ordered to be on a ship, aircraft, or deployed with a unit at a certain date or time and fails to show up is charged of either being AWOL or desertion. Whether it was intentional or by neglect the possible punishment is much harder if the member missed his orders on purpose.

Absence without leave commonly called AWOL or usually called Unauthorized Absence simply means *not being where you have to be at the time when you were supposed to be there*. If being late for work and missing a medical appointment is a violation of rules so is disappearing for a few days or months or years. Maximum possible punishments depend on the circumstances of absence.

Desertion on the other hand may result in the death penalty especially during the time of war. Desertion carries greater punishment compared to being AWOL. It is believed that being absent without authority for 30 days or more can be changed from AWOL to desertion. The main difference between the two offenses is that one is the intent to remain away permanently. If one intends to return under military control one day, then he is guilty of being AWOL. On the contrary, if a person is absent even for just one minute and captured, then he can be charged with desertion, if prosecution is able to prove that the member intends to stay away permanently from the military. [23]

Camp Roberts close combat training

Some aspects of basic training are psychological. The reasoning is that if a recruit cannot be relied upon to obey orders and follow instructions in routine matters it is unlikely that he or she will be reliable in a combat situation where there may be a strong urge to disobey orders or flee. The recruit who cannot work as part of a team (the unit) and comply with the routine tasks of basic training, therefore, is more likely to place him/herself, comrades, and the mission in jeopardy. A recruit who agrees to serve in a combat unit will experience a unique level of 'agreement' among participants, termed unit cohesion, that cannot be equaled with any other human organization as every team member's life may depend on the

---

[23] http://www.milpages.com/blog/460 Posted by: militaryone on July 13, 2011 in Military Concerns

actions of the recruit to his right or left. This unit cohesion is fully developed in Special Forces and commando units.[24]

There were thousands of ordinary criminals in ETO (*European Theater Of Operations*). Hundreds of them were caught, tried by court-martial, and sentenced to the stockade or, in the case of rape or murder, to death by firing squad. Sixty-five men were ordered shot. Eisenhower had to pass the final judgment. In sixteen cases he changed the sentence to life in the stockade; forty-nine men were shot.

Desertion was a serious problem on the ETO, partly because it was relatively easy to do in Europe, partly because of the never-ending nature of the combat, partly because the Army tried to get deserters back to their outfits and give them a second chance, meaning deserters could figure there wouldn't be any punishment if they were caught (there were no desertions on the Pacific islands)

In November 1944. Glenn Gray, on counter-intelligence duty, found a deserter in a French woods. The lad was from the Pennsylvania Mountains, he was accustomed to camping out, he had been there a couple of weeks living on venison, and intended to stay until the war ended. "All the men I knew and trained with have been killed," the deserter told Gray. "I'm lonely.... the shells seem to come closer all the time and I can't stand them."

He begged Gray to leave him. Gray refused, said he would have to turn him in, but promised he would not be punished. The deserter said he knew that; he bitterly predicted "they" would simply put him back into the line again -- which was exactly what happened when Gray brought him in. [25]

Martin mentions they will begin learning to shoot the mortar. In a future letter he indicates it is the 81 Mortar. The mortar is the infantry's own artillery, ready to go at a moment's notice at the order of the unit commander. The M1 81mm mortar was the largest weapon in the arsenal of the U.S. WWII infantry battalion. It provided the battalion commander with a powerful and flexible indirect fire capability. Sometimes called "infantry artillery," or "hip pocket artillery," mortars were capable of quickly laying down heavy barrages. These could stop

U.S. Soldiers fire an M1 mortar at Massa in Italy during WWII

enemy attacks under the worst conditions. Able to fire at high angles, mortars could

---

[24] http://en.wikipedia.org/wiki/Recruit_training

[25] http://www.worldwar2history.info/Army/deserters.html

fire at targets in defilade [a formation or position is "in enfilade" if weapons fire can be directed along its longest axis], either under direction of a forward observer, or firing off map coordinates. In the WWII Pacific campaigns, these weapons became an important part of the battalion's firepower, especially since they could be man-packed into positions that were inaccessible to artillery.

As an infantry weapon, the M1 mortar could be broken down into three separate loads. These were the barrel, weighing 44.5 lbs., the base plate, weighing 45 lbs., and the bipod, weighing 46.5 lbs. The M4 collimator sight fitted into a bracket on the bipod yoke, providing accurate laying for elevation and deflection. Aiming stakes were supplied in the basic issue items for each mortar, enabling the crew to lay their weapon on target for indirect fire. [26, 27]

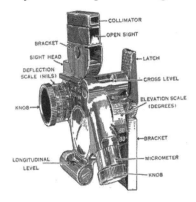

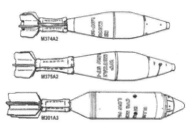

81mm high explosive, white phosphorus and illumination mortar rounds

The M4 collimator sight. The six was also used on the M2 60mm mortar. By laying the sight on aiming stakes, the mortar squad could fire indirect missions.

The open sight allowed the squad to fire direct lay missions.

U.S. Army Photo

Weight: 136 pounds
Length of tube: 49.5 inches
Elevation: 40 to 80 degrees
Rate of fire (normal): 18 rpm
Rate of fire (maximum): 30 to 35 rpm
Range: 100 to 3,290 yards

81mm MORTAR, M1, in firing position

26   http://www.ima-usa.com/81mm-mortar-parts-set-u-s-wwii.html
27   http://www.ww2gyrene.org/weapons_81mm_mortar.htm

Below is a list of Mortars used across the globe during World War II.[28]

Allied Nations:
United States:
– 60mm M2
– 81mm M1
Soviet Union:
– 50mm RM39/40
– 82mm BM41/BM43
Britain:
– 2-in Mortar
– 3-in Mortar
Axis Nations:
Germany:
– 5cm Granatwerfer 36 (Gr.W. 36)
• 50-mm Light Mortar - U.S. intel comparison of German 5cm mortar to U.S. 60-mm mortar (*IB, 1/43*)
• 5-cm Light Mortar, Model 365
– 8cm Granatwerfer 34 (Gr.W. 34)
• 8-cm Heavy Mortar, Model 34-8
– 12cm Granatwerfer 42 (Gr.W. 42)
– Other German Mortars:
• German 100-mm Mortar - Nebelwerfer, smoke and HE mortar (*T&TT, 5/43*)
• New Type 105-mm Mortar - Brief report on "new-type" 105-mm mortar (*T&TT, 5/43*)
• German 200-mm Spigot Mortar - Ladungswerfer, engineer weapon (*T&TT, 9/43*)
Italy:
– 45mm Model 35
– 81mm Model 35
• Italian 81-mm Mortar - Italian Model 35 compared to US 81-mm (*IB, 1/43*)
Japan:
– 50mm Model 89
– 81mm Model 97/99
– 90mm Model 94/97
– Other Japanese Mortars
• New Weapons Captured at Omoc - Japanese 120-mm mortar and 81-mm barrage mortar (*IB, 3/45*)
• Japanese 150-mm Mortar - Model 97 150-mm mortar with illustrations (*IB, 2/45*)

In his last letter Martin stated the U.S. "*had a gas*," but he could not recall what they called it. During WWII the use of poison gas was a very real fear as poison gas had been used in WWI, and many expected that it would be used in

---

[28] http://www.lonesentry.com/panzer/mortars.html

Gas mask drills

WWII. As a result people in Britain were issued gas masks and gas mask drills became a routine.

The gases used in WWI were crude but effective. In fact, technically, many of them were not gases but minute solid particles suspended in air like the spray from an aerosol can. Regardless of whether they were a true gas or not, they brought very great fear to the front line. By 1939, these gases had been refined and had the potential for being far more effective. Fighter planes had markedly changed by 1939, so it was believed a military's ability to deliver poison gas was a great threat.

The gases used to such effect in WWI were still potential weapons in WWII. *Mustard gas* had been used by the Italians in their campaign in Abyssinia from 1935 to 1936. *Chlorine* was a potential weapon but it had been overtaken in effectiveness by *diphosgene* and *carbonyl chloride*. Both of these were choking gases that damaged the respiratory system. *Tear gases* were also available – a more potent version of it was *Adamsite* which not only causes the classic symptoms of tear gas but also causes respiratory problems, vomiting, and general nausea.

German soldier in WWI with dogs equipped with gas masks

Mustard gas blistered the skin causing extreme pain. It was also capable of soaking through material onto skin beneath a uniform. A more severe version of it was *Lewisite* which had the same effect on skin but also caused respiratory problems and pneumonia.

Far more deadly than these gases were *cyanide, carbon monoxide* and *cyanogen chloride*. All of these impede the ability of blood to absorb oxygen. Unable to gain oxygen, the body quickly shuts down. "*Death is rapid, sure and relatively painless*" (Brian Ford).

Nerve gas was also available to governments in WWII. One of the first to be developed was *Tabun* by German scientists. Nerve gases attack the body's nervous system. The symptoms are nausea, vomiting, muscular twitching, convulsions, cessation of breathing, and death. *Sarin* and *Soman* were also developed as nerve gases. Of the three nerve gases named here, *Soman* was the most deadly. From inhalation, it is only a matter of seconds before a victim goes into convulsions. The US Army Manual TM 3-215 estimated that a victim of *Soman* would be dead within two minutes.

There is no doubt that most protagonists in WWII had stockpiles of poison gas. By 1945, the Germans had 7,000 tons of *Sarin* alone – enough to kill the occupants of 30 cities the size of Paris. The Americans also had sizable quantities of poison gases stockpiled. Britain experimented with *anthrax* on remote Scottish islands to see its impact on the animal population there. All countries that possessed poison gas in any form also had the potential to deliver it on an enemy.

With such potency and the ability to change the course of a battle why wasn't poison gas used in WWII – even as a last resource? It would appear certain that the *fear of retaliation* was the reason and the *fear that the enemy may well have*

developed a poison gas more virulent that anything the other side had. So in a war where atomic weapons were used, napalm, phosphorous, unrestricted submarine warfare etc., where civilians were seen by some as legitimate targets, no side was prepared to risk using a weapon that had been so feared in WWI. [29] [30]

Picture from WWI of actual gas battlefield

Below is an excerpt from a letter detailing the work Fr Doyle had to undertake in his work towards the end of April, 1916 in WWI. After reading this, you will understand the fear nations had in using gas in warfare.

Fr Doyle in uniform

"On paper every man with a helmet was as safe as I was from gas poisoning. But now it is evident many of the men despised the 'old German gas,' some did not bother putting on their helmets, others had torn theirs, and others like myself had thrown them aside or lost them. From early morning till late at night I worked my way from trench to trench single handed the first day, with three regiments to look after, and could get no help. Many men died before I could reach them; others seemed just to live till I anointed them, and were gone before I passed back. There they lay, scores of them (we lost 800, nearly all from gas) in the bottom of the trench, in every conceivable posture of human agony: the clothes torn off their bodies in a vain effort to

[29] http://en.wikipedia.org/wiki/Chemical_weapons_in_World_War_I
[30] http://www.firstworldwar.com/weaponry/gas.htm

breathe; while from end to end of that valley of death came one low unceasing moan from the lips of brave men fighting and struggling for life.

I don't think you will blame me when I tell you that more than once the words of Absolution stuck in my throat, and the tears splashed down on the patient, suffering faces of my poor boys as I leant down to anoint them. One young soldier seized my two hands and covered them with kisses; another looked up and said: 'Oh! Father I can die happy now, sure I'm not afraid of death or anything else since I have seen you.' Don't you think, dear father, that the little sacrifice made in coming out here has already been more than repaid, and if you have suffered a little anxiety on my account, you have at least the consolation of knowing that I have, through God's goodness, been able to comfort many a poor fellow and perhaps to open the gates of Heaven for them".[31]

After these stressful days were ended, Fr Doyle was given a few days' rest, and he was able to remove and change his clothes for the first time in over two weeks! Such was his exhaustion from serving the soldiers that he slept for 13 hours straight on his first night of rest.

Martin closes his letter with the food he got after missing the regular dinner time. Sounds like he hit gold! Again, ice cream is mentioned. Not just ice cream, but as Martin says, *"I mean good ice cream."* Can you imagine the appetites the men developed from all the training, drills, details, etc.? The enlistees were also extensively trained to eat the not-to-delicious *Ration Food* for battle situations. It was the military's policy to provide excellent food for the enlistees' at all military *training* institutions during WWII, and this included an abundance of *ice cream!*

---

[31] http://fatherdoyle.com/2011/04/

LETTER 8

Front & Inside of Christmas card

Pvt Martin Paulson	Mr & Mrs A Paulson	Postage: Free
Co A 88 Inf Tng Bn	Rt 1 Box 352	Posted: Dec 10, 1943 11:30 AM
Camp Roberts, Calif	Kent, Wash.	Camp Roberts, Calif.

LETTER 9

Martin hand wrote his Camp
Roberts address on the back of
this Western Union request.

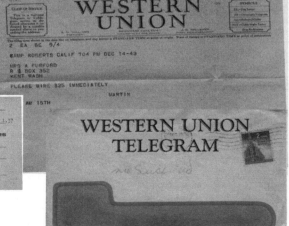

Auburn, Washington 12/15/43
Received from: Ruth D. Furford
$ 25.00 and 1.37
For: Telegraphic transfer to Pvt Martin Paulson, Camp Roberts, California
Note Postage: 2 cents

LETTER 10

Camp Roberts Letterhead Insignia

Pvt Martin Paulson
Co A 88 Inf Tng Bn
Camp Roberts, Calif

Mrs A. Furford
Rt 1 Box 352
Kent Wash.

Postage: Air Mail 6 cents
Posted: Dec 15, 1943 11 AM
Camp Roberts, Calif

Dear Ruth Curly & George,   *Dec ~~November~~ 14,*

I started writing one letter to you tonight. They came around and gave me a pass so I had to go down and wire for some money. I was down to Los Angles last weekend and I had so much fun that I am going back to take over where I left off. I have sure been lucky. I have been able to get a pass every week I havent had any guard or detail. I was going to buy some presents but I never did get around to. Ruth, could I get you to draw some money out and buy George, Curly, Sharon, Dad, and Bert a present. I cant find anything around here and it will be too late Saturday.

I saw the Lux Theater. They were doing 5 Graves to Cairo with Franchot Tone & Ann Baxter. We also went to the Hollywood Canteen. We saw Jane Wyman, Bob Cunningham, Cecil D DeMill, Pincky ᵖ Thomas, and a bunch more I cant remember right now.

I finished firing the 81 M. Mortar last week so now I am a mortar man. It cost $11 for every shell we shot so boy we sure shot up a lot of money shooting them.

I got the package from you the other day and thanks a lot. All the guys up here want me to open it because they think there is something to eat in it.

I am glad to hear George still likes school because as long as he likes it you wont have any trouble getting him to stay in school. I bet if he started not liking it he would be awful independent.

By the way I must have forgotten to tell you that Mrs. Matson's boy is getting a discharge.

Well thats all I can think of right now. I will be lucky if I get a chance to come home before next spring.

                                     Martin

PS. I sent a picture of myself to you.

Prior to this letter Martin had sent Ruth and her family a Christmas card and also sent a Western Union Telegram requesting Ruth to send $25. He also is requesting Ruth to purchase some Christmas presents he was not able to purchase. He mentions George, Curly, Sharon, Dad, and Bert. You have met George (Martin's nephew) and Curly (Ruth's husband). Martin's Dad is Adolph Manuel Paulson. Bert is married to Martin's sister, Myrtle. Sharon is Martin's niece (sister Carnie's [Karen] daughter).

Sharon Bauder &   *Arvid (Curly)*   *Adolph Paulson*   *Bert & Myrtle Rae*
George Furford   *Furford 1938*   *1944*   *1937*
1943

Camp Roberts - field firing the mortar

The above picture of *Mortar field firing* is from a Camp Roberts training brochure Martin had in his Photo Album. Martin said in his letter that each shell they shot cost $11!

Lux Radio Theater was broadcast on NBC Blue Network from 1934-1935, CBS from 1935-1954 and NBC from 1954-1955. The show was moved from NY to Hollywood in 1936. Initially, the series adapted Broadway plays during its first two seasons before it began adapting films. These hour-long radio programs were *performed live before studio audiences.* It became the most popular dramatic anthology series on radio, broadcast for more than 20 years and continued on television as the Lux Video Theatre through most of the 1950s. **Cecil B. DeMille** took over as the host on June 1, 1936, continuing until January 22, 1945. On several occasions, usually when he was out of town, he was temporarily replaced by various celebrities, including Leslie Howard and Edward Arnold.

Lux Radio Theater strove to feature as many of the original stars of the original stage and film productions as possible, usually paying them $5,000 an appearance. In 1936, when sponsor *Leve*r *Brothers* (who made "Lux" soap and detergent) moved the show from New York City to Hollywood, the program began to emphasize adaptations of films rather than plays. The first *Lux* film adaptation was *The Legionnaire and the Lady*, with Marlene Dietrich and Clark Gable, based on the film Morocco. That was followed by a *Lux* adaptation of *The Thin Man*, featuring the movie's stars, Myrna Loy and William Powell.[32]

Five Graves to Cairo[33]

Film poster

Directed by: Billy Wilder
Produced by: B. G. DeSylva
Written by: Biro (play), Brackett, & Wilder
Starring: Franchot Tone, Anne Baxter, Akim Tamiroff, & Erichvon Stroheim
Music: Miklos Rozsa
Cinematography: John F. Seitz
Editing by: Doane Harrison
Distributed by: Paramount Pictures
Release date: May 4, 1943
Running time: 96 min.
Country: United States
Language: English
budget: $855,000 (estimated)

[32]http://en.wikipedia.org/wiki/Lux_Radio_Theater
[33]http://en.wikipedia.org/wiki/Five_Graves_to_Cairo

During WW II, *THE HOLLYWOOD CANTEEN* was set up to help keep up the morale of young soldiers. It operated at 1451 Cahuenga Boulevard in Hollywood,

California between October 3, 1942 and November 22, 1945 (Thanksgiving Day) as a club offering food, dancing and entertainment for servicemen, usually on their way overseas. Even though the majority of visitors were U.S servicemen, the Canteen was open to servicemen of allied countries as well as women in all branches of service. The serviceman's ticket for admission was his uniform and everything at the Canteen was free of charge.

Jane Wyman signs autographs at the Hollywood Canteen 1943

The driving forces behind its creation were *Bette Davis* and *John Garfield*, along with composer *Jules Stein, President of Music*

Bette Davis serving service men at the Canteen

Corporation of America, who headed up the finance committee. Bette Davis devoted an enormous amount of time and energy to the project and served as its president. The various guilds and unions of the entertainment industry donated the labor and money for the building renovations. The Canteen was operated and staffed completely by volunteers from the entertainment industry. By the time the Canteen opened its doors, over 3000 stars, players, directors, producers, grips, dancers, musicians, singers, writers, technicians, wardrobe attendants, hair stylists, agents, stand-ins, publicists, secretaries, and allied craftsmen of radio and screen had registered as volunteers.

Glamorous stars volunteered to wait on tables, cook in the kitchen and clean up. On September 15, 1943 the one millionth guest walked through the door of the Hollywood Canteen. The lucky soldier, Sgt. Carl Bell, received a kiss from *Betty Grable*.

A Hall of Honor at the Hollywood Canteen had a wall of photos which honored the film actors who served in the military. Most of those actors, while on shore leave, came out to help the Canteen. [34, 35]

Jane Wyman, Marlene Dietrich, Bob Hope, Mervin LeRoy, Bette Davis & Joan Leslie looking at the Hall of Honor at the Hollywood Canteen

---

[34] http://rustyfrank.com/beso/beso-0808.asp

[35] http://martinturnbull.wordpress.com/2012/01/28/hollywood-canteen-where-the-soldiers-met-the-stars/

HOLLYWOOD CANTEEN, HOLLYWOOD, CALIFORNIA

*A Sunday afternoon at the Hollywood
Canteen*

Hollywood Canteen Postcard

Martin appreciates very much the package received from home...and the other fellows would love to have had him open it right away! Think they miss home cooking?!!

No information was found on Mrs. Matson's son. He was not listed in the names of those whom Martin trained with so he must have been in another Company.

Again, we are not sure what picture Martin sent home, but you are sure to enjoy this picture of Martin in his younger years with his Mother and sisters.

Rakel (Mother), Carnie, Martin, Ruth & Myrtle Paulson
Note the 1922 Studebaker!

LETTER 11

Pvt Martin Paulson
Co A 88 Inf Tng Bn
Camp Roberts, Calif

Mr. A. Furford
Rt 1 Box 352
Kent, Wash.

Postage: Free
Dec 26, 1943 3:30 PM
Camp Roberts,
California

Dear Ruth, Curly & George,   *December 25, 1943*

They have been telling us ever since we got here that this is the toughest training center in the country and I sure know they arn't fooling. We get more training in 17 weeks here now than they used to get in a years training. Im in better shape now than I have <u>ever</u> been in. We always work from 12 to 20 hours every day. And I mean work. We have the toughest platoon in the company and so the other day the other 3 platoons thought they were going to take us. They charged us without any of us knowing anything about it in a free for all. Even with 3 to 1 we took care of ourself.

We shot the famous Bazooka the other day and I am telling you it is really something. No one knows what is in the charge, but any tank or anything you hit with it is defeantely put out of action. It can be fired effectively, I mean with accuracy, up to 300 yards and it will penatrate steel 6 inches thick. They sure have taught us how to fire almost every weapon in the Army. The other day we fired anti-tank gernades with a rifle. They kick so hard that you cant put the rifle to your shoulder and after you fire it it is so smoking you cant see your target. They have the same charge as a bazooka but you cant fire them as far.

Dont let any of this propaganda about sunny California fool you. We have to carry overshoes with us all the time because it really rains. And a lot of mornings the ground is white with frost. We always wear gloves and field jackets. That reminds me. If curly, you want a darn good coat for $7.00 I can get you a field jacket and boy they are a real good coat and I would get one if I needed one. They even have a zipper. It is almost time to go over and have a big turkey dinner and afterwards I am going to town and <u>take off</u>. I cant start smoking now. We can get cigaretts for 13 cents a package but I cant afford it now.

I didnt have much time to explain about those presents I asked you to buy. I meant for you to get something for them and draw $10 or $15 out of the bank to cover them. I couldnt find anything around here and by the time I got a chance to *get to town they would have been late. I hate to put you to all the trouble though. Another thing. The next time if you havent been doing it, draw out enough money to cover the cost of the money orders and everything.*

My Basic Training is half over now and I might get a furlough after 8 more weeks.

Martin

PS. Did you get the picture? I sent Ruths present to Karen. Everyone enjoyed the candy and all of them want to say thanks.

The following pictures are from Camp Roberts in Post Cards[36] and of those Martin took from a Camp Roberts booklet in 1943 which he had in his personal photo album. All pictures are of Camp Roberts Infantry Replacement Training Center in California and show the extensive training the enlistees endured.

Each soldier had to be efficient in bayonet fighting

37 millimeter gun drill

Packs and Rifles

Artillery men clean rifles

---

[36]http://www.militarymuseum.org/CpRobertsPostcards.html

All trainees fire the M1 rifle and the carbine either for qualification or for familiarization with the weapon

On the 100-inch machine gun range, men learn confidence in their weapons and in firing them

Returning to camp

37 mm gun in action

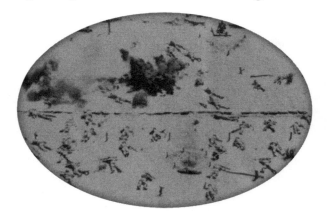

Soldiers moving (crawling) forward through mine fields under overhead machine gun fire

Remember the statement Martin made in an earlier letter,
"I competed with the moles that were underground!"

HISTORY OF THE BAZOOKA

Robert H. Goddard (rocket pioneer scientist) developed the basic idea of the bazooka at the end of World War I. On 6 November 1918, at Aberdeen Proving Ground, Maryland, he demonstrated a tube-launched, solid-propellant rocket.

Bob Burns & his Bazooka

In 1942, early in World War II, an Army first lieutenant with an engineering degree named Edward Uhl helped develop the shoulder-fired rocket launcher. The Bazooka went from the drawing board into combat within 30 days, setting a record for effective procurement. The 2.36 inch M1 rocket launcher was introduced in June 1942, and the improved M1A1 in August 1943. It was named the "Bazooka" after a custom-made musical instrument used by then-popular radio comedian Bob Burns. The M9 bazooka, introduced in June 1943, was a major redesign and improvement of the original weapon. It was replaced in turn by the M9A1 in September 1944.

WWII Bazooka Team

All bazooka rocket launchers feature a smooth bore steel tube, a shoulder frame and a trigger mechanism. Each of the models differs in details as briefly described in the following paragraphs. Bazookas are a crew served weapon with a two-man team, gunner (aim/fire) and loader (ammo prep/loading). It was effective against tanks to about 100 yards and could be used at longer distances against softer targets.

The original M1 bazooka was 2.36 inches in diameter. It had a wooden stock and hand grips. It used the same sling as the M1 Garand rifle. The rocket is loaded in the rear of the tube and a wire is connected. Pressing the trigger energizes the rocket from two BA-30 1.5 volt D-cell batteries in the stock, connected through an off/on switch.

The bazooka ammunition was a small, fin-stabilized rocket-propelled grenade. The original model cost only $19 to produce. While useful, the first bazooka had many limitations. Among other deficiencies, it was extremely inaccurate in combat and the back-blast tended to expose the location of positions.

Actual WWII inert round for the M1A1 Bazooka

The first successor model was the M1A1. The tube was still a single piece, but it had improved sights. The forward hand grip and the off/on switch was eliminated. A small disc made of mesh wire could be clamped to the muzzle to protect the gunner from back-blast. The mesh wire was ineffective and was mostly ignored by the troops. In later production, a solid metal funnel at the muzzle replaced the mesh with much better effect.

The next evolution was the M9 bazooka, introduced in June 1943, and replaced by the M9A1 in September 1944. This was a major redesign of the original weapon with many improvements. The tube was made from lighter metal in two parts that could be separated for convenient transport. A metal shoulder stock replaced the wood of the M1 series and the tube featured a metal funnel like the late production M1A1. The unreliable batteries were replaced by a small magneto-generator in the trigger and the fixed

Bazooka - Okinawa 1945

iron sights replaced by optical ones. The M9A1 (and other 2.36" models remaining in inventory) were withdrawn from service at the end of WW II.[37]

In the years just prior to World War II, the United States adopted the spigot-type 22mm rifle grenade launchers. Having come into wide acceptance during World War II, these rifle grenades were increasingly used in the years after the war. These 22mm grenade types range from powerful anti-tank rounds to simple finned tubes with a fragmentation hand grenade attached to the end. They come in "standard" type which are propelled by a blank cartridge inserted into the chamber of the rifle. And, the newer "bullet trap" and "shoot through" types, as their names imply use live ammunition.[38]

After World War II, more and more countries began to adopt 22mm anti-tank rifle grenades with shaped-charge or HEAT warheads. The bullet-trap rifle grenade design saw increasing use during the years after World War II, most notably the French AC58 anti-armor and APAV40 multipurpose grenades. The 22mm rifle-grenade launchers were further simplified, becoming an integral part of the rifle itself with the use of an adapter.

---

[37]http://olive-drab.com/od_infweapons_bazooka.php
[38]http://grenadelauncher.com/

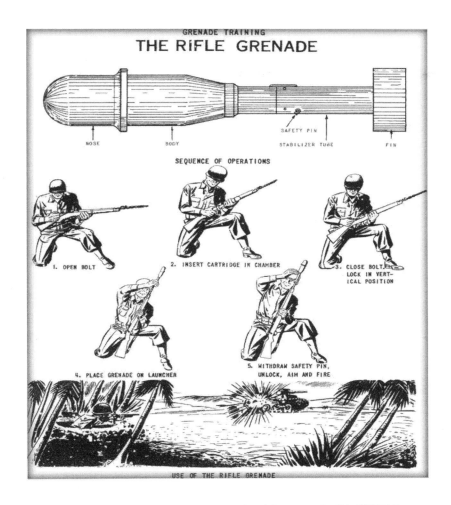

THE $7.00 FIELD JACKET

Field Jacket

Although the M41 Parson's Jacket was widely used in World War II, it was not really a satisfactory solution for the soldier. The Field Jacket M-1943 was an integral part of a combat uniform being developed by the War Department based on the layering principle to give great flexibility for conditions encountered in the world-wide war.

The Jacket, Field M-1943 (formal name) consisted of an olive drab cotton outer shell with layers added inside as more warmth was needed. There was a pile jacket liner for extremely cold areas, while the short wool jacket (the "Ike" jacket) was worn in milder temperatures. An olive drab cotton cap, also designated M-1943, was the head cover and was worn inside the helmet liner when the M-1 helmet system was used. A fur-edged hood was also added as an accessory. The wide-cuff double-buckle combat boots were adopted at the same time.[39]

The new M43 Field jacket is dutifully made to the specifications of the original Jacket, Field M-1943 worn by U.S. soldiers during World War II. [40] Today's prices range from $59.95 to $109.95 depending on the manufacturer.

Martin indicated cigarette's cost 13 cents a pack. Today's generation would be surprised to see Cigarette Ads from WWII showing military men & women, animals, housewives, Santa's, and more! Most encouraged the purchase of *War Bonds* to help *"our fighting men and women"* and the war effort in general. Below is a sample of the Ads.[41]

Chesterfield Christmas Santa Cigarette Ad 1943

Chesterfield Cigarette Ad, Life Magazine, May 10, 1943

1943 Camel Cigarette Ad - US ARMY Fighting Engineers

---

[39]http://www.found-nyc.com/blog/2008/01/16/original-design-02-m-1943-field-jacket/
[40]http://www.hammacher.com/Product/
[41]https://www.google.com/search?q=1943+cigarette+ads

LETTER 12

Pvt Martin Paulson
Co A 88 Inf Tng Bn
Camp Roberts, Calif

Mrs. A. Furford
Rt1 Box 352
Kent, Washington

Postage: Free
Jan 7, 1944 3:30 PM
Camp Roberts, Calif

Dear Ruth, Curly, & George   *January 6*

I know I wont have time to write to you for about a week. I looked at the program and we are going to have a lot of night work. Last weekend I was in Frisco and another guy wants me to go back again with him this week. We sure had a good time.

We have just finished the easiest part of the training we get. I am now qualified to drive an Army truck if they give me some license. They dont give everyone that passes a license.

I sent a birthday present to you Ruth. I dont know if you will get by your birthday though. I didnt get time to take it over to the post office right away.

My basic training will be over in a couple of months, then I will probably get a furlough to come home. Everyone doesnt get one though. If I dont it will probably be six more months before I get one. I got the last money you sent in plenty of time. It really surprised me how soon it did come. I will need some more after next weekend, but I dont know how much until I come back so I will let you know next week.

There really isnt much to write about today. It seems that we do the same old thing every day. One thing we are going to fire this week that really surprised me is the twenty two. I dont know yet why we fire them but we do. I have fired so many different weapons on different ranges that I can hardly keep tract of all of them myself. I eaven fired a 45 pistol.   *Martin*

Martin talks about the fun he had in *"Frisco"* (San Francisco, CA). Below are excerpts from a chronology of San Francisco's WWII events in 1943. Though it is extensive, it is worth the read. [42] It is important to note, this is just one city's contribution to the war.

---

[42]http://www.sfmuseum.org/war/43.html

CHRONOLOGY OF 1943 SAN FRANCISCO WAR EVENTS

January 1, 1943 – Examiner launched the "Save a Life With a Knife" campaign and urged readers with sturdy hunting knives, with blades at least four-inches long, to bring them to campaign headquarters at 1025 Columbus Ave., or to the Examiner Want Ad Lobby at Third and Market streets. The knives were to be shipped to the jungle fighting fronts by airplane.

January 17, 1943 – Tin Can Drive Day for scrap metal.

January 26, 1943 – Japanese aircraft strafed Constantine Harbor on Amchitka Island in the Aleutians.

January 30, 1943 – B-17 crew attacks unidentified submerged object in Alaskan waters, and dropped four depth charges and one bomb. The unidentified object was a whale.

February 1, 1943 – Three hundred soldiers appear in Irving Berlin's "This is the Army," at the Opera House. Personal appearance by Irving Berlin. Proceeds to the Army's Relief Fund.
– Mayor Rossi has asked San Francisco hotels to provide more sleeping space for soldiers by putting cots in dining rooms and ballrooms.

February 16, 1943 – James Waterman Wise speaks of "The Jew in a Warring World," at the Jewish Community Center.

February 28, 1943 – Life Magazine photographer William Vandivert's "Two Years of War in England" exhibition closes at the San Francisco Museum of Art, Civic Center.

WWII Poster

March 3, 1943 – Adm. Thomas C. Kincaid, commanding officer of the Alaska Defense Command, begins planning for the invasion of Attu.

March 5, 1943 – Pepsi-Cola Center, 948 Market Street, opened for servicemen.

March 26, 1943 – Navy engaged the Japanese in the Battle of Komandorskies, 150 miles west of Cape Wrangell, Alaska. B-25 Mitchell Bombers attacked Japanese positions on Kiska.

April 1, 1943 – Gen. DeWitt orders preparations for Operation Land Grab, the invasion of Attu Island. American planes strike Japanese targets on Kiska.

April 14, 1943 – United States War Food Administration, Office of Distribution, regional poultry and egg conference in San Francisco.

May 2, 1943 – Civilian Defense held the first Water Evacuation Drill for 1500 wardens at the foot of Van Ness Ave.

May 7, 1943 – U.S. Senate adopted Senate Resolutions 101 and 111 authorizing the Committee on Military Affairs or any subcommittee thereof to visit Japanese Relocation Centers in the United States.

May 11, 1943 – Attu and Kiska in Aleutian Islands were retaken by a military expedition launched from San Francisco. The campaign lasted until May 30.

May 27, 1943 – U.S. Senate Committee on Naval Affairs hearing on the Navy's current and prospective occupancy of Treasure Island.

May 30, 1943 – All organized Japanese Army resistance ended in the Aleutians.

May 30, 1943 – Dies Committee on Un-American Activities reported that 40,000 Japanese are still at large in the U.S. And an uncertain number were trained in Japan as saboteurs. The committee also criticized the War Relocation Authority for releasing 1000 Japanese per week from relocation camps.

June 8, 1943 – Civil Defense officials began *V-Home Campaign* because of the continued possibility of enemy attack. The objective was to award "*V-Home, We Are Prepared*" stickers to qualified

WWII Poster

households. These stickers were made available by the United States Office of Civilian Defense as part of a national campaign which is already underway.

June 17, 1943 – Liberty ship "Fremont Older" launched today at Richmond Shipyard No. 2.

July 3, 1943 – When it is necessary for a Civilian Defense Warden to enforce blackout regulations by unusual action - such as breaking a window, gaining entrance to a building, or other such occurrence, or in the event of an injury to a Warden in the performance of his duty, the Sector Warden was to, immediately after the "All Clear," telephone the incident to the Battalion Headquarters in his district giving the name and address of the violator as well as a description of the violation and action taken.

July 29, 1943 – Office of Civilian Defense, at Washington, D. C., ordered Fire Guard watches in San Francisco because of the fear of Japanese incendiary bomb raids.

August 2, 1943 – Civilian Defense officials established War Gas Self-Aid Stations in San Francisco in preparation for gas attacks by the Japanese.

August 18, 1943 – Construction began on barracks for servicemen in Civic Center.

September 9, 1943 – Roy Rogers, King of the Cowboys, and his horse Trigger, appeared in the Admission Day Parade on Market St.

November 1, 1943 – Dimout order lifted. (a restriction limiting the use or showing of lights at night especially during the threat of an air raid)

November 21, 1943 – Dies Committee found that the Japanese internment camp at Rivers Camp, Arizona was not well- run, and the Japanese there are in control. Land for the internment camp had been leased to the Government by the Pima

Indian tribe. Undercover investigators found bootleggers selling liquor there at $6 per pint, and that Caucasian employees were chummy with the Japanese.
November 24, 1943 – Leopold Stokowski conducted all-Russian Program with the San Francisco Symphony.

Again, Martin mentions the possibly of getting a furlough. One must remember that these men were taken from their daily lives directly into intense war-like training and they looked forward to getting back home before being shipped out. It must have been discouraging to realize that not everyone got furlough and, therefore, you *may not* get furlough. Camp Roberts was a "*Replacement*" training center and men were shipped out to fill the ranks of those who died in battle on a regular basis and you never knew when it would be your turn.

World War II was a global war that was underway by 1939 and ended in 1945. Estimates for the total casualties of the war vary as many deaths went unrecorded. Most suggest that some 60 million people died in the war, including about 20 million soldiers and 40 million civilians.

Martin is surprised in having to shoot the .22 rifle in training. Research indicates it was an exceptionally accurate rifle, great for night time accuracy, and bullets were much more inexpensive than others. According to the War Department Technical Manual dated 16 March 1942 the purpose was to "*provide an accurate small-bore weapon for training purposes,*" and the six types of these rifles produced were three U.S. military rifles and three commercial rifles. [43]

Rifle: U.S. Cal .22 M1922
Rifle: U.S. Cal .22 M1
Rifle: U.S. Cal .22 M2
Rifle: U.S. Cal .22 Remington Model 513T
Rifle: U.S. Cal .22 Stevens, Model 416-2
Rifle: U.S. Cal .22 Winchester, Model 75

War Department Technical Manual 1942

---

[43]http://www.scribd.com/doc/12980693/1942-US-Army-WWII-Rifles-22-Caliber-144p

Martin says,
"I have fired so many different weapons on different ranges that I can hardly keep track of all of them myself. I even fired a 45 pistol".
Below are some of the Infantry weapons of WWII.[44,45,46]

U.S. WWII Infantry weapons

U.S. WWII Carbine with rifle case; M19aaA1 .45 pistol with holster; soldiers helmet; and bayonet

WWII pistol training

WWII Infantry Weapons

[44]http://www.antiquemilitaryshooter.com
[45]http://dailygunpictures.blogspot.com/2009/06/ww-2-collection.html
[46]http://www.calguns.net/calgunforum/showthread.php?t=402112

LETTER 13

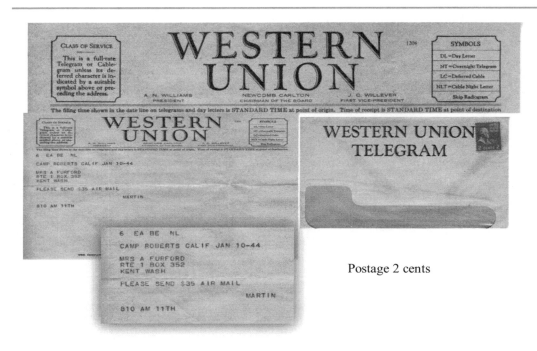

Postage 2 cents

LETTER 14

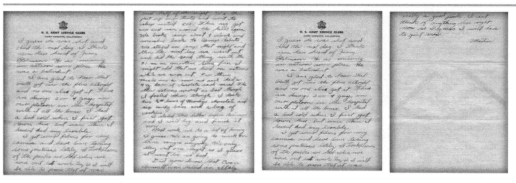

Postage: Free
Jan 17, 1944   3:30 PM
Camp Roberts, Calif

Pvt Martin Paulson
Co A 88 Inf Tng Bn

Mrs. A. Furford
Rt 1 Box352
Kent, Wash.

Dear Ruth, Curly & George,   *January 16*

I will write and let you know right away that I got the money allright. About the next time I send for some it might be for a train ticket. My training, basic, is over the nineteenth of next month.

We sure had a rough week last week. We had to march seven or eight miles with about a eighty five pound pack, a rifle, and half of the time I had a part of a machine gun which weighed 51 pounds. Some fun. Then when we got there we made light packs and ran all over the hills putting the machine gun in action. I was no 1 man, which is the man behind the gun. We did this all the rest of the day and half of the night. We then put up our tents and went to sleep until 5:00. Then we got up and ran around the hills again. We broke camp about 9 oclock and marched back to Camp Roberts. We stayed in camp that night and then the next day we went out and did the same thing with the 81 mm mortar. Some fun. I might add that we lived on rations while we were out. For three meals in a row we each had a 4 oz bar of chocolate each meal. The other rations werent as bad though. I fooled them though. I took two 1/2# bars of Hersheys chocolate and six candy bars and a bag of cookies.

I started this letter before dinner and I will try and finish it now.

Next week we do a lot of firing I guess. We are going to work on three ranges anyway. We only stay out one night so I guess it wont be so bad.

Did you know that Evan Bennett was killed in Italy. I guess he was shot and died the next day. I think you have heard of Jerry Robinson. He is missing in action some place. He was a Lieutenant.

I am glad to hear that Ruth got over the flue allright and no one else got it. There are always 3 or 4 guys in our platoon in the hospital with it all the time. I had a bad cold when I first got down here, but since then I havent had any trouble.

I got some films for my camera and have been taking some pictures lately. I took some of the packs we had when we were out last week too, so I will be able to prove that it was really a good pack. I cant think of anything else right now so I guess I will have to quit now.

                                                Martin

Sounds like Martin had a rough week of training. Imagine the large pack on their backs, carrying rifles, and then having to pack an additional weight of 51 lbs. for 7-8 miles up and down hills! Then when arriving at location running around setting up and firing of the equipment.

Martin said, *"When we got there we made light packs and ran all over the hills putting the machine gun in action. I was #1 man, which is the man behind the gun."* In the pictures of the machine gun, you can almost picture Martin behind the gun as #1 Man.

Type:	Medium **machine gun**[47]
Weight:	31 lb.
Length:	37.9 in (M1919A4)
	53 in (M1919A6)
Barrel length:	24 in
Caliber:	Various
Action:	Recoil-operated/short-recoil
operation	
Rate of fire:	400-600 round/min
Muzzle velocity:	2,800 ft. /s
Effective range:	1,500 yd. (maximum effective range)
Feed system:	250-round belt

Machine gun training, Camp Roberts

Type:	Infantry **mortar**[48]
Weight:	Tube 44.5 lb.
	Mount 46.5 lb.
	Base plate 45 lb.
	Total 136 pounds
Length:	3 ft. 11 in
Caliber:	81 millimeters (3.2 in)
Rate of fire:	18 rpm sustained
	30-35 rpm maximum

Muzzle velocity:	700 ft./s
Effective range:	3,300 yd.
Sights:	M4

U.S. Soldiers fire an M1 mortar during WWII

It brings a smile to ones face when you hear..."*I fooled them though. I took two 1/2^{lb} bars of Hershey's chocolate and six candy bars and a bag of cookies.*" Boys will be boys! Martin said there was a 4 oz. bar of chocolate with each meal/ration, but that it was not enough. Below is some very interesting WWII history on the Hershey Bar.

Hershey Chocolate Corporation's involvement with the production of military ration bars began when Captain Paul Logan, from the office of U.S. Army Quartermaster General, met with William Murrie, President, Hershey Chocolate Corporation and Sam Hinkle, Chief Chemist, in April 1937. This initial visit started the experimental production of a ration bar which was to meet the needs of soldiers involved in a global war.

When Murrie and Hinkle told Milton Hershey about the visit by the Army

---

[47]http://en.wikipedia.org/wiki/M1919_Browning_machine_gun
[48]http://en.wikipedia.org/wiki/M1_Mortar

Quartermaster Captain, he was very interested in hearing every detail and instructed them to get started on the project right away.

The standard chocolate bar, which melted readily in summer heat could never be adapted to being carried in a soldier's pocket. In addition, *it was thought to be too tempting in taste to be used as an emergency ration to be eaten only when on the verge of starvation.* Captain Logan explained his requirements: a bar weighing about four ounces, able to withstand high temperatures, high in food energy value, and tasting just a little better than a boiled potato.

The original formula and shape of the ration bar were altered slightly when thiamine hydrochloride was added as a source of Vitamin B1 to prevent beriberi, a disease likely to be encountered in the tropics. These bars were originally called "Logan bars" and later were referred to as Field Ration D.

After the attack on Pearl Harbor by the Japanese on December 7, 1941, the Quartermaster felt it necessary to protect Field Ration D as well as other rations, from possible damage by poison gas.

New specifications called for the placing of each bar in a heavy cellophane bag, closing the bag by means of a heat seal, inserting this into an individual cardboard carton, securely gluing the carton ends, dipping the cartons in a wax mixture, packing twelve waxed cartons in a master carton, gluing the master cartons top and bottom, packing twelve master cartons in a wooden case, and nailing and steel stripping the case.

In 1939, Hershey was able to produce 100,000 units per day. By the end of 1945, production lines on three floors of the plant were producing approximately 24 million units per week. It has been estimated that between 1940 and 1945, over three billion ration units were produced and distributed to soldiers around the world. In addition to the individual bar, Hershey Chocolate produced a THREE-PACK OF THE FOUR OUNCE BARS intended to furnish the individual combat soldier with the 1,800 calorie minimum sustenance recommended each day.

In 1943, the Procurement Division of the Army inquired about the possibility

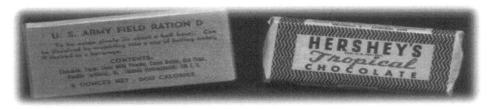

Ration D bar and Tropical Chocolate bar, ca. 1942-1944

of obtaining a heat resistant chocolate confectionery bar with an improved flavor. After a short period of experimentation, Hershey's Tropical Chocolate Bar in both one and two ounce sizes was added to the list of war production items. This bar was destined to exceed all other items in the tonnage produced and along with the Field Ration D bar, became part of Hershey Chocolate's history. [49]

Pictures below of which Martin mentions in his letter are of *full packs*. Martin is on right in the first picture. He does not remember the name of the other soldier (it has been over 70 years!) -- both memories and pictures fade with time. Though Martin may not remember all the names, at 94 years of age, his memory is fantastic. His memories and researched facts have matched consistently! The pictures in Martin's photo album are of great interest as they are of HIS experiences, and therefore will be included even though they may not be the best of quality.

One wonders what goes through the trainees' minds while in Basic Training when hearing of the loss of those they knew who were killed or missing in action in current overseas wartime fighting. Martin mentions Evan Bennett being killed in Italy, and Jerry Robinson missing in action.

Full packs (front view)
Martin on right

Full packs (back view)

Missing in action (MIA)

...is a casualty category assigned under the Status of Missing to armed services personnel who are reported missing during active service? They may have been killed, wounded, become a prisoner of war, or deserted. If deceased, neither their remains nor grave can be positively identified. Becoming MIA has been an occupational risk for service personnel for as long as there has been warfare. [50]

---

[49]http://www.hersheyarchives.org/essay/details.aspx?EssayId=26
[50]http://en.wikipedia.org/wiki/Missing_in_action

LETTER 15

Pvt Martin Paulson
Co A 88 Inf Tng Bn
Camp Roberts, Calif

Mrs. A. Furford
Rt 2 Box 352
Kent, Wash

Postage: Free
Jan 27, 1944 1:30 PM
Camp Roberts. Calif

Camp Roberts, Calif

Dear Ruth & Curly,   *January 26,*

 Well it sure looks like I will soon be seeing you. I havent as yet, but I am going to sign up for a furlough tonight. If nothing goes wrong I will be on my way up there the last of next month, about the 27th.

 Next week we go out and stay for 2 weeks on a Bivouac. We stay out all the time and live like we would on the front lines. Some fun. It is sure cold down here and now it has started raining so I guess we are really in for it.

 Yesterday afternoon we had to crawl under machine gun fire. They were firing a couple of feet off the ground then we had to go over logs and through barbed wire. They also had mines blowing up around us. Last night we had to go through it again. They used all tracers with the machine guns and used a lot of flares and mines. From a distance it sure looked pretty but I am telling you I sure gave a mole a lot of compatition sp. I have some tracer shells. I mean just the lead part, and a lot of things like that I will bring home with me. I also have one of those famous D rations and I am going to make you eat some. They sure taste like the devil.

 Well thats all the time I have now.

            Martin

Do you think Martin is wanting to go home for a visit? I wonder if the readers are as surprised as I that Martin had to sign up for furlough. You would think the soldiers would automatically get a furlough to see family before shipping out. But then again the U.S. was at war. Research did reveal that if an "event" occurred all furloughs were automatically canceled. For example after the attack on Pearl Harbor all furloughs were canceled. However, no such 'event' was taking place at this time. Research also inferred that the amount of time one could take for furlough after basic training depended on the length of the basic training and intensity of the training. We have learned through Martin's letters that he would be having 17 weeks of basic training which is the longest training given during basic training.

Martin doesn't sound too happy about going out on Bivouac for two weeks. How many Hershey bars, candy and cookies will he sneak out this time?!

biv·ouac: (biv-oo-ak, biv-wak) ...a military encampment made with tents or improvised shelters, usually without shelter or protection from enemy fire. And as Martin explains, *"live like we would on the front lines."*

Army manual bivouac tent set up Instructions:[51] [52]

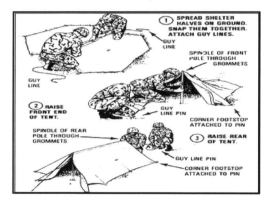
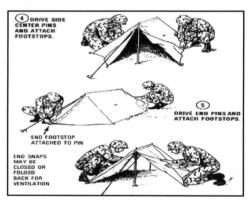

Proper food preparation, storage and handling, and preservation became a top priority for the military. The science of nutrition expanded greatly during

D-Rations

WWII. In the United States, scientists worked to identify which vitamins and minerals were most essential to a healthy body and in what amounts, and studies were conducted to determine how many calories were burned doing various activities. Soldiers' rations were carefully formulated to supply the maximum amount of nutrition and energy, while providing for variety and taste. Meeting these challenges meant working first in the laboratory before working in

[51]   http://www.armystudyguide.com/
[52] http://www.ww2rationtechnologies.com/MainPage.html

the kitchen. The development of the D-ration provides a great example.

The "D" ration was a high-calorie emergency ration that came in the form of a fortified chocolate bar. By the end of the war, millions of these rations had been produced in the United States and delivered around the world, along with billions of other rations for the military.

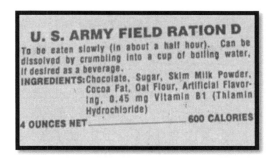

D-Ration ingredients

Note that Martin is going to make his sister (and I am sure other family members) taste *"one of those famous D rations"* so they know what he will be eating in battle situations. His comment is that *"they sure taste like the devil."*

Martin again talks about crawling under machine gun fire. When interviewing him, he said pretty much what he said in the letter only a little more graphically, *"I most definitely competed with the moles in digging as much into the dirt as I could. It was a terrifying experience!"* He says in the letter he had to go over logs and through barbed wire, and that they had mines blowing up around them. What must be going through the soldiers minds? Especially knowing they may be facing this or worse in real battle situations. *Boys growing into men overnight!*

Soldiers crawling under gunfire at Camp Roberts (from training manual)
– Martin's photo album

Close-up of soldier crawling under fire - from Martin's photo album - notice the trail he is leaving behind!

"They used tracers with the machine guns and used a lot of flares and mines. From the distance it sure looked pretty but I am telling you, I sure gave a mole a lot of competition."   *Martin*

LETTER 16

Pvt Martin Paulson
Co A 88 Inf Tng Bn
Camp Roberts Calif

Mrs A. Furford
Rt 1 Box 352
Kent Wash

Postage: Free
Feb 3, 1944 11:30 AM
Camp Roberts, Calif

Dear Ruth & Curly & George,   *February 2,*

    Here I am out on Bivouac. We have to stay out in the field for 2 weeks. We started in this Monday and we end up around the 14th, anyway a week from this Saturday. We cant buy anything to eat out here and they arnt feeding very well. I brought along a lot of candy but it is running short. Is there any chance of having you send something to eat. If you can, get it here before we go in.

    Another thing would you send me about $15 in about 10 days. I will need it if the furlough I asked for comes through.

    I sure hit it lucky out here on bivouac. The lieutenant picked me out to be his as he calls me orderly messenger and record in command. Some fun. I dont get any guard or any details.

    Thats all I have time to write now. Be seeing you pretty soon. I hope.

Martin

    Sounds like Martin is hungry! Apparently the candy he took wasn't enough to appease his appetite. If we put ourselves in his place and realize how the Army is preparing them for war-time battle situations -- which included not only teaching them to eat D-rations, but also included very intensive training -- ever wonder how you would hold up? He must have been so hungry he wasn't thinking straight as mail delivery was not what it is today so it would be very unreasonable to expect food from home in such a short time. Martin said he doesn't remember much about Bivouac except being hungry, eating D-rations, and just getting through it. He said,

    "When you look back on it, it was EASY compared to the real thing."

    Martin must also be a little homesick! The letter's closing:
"Be seeing you pretty soon. I hope"
- speaks loudly to how homesick he was.

Martin was chosen as "orderly messenger" and "record in command." One of the perks was not having to stand guard duty and detail. The following from *"Tales of Soldiers and Civilians"* provides an interesting insight into the meaning of orderly:

"Orderly" is a word covering a multitude of duties. An orderly may be a messenger, a clerk, an officer's servant—anything. He may perform services for which no provision is made in orders and army regulations. Their nature may depend upon his aptitude, upon favor, upon accident. [53]

Ruth, Rakel (Mother), little Carnie (Karen),
Myrtle, and Martin - Cascade Mountains,
Washington State
1927

---

[53]http://www.ambrosebierce.org/missing.html

LETTER 17

Pvt Martin Paulson	Mrs. A. Furford	Postage: Free
Co A 88 Inf Tng Bn	Rt 1 Box 352	Feb 9, 1944 11:30 AM
Camp Roberts, Calif	Kent, Wash	Camp Roberts, Calif

Dear Ruth & Curly,   *February 7,*

Well our bivouac is over half finished and I am still alive so I guess it isnt quite as bad as they said it would be. They havent been giving us much to eat and we have been getting a lot of rations. If you want a candy bar it cost you twenty five cents and the guys that bring or brought them out sell all they can get ahold of. None of us can get into camp and about the only way we can get them is buy them from truck or jeep drivers.

We have to stay up all night Thursday night and then we get a hour and one half rest Friday morning. We then work all day Friday. We go to bed about eight Friday night and then get up at midnight and march 25 miles in eight hours. That is really something to look forward to isnt it. We have to carry full field packs and rifles too.

It looks like I will get my furlough. If I do I have a chance to ride up in a 42 chevolet (sp)*. They have a rule that only the guy that has the car can go in the car so if I go I will have to buy a train ticket then get off the train at the first stop and get in the car.*

Almost all the guys in our platoon (that can) are growing a mustache so I am too. Mine isnt so hot though. My wiskers are too light so it doesnt show up very well. When everyone started to let their mustache grow and the corporal noticed it he was going to make us shave them off. We then politely informed him that our liutendent was growing one and said he didnt care if we did. So that sure put him in his place in a hurry.

Boy is everyone cranky out here. Someone is always blowing off. Without enough to eat and sleep you get so that if anyone says or does anything you dont like you tell them off. That is if you are bigger then he is. Otherwise you might get hurt.   *Martin*

5 ^C Hershey Bar

The following chart shows Hershey Company's price/weight data for their famous Hershey Bar from 1908-1986.

Martin indicated he was having to pay 25 cents for a Hershey Bar from the truck & Jeep drivers. Note that the price for a Hershey Bar in 1944 was 5 cents! A side business with profit for the drivers?

The real Hershey Bar tasted a whole lot better than the Hershey D-ration Bar.[54] The D-ration bars were made of chocolate liquor, sugar, skim milk powder, cocoa butter, oat flour, and vanilla – a concoction that would withstand temperatures up to 120°F. Vitamin B1 was also an added supplement. A reduced sugar component left the bars tasting *"a little better than a boiled potato."*

Hershey D-Ration Bar was often referred to as the "Logan Bar"

1908	9/16 oz.....2 cents	**1944**	**1 5/8 oz.....5 cents**	**1970**	1 3/8 oz.....10 cents
1918	1 6/16 oz.....3 cents	**1946**	1 1/2 oz.....5 cents	**1973**	1.26 oz......10 cents
1920	9/16 oz.....3 cents	**1947**	1 oz.....5 cents	**1974**	1.04 oz.....15 cents
1921	1 oz.....5 cents	**1954**	7/8 oz.....5 cents	**1975**	1.05 oz.....15 cents
1924	1 3/8 oz.....5 cents	**1955**	1 oz.....5 cents	**1976**	1.02 oz.....15 cents
1930	2 oz.....5 cents	**1958**	7/8 oz.....5 cents	**1977**	1.02 oz......20 cents
1933	1 7/8 oz.....5 cents	**1960**	1 oz.....5 cents	**1978**	1.02 oz.....25 cents
1936	1 1/2 oz.....5 cents	**1963**	7/8 oz......5 cents	**1980**	1.05 oz.....25 cents
1937	1 5/8 oz.....5 cents	**1965**	1 oz......5 cents	**1982**	1.45 oz.....30 cents
1938	1 3/8 oz.....5 cents	**1966**	7/8 oz......5 cents	**1983**	1.45 oz.....35 cents
1939	1 5/8 oz.....5 cents	**1968**	3/4 oz.….5 cents	**1986**	1.45 oz.....40 cents
1941	1 1/4 oz.....5 cents	**1969**	1 1/2 oz.....10 cents	**1986**	1.65 oz.....40 cents

We get a further look into WWII Bivouac training when Martin tells of their daily schedule:

"We have to stay up all night Thursday night and then we get a hour and one half rest Friday morning. We then work all day Friday. We go to bed about eight Friday night and then get up at midnight and march 25 miles in eight hours."

---

[54]foodtimeline.org/foodfaq5.html

And at the end of the letter it is obvious the strain the trainees are under from Martin's comment:

"Boy is everyone cranky out here. Someone is always blowing off. Without enough to eat and sleep you get so that if anyone says or does anything you dont like you tell them off. That is if you are bigger than he is. Otherwise you might get hurt."

Martin

Photo Martin took of fellow soldier in 'Full Field Pack' with rifle

Martin is really looking forward to his furlough! And excited about riding in a 1942 Chevrolet. After reading the interesting facts below you will understand his excitement of getting to ride in a 1942 Chevrolet.[55] [56]

Priced at $880, just $35 higher than the Special DeLuxe five-passenger coupe, this 1942 Chevrolet Fleetline Aerosedan proved to be Chevy's best-seller for 1942.

Chevrolet offered three models in 1942: the Master Deluxe, the Special Deluxe, and the Fleet-line. It is estimated less than 2,350 Chevrolet's were built.

Some of Chevrolet's color choices reflected the mood of the time: Volunteer Green, Ensign Blue, Torpedo Gray, and Martial Maroon. After Pearl Harbor, the industry began complete conversion to war production. On December 14, the government decreed that to conserve scarce metals, all cars built after January 1, 1942

1942 Chevrolet doghouse shows off an increasingly modern look, with a nearly full-width, horizontally oriented 'American Eagle'grille and headlamps fully enclosed in the fenders.

[55]http://auto.howstuffworks.com/1941-1942-chevrolet-fleetline.htm
[56]http://www.macsmotorcitygarage.com/2012/11/06/mcg-car-spotters-guide-to-the-1932-to-1942-chevrolet/

could not use any bright work apart from chrome-plated bumpers. These cars were known as "blackouts." The grille, medallions, hubcaps, all window and body trim,

were painted metal instead of chrome. Blackouts of any make are rare; they were only made during January 1942. The 1942 Chevrolets were equipped with a 216 cid engine which produced 90 hp. They were priced from $799.

On January 1, 1942, the *Office of Production Management* (OPM) froze dealer inventories, halting all new car and truck sales pending a rationing program to be implemented in March. All passenger car production had ended by February 11. Nationwide, there remained 340,000 new 1942 cars in dealer inventories, including all the January 1942 blackouts.

The 1942 Chevrolet's front fenders faded halfway into the doors, with only vestigial running boards. Civilian passenger car production at Chevrolet ended early in 1942, following Pearl Harbor, and would not resume again until the 1946 model year.

During the war, Chevrolet and GMC made military trucks and ambulances, armored artillery and shells, airplane engines, and amphibious DUKW's. Chevrolet's car production resumed on October 3, 1945. After the War, the local ration boards authorized each new car sale at OPM-controlled prices. Used car prices nearly doubled. New tires were not available; recaps were rationed. Gas was rationed. The national speed limit was reduced to 35 mph.[57]

Army landings in South Pacific in amphibious 'Duck'

The **DUKW** (colloquially known as **Duck**) is a six-wheel-drive amphibious truck that was designed by a partnership under military auspices of Sparkman & Stephens and General Motors Corporation (GMC) during World War II for transporting goods and troops over land and water and for use approaching and crossing beaches in amphibious attacks. [58]

[57]http://www.lemaymuseum.org/vehicles.php?vid=628
[58]http://en.wikipedia.org/wiki/DUKW

LETTER 18

Pvt Martin Paulson
Co A 88 Inf Tng Bn
Camp Roberts, Calif

Mrs. A. Furford   Postage: 6 cents airmail
Rt 1 Box 352   February 16, 1944 11 AM
Kent, Wash.   Camp Roberts, Calif

Dear Ruth & Curly,   *February 15, 1944*
I havent much time to write as usual but I will try to write a short letter. We made the bivouac all right and then coming in we set a new record for the camp. Twenty five (25) miles in seven hours. We did that after staying up two nights in a row. Some fun. Thanks a lot for the candy. I got it just when we got back to camp after the hike so you can imagine how long it lasted when I opened it up. You said you were going to send some money to me at the same time you sent the candy. I havent got the money yet and if I havent got it by next Monday I wont be able to go on my furlough if they give it to me. Would you send $15 more just in case I dont get the other money. That is if it is lost or anything. Maybe it would be best to wire it. Dont make a special trip to town to wire though. Just so I get it by Monday it will be all right. I have to have my teeth worked on a little bit so I might not get my furlough for two or three weeks more now. I graduate from training Saturday. No more basic training thank God. By the way they said they were going to give us a metal for making such good time on the hike. I dont know if I told you we have to carry full field packs and rifles on that hike.

Martin

Martin mentions setting a new record on the 25 mile hike when returning from Bivouac to Camp Roberts. Twenty-five miles! In seven hours! And they did this after staying up two nights in a row! I love his sarcastic *"Some Fun"* comment. And note that at the end of the letter he comments on them having to do the hike in *"full field Packs and rifles."*

His sister, Ruth, responded to Martin's request and sent candy! Martin had sounded so hungry it must have pulled on her heart strings! But notice, he didn't get it till he got back from Bivouac. If you had gotten that letter asking for Candy, wouldn't you have done everything you could to send a large box of his favorites. Martin says it was the best tasting candy ever! ...and that he had a lot of help eating it! He doesn't remember names, but he remembered getting that candy! Candy and thoughts of home. After two weeks of Bivouac who wouldn't want to go home.

He must have felt discouraged to have furlough moved back for the dental work he needed. Regarding his basic training, his comment in this letter says it all....

"No more basic training thank God."

LETTER 19

Pvt Martin Paulson
Co A 88 Inf Tng Bn
Camp Roberts, Calif

Postage: 6 cents airmail
Feb 25, 1944 11 AM
Camp Roberts, Calif

Mrs. A. Furford
Rt 1 Box 352
Kent, Wash

Dear Ruth, Curly & George,   February 21
I just found out today that I probably wont get a furlough for awhile, maybe. I mean I dont think I will but I may. I got the $15 allright. We finished our training Saturday and I now have a diploma saying I am a heavy weapons man for the infantry.
There isnt anything else to write about. If anything comes up I will let you know. I may get shipped any time to some other outfit, but I am pretty sure they wont send me over.

Martin

Martin graduated from Basic Training and says he is now a heavy weapons man for the Infantry. Here are more pictures of the training at Camp Roberts during WWII from Martin's photo album. [59] [60]

---

[59]http://www.militarymuseum.org/CpRobertsPostcards.html
[60]Bottom two photos from Martin's photo album

Parading to the target range

37 millimeter on 1,000 inch range

Keep them flying

Artillery Drill

155 millimeter Howitzer artillery training

Firing the 75 millimeter gun

LETTER 20

Pvt Martin Paulson
Co A 88 Inf Tng Bn
Camp Roberts, Calif

Mrs. A. Furford
Rt 1 Box 352
Kent, Wash

Postage: Free
Mar 3, 1944 3:30 PM
Camp Roberts, Calif

Dear Ruth & Curly,   *Mar ~~February~~ 2*

I guess I had better let you know that I got both checks allright and that it will probably be another befor I get my furlough from what I can find out. It sure seems funny around here. Only a few of us are left and now the rookies have started coming in for the next cycle. We dont do any training now. All we do is try to keep off details and loaf when we get on one. I am sure getting lazy.

I went into Sam Magile last night and really had a good time. Every time I went out before I always went at least as far a Paso Robles because I thought that San Magile was too small to have any fun at. Believe it or not there was just as many women there as soldiers. In Paso Robles there are a least 50 soldiers to every woman.

I cut an article out of the paper about our 25 mile hike I will send to you. I would like to have you save it for me though. I have been taking some pictures with my camera and they gave me some doubles of some of the pictures. I will put some of them in this letter that you can have.

Well I guess thats about all I can think of now. There really isnt much happening around here.   *Martin*

PS Curly, I saw Olson the other day. He said he was going to the hospital for an operation for hernia.

On the next page is the article mentioned in Martin's letter regarding the march back to camp after Bivouac. What an honor!! And what an interesting read!

Martin tells of going to San Miguel instead of Paso Robles. Below is a map showing Camp Roberts in relation to the surrounding area.

A) Camp Roberts
B) Paso Robles with San Miguel between

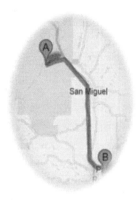

Today, the 18.4 mile trip from Camp Roberts to Paso Robles takes 27 min. In 1944 roads were not what they are today so travel would have taken longer and often by train.

It must have been wonderful to be able to get off base to enjoy female company and have a good time after such long intense training.

FRIDAY, FEB. 25, 1944

Record Made By 88th Men On Bivouac

By PVT. MILTON C. JONES
Co. A, 88th Inf. Tng. Bn.

A record of endurance and stamina was set by trainees of the 88th Inf. Tng. Bn. last week when they completed a 25-mile bivouac march in seven hours.

"Brother, I sure feel sorry for the next cycle if they try to beat our record."

This statement made by many of the men expresses their opinion of the battalion's feat.

The march in from a two-week bivouac marked the first time the 25-mile distance was covered here by Infantry trainees. It was made in conformance with War Department regulations prescribing the requirements for awarding the "Expert Infantryman Badge." These regulations allow a time of eight hours for the march.

The opinion of the battalion officers regarding the march was expressed by one of them when he said, "This march certainly proves that the men are entitled to be called soldiers. They have graduated from the class of rookies."

Winding up two weeks of strenuous training, the march started at 0300 Feb. 12, from the bivouac area on P-17. Only three breaks, totaling 35 minutes, were taken, so the marching time amounted to six and one-half hours. This required maintaining a cadence of about 116 steps a minute over all types of terrain. Which, if you ask any of the men of the 88th, is "hitting the ball," especially when you're wearing a full field pack with gas mask, rifle and other equipment.

The pace was set by Sgt. Arthur H. Cunningham, Co. B, under the supervision of his company commander, Captain Barham.

During bivouac, carefully-planned problems simulating battle conditions as closely as possible provided much valuable training and proved highly interesting to the men. The problems had been arranged by Lt. Col. Louie C. Aston, battalion inspector of training, who was in the fighting on Guadalcanal.

Much realism was added t[o]

Guadalcanal.

Much realism was added to the execution of the problems by the fact that many of the officers have seen overseas service. They were able to give their men many sidelights and combat suggestions based on their personal experiences. Lt. Col. H. F. Newell, battalion CO, as well as all of the company commanders have been engaged in active duty in the Pacific area. Lt. Henry R. Peterson, Co. A, was on Guadalcanal; Capt. G. S. Barham, Co. B, Guadalcanal; Lt. Lewis C. Allen, Co. C, New Guinea, and Capt. Joel B. Wood, Co. D, Alaska.

One problem presented itself though which hadn't been scheduled by Capt. James Schults, Bn. S-3, and called for an entirely new brand of tactics.

One morning Pvt. Sing B. Gin, trainee of Co. C, dashed into Co. HQ to report that something strange was going on in the slit trench which he had so carefully dug two-by-two-by-six-Golly.

Queenie, a friendly little dog who had attached herself to the company, had just brought into the world seven little additions for the company roster.

Lieutenant Cross, assistant S-3, assumed the responsibility of arranging transportation and a guard detail to bring the family back to the battalion area. The latest reports are that the new members of Co. C are quite content with Roberts life.

Mid-bivouac Sunday provided time for a much needed clean-up and recreation period. Blessed with a bright, sunny day, the bivouac area took on the appearance of a nudist camp. Pinkish-skinned G.I.'s experimented in the nimble art of bathing in a quart of water—one pint in a helmet for soaping, then a second pint for rinsing.

An open-air barber shop set up under a tree by Pvt. Virgil Harris, Co. A, did a land-office business.

The acme of camouflage must have been reached on at least one slit trench as it is said to have accidentally claimed none other than the battalion commander, Colonel Newell.

—— Buy War Bonds ——

LETTER 21

Pvt Martin Paulson Co A 88 Inf Tng Bn Camp Roberts, Calif	Postage: 6 cents airmail Mar 8, 1944 3:30 PM Camp Roberts, Calif

Mrs. A. Paulson
Rt 1 Box 352
Kent, Wash

Dear Ruth & Curly,   *Mar ~~February~~ 7,*

Here I go again. How about sending me $50 as soon as you can. I just filled out my income tax return and as I was afraid of I owe the government a little money. If I didn't have any money I could get out of paying but there is more red tape and I would have to swear I was broke and everything so I guess I had better pay.

I found out that I had to have some dental work done and that was why they held me up. It took them 2 weeks after the training before they eaven said anything and a couple of days more before they did anything. I will be luck if I get home on furlough in another month.

There isnt much to do now except try to keep off details which I have been pretty lucky in doing lately. We dont get any more training now. Did I mention to you before that I got a diploma. It says I have satisfacoraly completed seventeen weeks of basic training and that I am heavy weapons trained.

The lights are going out pretty soon so I guess I will have to stop.

Martin

I just thought of a better idea. Instead of sending me the money would you draw out the money and mail my return for me. I am including the forms in this letter.

The mention of having to pay on his "income tax return" for 1943 brought up an interesting question: *what were the tax policies during WWII?*

THE PRESIDENT, THE CONGRESS, & TAXES

Federal tax policy was highly contentious during the war. President Franklin D. Roosevelt worked with congress and both sides agreed on the need for high taxes (along with heavy borrowing) to pay for the war. Top marginal tax rates ranged from 81%-94% for the duration of the war, and the income level subject to the highest rate was lowered from $5,000,000 to $200,000. Roosevelt tried unsuccessfully to impose a 100% surtax on after-tax incomes over $25,000 (equal to roughly $335,769 today). Congress also enlarged the tax base by lowering the minimum income to pay taxes, and by reducing personal exemptions and deductions. By 1944 nearly every employed person was paying federal income taxes (compared to 10% in 1940).

Many controls were put on the economy. The most important were price controls, imposed on most products and monitored by the Office of Price Administration *(OPA)*. Wages were also controlled. Corporations dealt with numerous agencies, especially the War production Board (WPB), and the War and Navy departments, which had the purchasing power and priorities that largely reshaped and expanded industrial production.

Even before the United States entered the Second World War, increasing defense spending and the need for monies to support the opponents of Axis aggression led to the passage in 1940 of two tax laws that increased individual and corporate taxes, which were followed by another tax hike in 1941. By the end of the war the nature of the income tax had been fundamentally altered. Reductions in exemption levels meant that taxpayers with taxable incomes of only $500 faced a bottom tax rate of 23 percent, while taxpayers with incomes over $1 million faced a top rate of 94 percent! These tax changes increased federal receipts from $8.7 billion in 1941 to $45.2 billion in 1945. Even with an economy stimulated by war-time production, federal taxes as a share of GDP grew from 7.6 percent in 1941 to 20.4 percent in 1945. Beyond the rates and revenues, however, another aspect about the income tax that changed was the increase in the number of income taxpayers from 4 million in 1939 to 43 million in 1945.[61] [Bottom line: EVERYONE, including soldiers who earned wages paid taxes]

RATIONING - continuation of report

In 1942 a rationing system was begun to guarantee minimum amounts of necessities to everyone (especially poor people) and prevent inflation.

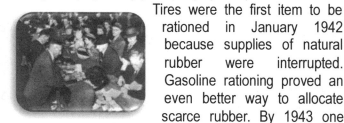

Tires were the first item to be rationed in January 1942 because supplies of natural rubber were interrupted. Gasoline rationing proved an even better way to allocate scarce rubber. By 1943 one needed government issued ration coupons to purchase typewriters, coffee, sugar, gasoline, bicycles,

Families registering for Ration Books

Buying goods with Ration Coupons

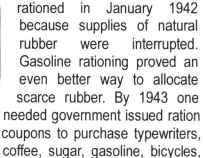

clothing, fuel oil, silk, nylon, stoves, shoes, meat, cheese, butter, lard, margarine, canned foods, dried fruits, jam, and many other items. Some items—like new automobiles and appliances were no longer made. The rationing system did not apply to used-goods (like clothes or cars).

---

[61]http://www.policyalmanac.org/economic/archive/tax_history.shtml

To get a classification and a book of rationing stamps, one had to appear before a local rationing board. Each person in a household received a ration book, including babies and children. When purchasing gasoline, a driver had to present a gas card along with a ration book and cash. Ration stamps were valid only for a set period to forestall hoarding. All forms of automobile racing were banned, including Indianapolis. Sightseeing driving was banned, too.[62]

PERSONAL SAVINGS - continuation of report

War Bond

WWII Poster – "Drive the Axis to Decay by Buying War Stamps"

Personal income was at an all-time high, and more dollars were chasing fewer goods to purchase. This was a recipe for economic disaster that was largely avoided because Americans—cajoled daily by their government to do so—were also saving money at an all-time high rate, mostly in War Bonds but also in private savings accounts and insurance policies. Consumer saving was strongly encouraged through investment in War Bonds that would mature after the war. Most workers had an automatic payroll deduction; children collected savings stamps until they had enough to buy a bond. Bond rallies were held throughout the U.S. with famous celebrities, usually Hollywood film stars, to enhance the bond advertising effectiveness. Several stars were responsible for personal appearance tours that netted multiple millions of dollars in bond pledges—an astonishing amount in 1943. The public paid 3/4 of the face value of a war bond, and received the full face value back after a set number of years. This shifted their consumption from the war to postwar, and allowed over 40% of GDP to go to military spending, with moderate inflation.

WWII Poster

Americans were challenged to put "at least 10% of every paycheck into Bonds." Compliance was very high, with entire factories of workers earning a special "Minuteman" flag to fly over their plant if all workers belonged to the "Ten Percent Club."

---

[62] https://www.google.com/search?q=pictures+of+rationing+books

<u>LABOR</u> - continuation of report

The unemployment problem ended in the United States with the preparations leading up to World War II. Greater wartime production created millions of new jobs, while the <u>draft</u> reduced the number of young men available for civilian jobs. So great was the demand for labor that millions of retired people, housewives, and students entered the labor force, lured by patriotism and wages. Roosevelt stated that the efforts of civilians at home to support the war through personal sacrifice was as critical to winning the war as the efforts of the soldiers themselves. [63]

THE DEVELOPMENT OF THE UNITED STATES LABOR FORCE, THE ARMED FORCES AND UNEMPLOYMENT DURING THE WAR YEARS:

Year	Total labor force (*1000)	Armed forces (*1000)	Unemployed (*1000)	Unemployment rate (%)
1939	55,588	370	9,480	17.2
1940	56,180	540	8,120	14.6
1941	57,530	1,620	5,560	9.9
1942	60,380	3,970	2,660	4.7
1943	64,560	9,020	1,070	1.9
1944	66,040	11,410	670	1.2
1945	65,290	11,430	1,040	1.9
1946	60,970	3,450	2,270	3.9

Additional pictures, posters and advertisements of War Bonds and Rationing.

---

[63]http://en.wikipedia.org/wiki/United_States_home_front_during_World_War_II

LETTER 22

Paso Robles (written under return address)

Pvt Martin Paulson	Mrs. A Furford	Postage: 6 cents airmail
Co A 88 Inf Tng Bn	Rt1 Box352	Mar 14, 1944 11:00 AM
Camp Roberts, Calif	Kent, Wash	Camp Roberts, Calif

Dear Ruth & Curly,   *March 13,*

I suppose you will really be surprised to get this letter so soon after the last one. Well the trouble is that now I can go in to town every night and when I get in there I always spend more than I intend to, and I want enough money on hand to buy a ticket if I get a furlough. I really hate to bother you again so soon but would you send me $25 more. I bet you are sure sorry I appointed you my banker.

You can tell George that I have some shells that have been fired that look like real shells that I will give him when I come home. I also got a 81 MM mortar shell that I am going to make a lamp out of. I got a chance to buy some of these C & D rations. I am going to make you eat some D rations eaven if I have to use a club. Im telling you, you really have to be hungry to eat them. When I thought I was going to get my furlough I bought 25 of these big hershey bars to bring home. You know I can get them for 10 cents each here. If I get a chance to get any before I leave I will bring some up with me.

How do you like the pictures my camera takes. They are pretty good some times. That is if I am lucky enough to get every thing set right. I took a lot of pictures while we were on bivouac and some of them came out real good.

Curly, if they ever start to draft you dont go in the Army. Take the Sea Bees. If you get in the army about the only chance you have to get into anything is the infantry now. They have every type of person you ever heard of in the company I was in. We had one of the best vioulinist in the country, George Swagart of Chicago, lawyers, proffesor, fruit tramps and everything. It doesnt make any difference what you are qualified to do. The infantry is where they need the men. You might not realize it now but you will sure be sorry if you ever get in the infantry.

I want to get this off tonight so I guess I will have to quit.   *Love   Martin*

City of Paso Robles 'The Pass of the Oaks'

Paso Robles (where Martin was going almost every evening) has a very rich history. As we look into its history we will get a small look into what the area was like when Martin was there. Although there is a lot of history on Paso Robles prior to 1940 and after WWII, there is not much during 1941-1946.

The Salinan Indians lived in the area thousands of years even before the mission era. They knew this area as the "Springs" or the "Hot Springs." As far back as 1795, Paso Robles has been spoken of and written about as *"California's oldest watering place"*—the place to go for springs and mud baths. By 1868 people were coming from as far away as Oregon, Nevada, Idaho, and even Alabama. Besides the well-known mud baths, there were the Iron Spring and the Sand Spring, which bubbles through the sand and was said to produce delightful sensations.

1942 Paso Robles Garden Inn Hotel

Wine grapes were introduced to the Paso Robles soil in 1797 by the Spanish conquistadors and Franciscan missionaries. Spanish explorer Francisco Cortez envisioned an abundant wine-producing operation and encouraged settlers from Mexico and other parts of California to cultivate the land. The first vineyard artists in the area (as they were called then) were the Padres of the Mission San Miguel. Their old fermentation vats and grapevine artwork can still be seen at the Mission north of the city of Paso Robles.[64]

A Paso Robles Vineyard

The ranches in the outlying areas were very important to the Paso Robles area. On these ranches could be found large herds of cattle and horses, grain

---

[64]http://en.wikipedia.org/wiki/Paso_Robles,_California

crops, garden produce, and fruit and nut orchards. At one time, Paso Robles was known as "Almond City" because the almond growers created the largest concentration of almond orchards in the world. Some of these orchards can still be seen in the area and many of these ranch lands have become vineyards for many wineries. To show their appreciation to the ranchers, the business people established Pioneer Day in October 1931 as an annual city holiday. This is still celebrated today.

In November 1940, construction on a new Army base began 13 miles north of Paso Robles. Camp Roberts opened in February 1941 and the war years began in December of 1941. In 1942 Estralle Army Air Field was built northeast of the city. When it was decommissioned in 1944, it became an airport. Changes in Paso Robles came through the influx of workers, Army officers, trainees and USO entertainers. The USO was an

1906 Carnegie Library, Paso Robles

active place in Paso Robles. WWII brought an influx of military personnel and families into the area. In 1940 there were 3,045 residents in the city. The 2010 census reported 29,793 residents. [65]

Army Field Ration Type C

Martin mentions bringing home shells of various sizes and C & D rations that he is going to *make* his family eat. George does not remember getting the shells (he was 6 years old then). As for the C & D rations further research revealed that with advances in food technology more than 23 different rations and supplements were developed during WWII, and over 8 million personnel were fed with *one billion* individual rations. Troops ate C-Rations for up to 90 days. The rations were generally disliked by soldiers. C-Ration:

M units (meat and vegetables) - *6 of 11 M-units contained beans!*
B units (bread, sugar and coffee)

---

[65]http://www.pasorobleshistoricalsociety.org/a-history-of-paso-robles/

RATIONS OF WWII:

Life Raft Ration - included C biscuits, pemmican, chocolate tablets, and milk tablets

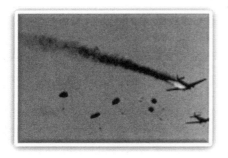

Bail-Out Ration (example: 2 - 2Oz. Pkgs. Malted Milk Dextrose and Dextrose tablets
2 – 2 oz. Ration D Bars
2 - Sticks Chewing Gum
1 - Pkg. Bouillon Powder)

Parachute Ration - included a combination of D bars, fruit bars, hard candy, lemon-juice powder, and K biscuits

Airborne Life Boat Ration - the packaged ration contained food for two men for one meal, each package including a breakfast and supper unit.

A-Ration - rations were generally whatever meat and produce could be obtained locally, so there could be great variety from one theater of operations to the next.

B-Ration - modified to reduce bulk and weight

C-Ration - the early waves of criticism from the field were aimed at the monotonous meat diet offered by the first C ration. By 1939 the six-can ration contained 4,437 calories and weighed five pounds ten ounces including 6 different meat combinations

D-Bar - the D bar led the way to intensive research in Army subsistence during the war. Over 450 million bare were produced and stockpiled overseas by 1944.

K-Ration - was the Laboratory's answer to the demand for an individual, easy-to-carry ration that could be used in assault and combat operations. The most famous ration of WWII was the K-Ration, it was first requested for paratroopers to carry in their pockets. Its components were the most nutritionally balanced of any ration available at the time. One of the 9 requirements for the K-Ration:[66] *"it should not disrupt normal elimination from the bowel or derange the chemistry of the body!"*[67]

Three WW II paratrooper buddies enjoy a quick lunch consisting of the Field Ration K developed by the Quartermaster Corps.

Assault Lunch - the need for a lightweight, small, and concentrated ration to provide assault troops with an easily

carried prepared food, which would bridge the gap between the beginning of actual combat and the restoration of normal supply functions, became evident during the amphibious campaigns in the Pacific in 1944

---

[66] http://www.qmfound.com/army_rations_historical_background.htm
[67] http://nsrdec.natick.army.mil/about/f food/history/Historical_Rations.pdf

5 in 1 & 10 in 1 - A small-group field ration composed of components of the standard field ration type B packed in basic packages of five (or ten) complete rations each.. The inner and outer packages are to be proof against water, vapor, moisture, and chemical agents. They are to be of such shape and dimensions as to be suitable for either animal-pack or man-carry, and sufficiently sturdy as to material and construction to withstand normal handling and transportation in motor vehicles, on pack animals or by man carry

Air Crew Lunch - the Aircrew Lunch contained a selection of small loose candies, candy bars, and gum packaged in a two-compartment box with sliding sleeve

Mountain Ration - specification in November 1942 proposed that the mountain ration consist of food for four men for one day. The basic components of three menus making up the ration included Carter's spread (a butter substitute), soluble coffee, dry milk, biscuits, hard candy, cereal (three varieties), dehydrated cheese, D ration bars, fruit bars, gum, lemon-juice powder, dehydrated soup, salt, sugar, tea, cigarettes, and toilet paper. Menu 1 offered variety with luncheon meat and dehydrated baked beans; menu 2 added corned beef and dehydrated potatoes; and pork sausage meat and precooked rice were included in menu 3. The components were assembled in a solid fiber carton labeled "U. S. Army Mountain Ration." Three cartons, one of each menu, were over-packed in a similarly labeled outer carton.

10th Mountain Division - (in Italy, part of the U.S. Fifth Army) photograph was taken near Bologna, Italy on the morning of 14 April 1945

Jungle Ration - Assembled especially for jungle troops it consisted of the basic pattern – food for four men for one day – which followed the mountain-ration design. The Jungle ration included canned meat, dry milk, peanuts, biscuits, precooked cereal, gum, cigarettes, hard candy, cocoa beverage powder, soluble coffee, fruit bars, lemon powder, raisins, salt, sugar, and toilet tissue. Components were compactly assembled in a specially constructed solid fiber carton.

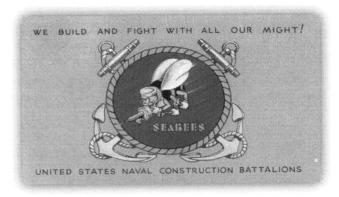

WE BUILD AND FIGHT WITH ALL OUR MIGHT!

SEABEES

UNITED STATES NAVAL CONSTRUCTION BATTALIONS

SEABEES Logo

Martin suggests to Curly (Ruth's husband, Arvid Furford) that if they drafted him to choose Seabees. The following is a short history of who the Seabees were and the role they played in WWII.

After the December 7, 1941 Japanese attack on Pearl Harbor and the United States entry into the war, the use of *civilian labor* in war zones became impractical. The need for *a militarized Naval Construction Force* to build advance bases in the war zone was self-evident. Therefore, Rear Admiral Ben Moreell determined to activate, organize, and man Navy construction units. On December 28, 1941, he requested specific authority to carry out this decision, and on January 5, 1942, he gained authority from the Bureau of Navigation to recruit men from the construction trades for assignment to a Naval Construction Regiment composed of three Naval Construction Battalions. This is the actual beginning of the renowned *Seabees*, who obtained their designation from the initial letters of **C**onstruction **B**attalion. Admiral Moreell personally furnished them with their official motto: *Construimus, Batuimus* – "We Build, We Fight."

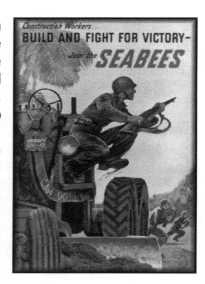

SEABEES Poster WWII

The first recruits were the men *who had worked in shipyards* and built docks and wharfs and even ocean liners and aircraft carriers. By the end of the war, 325,000 such men had enlisted in the Seabees. They knew more than 60 skilled trades, not to mention the unofficial ones of souvenir making and "moonlight procurement." Nearly 11,400 officers joined the Civil Engineer Corps during the war, and 7,960 of them served with the Seabees.

As the war progressed and construction projects became larger and more complex, more than one battalion frequently had to be assigned to a base. For example, 55,000

Seabees with the 4th Naval Construction Brigade build an incinerator out of spare parts and 55 gallon drums

Seabees were assigned to Okinawa and the battalions were organized into 11 regiments and 4 brigades, which, in turn, were all under the command of the Commander, Construction Troops, who was a Navy Civil Engineer Corps officer, Commodore Andrew G. Bisset. Moreover, his command also included 45,000 United States Army engineers, aviation engineers, and a few British engineers. He therefore commanded 100,000 construction troops in all, the largest concentration of construction troops during the entire war. [68]

---

[68]http://en.wikipedia.org/wiki/Seabees_in_World_War_II

Martin mentioned various men within his company who were drafted into the Army... a well-known violinist (George Swagart of Chicago), lawyers, professors, fruit tramps and many others. He says, *"It doesnt make any difference what you are qualified to do. The infantry is where they need the men."*

Then: *"You might not realize it now but you will sure be sorry if you ever get in the infantry"*

His comments tell you he realizes ...
- what his training is preparing him for,
- the seriousness of this training,
- that it didn't matter the standing you had in the community, and
- that *all* men were called to serve their country.

Martin at Camp Roberts with items in his hands which he purchased for home... if, and when, he gets furlough!

LETTER 23

Pvt Martin Paulson
Co A 88 Inf Tng Bn
Camp Roberts, Calif

Postage: Free
Mar 27, 1944 5:30 PM
Camp Roberts, Calif

Mrs A. Furford
Rt 1 Box 352
Kent, Wash

Dear Ruth & Curly,

Thanks a lot for sending the money. Whenever they get around to giving me my furlough they will just tell me and then if I havent got the money to buy my ticket right away, no furlough. I am going to be smart this time and not cash the money order until I get the furlough, that way I will be sure to have the money.

Did I ever tell you that I am staying in a company where most of the men are overseas men. That is I sleep and eat here but I still belong to the 88th. Most of them were in the 164th infantry that fought at Guadicanal. I have heard so many stories that I bet I could fool eaven a expert that I was over there if I had all their ribbons. A fellow hasnt been in anything around here if he can get all his ribbons on his blouse at the same time. One guy that sleeps pretty close to me has a D.S.C.

You havent mentioned much about George lately. How is he getting along. I bet he has changed a lot since I left. Is he just as indepentant in school as he was.

You probably wont know me when I come home. I dont look like it but I weigh over 180 now. If I do anything to work up an appetite when I get home on furlough I guarantee to eaven give Curly some close competition.

Thats all I can think of now.

Martin

Martin mentions bunking with guys from the 164th. The 164th Infantry Regiment was the first United States Army unit on Guadalcanal. The following helps one understand more of what Martin learned from their stories.

Commanded by Colonel Earle Sarles, the 164th transited the South Pacific ferry route in January 1942 to New Caledonia. There they joined the 182nd Infantry Regiment and the 132nd Infantry Regiment, in addition to artillery, engineer and other support units to form a new division on May 24, 1942, designated the *American Division*. The name *Americal* was derived from a combination of the words America and New Caledonia. The regiment spent nearly five months in combat training. In September, Colonel Sarles, a National Guard officer, was replaced as commander of the regiment by Colonel Bryant E. Moore, a West Point graduate. Moore would subsequently be promoted to command an infantry division in Europe, and the regiment would serve under other commanders, almost all of whom advanced to general's stars.

3rd Battalion 164th Infantry North Dakota National Guard

Arriving at Guadalcanal on October 13, 1942 ahead of its brother regiments as emergency reinforcement for the 1st Marine Division, the Regiment was the first U.S. Army unit to engage in offensive action during World War II in the Battle of Guadalcanal. Between October 24 and October 27, elements of the regiment withstood repeated assaults from Japanese battalions and inflicted some two thousand enemy casualties. The First Marine commander, Major General A. Vandegrift, was so impressed by the soldiers' stand that he issued a unit commendation to the regiment for having demonstrated *an overwhelming superiority over the enemy.* In addition, the marines took the unusual step of awarding Lt. Colonel Robert Hall, commander of the 3rd Battalion, 164th, with the Navy Cross for his role in these battles.

U.S. troops with the 164th Infantry Regiment, Americal Division, pass a truck made into an armored truck by the Japanese on Dumaguete, Negros Island, P.I., on April 29, 1945

Until the Americal Division commander, Major General Alexander M. Patch, and other units of the division arrived, the 164th fought alongside the Marines in a series of encounters with Japanese units in the Point Cruz area where they successfully dislodged enemy troops from two hilltop strong points. The action earned them the nickname *"The 164th Marines."* Members of the 164th were also known as *Jungle fighters"* within the U.S. media because of the terrain on which they fought.

Later, the 164th participated in extensive jungle patrols as well as organized offensive sweeps of the island to eliminate remaining Japanese resistance. This experience gained the regiment valuable combat experience in jungle travel and navigation, ambush and counter-ambush, and small-unit tactics using small arms and light support weapons. After the Battle of Guadalcanal, the regiment returned to Fiji with the rest of the Americal Division to refit and replenish losses. At this point, many veteran officers and men of the 164th volunteered to join the 5307th Composite Unit, better known as *Merrill's Marauders,* for service in Burma. With the rest of the Americal, the Regiment later participated in the Bougainville campaign, then fought to secure the islands of Leyte, Cebu, Negros, and Bohol in the Philippines. The regiment was slated to be part of the invasion of Japan when the war ended in August. [69, 70]

Martin said one soldier of the 164th Infantry had received the D.S.C. (Distinguished Service Cross). Research discovered the following individual in the 164th who met the criteria to receive this medal prior to March 1944 (when Martin wrote this letter). It may or may not be that person, but he deserves recognition.

CLARK, WILLIAM A.

SYNOPSIS: Sergeant William A. Clark (ASN: 37035020), United States Army, was awarded the Distinguished Service Cross for extraordinary heroism in connection with military operations against an armed enemy while serving with Company M, 164th Infantry Regiment, Americal Division, in action against enemy forces on 25 October 1942. Sergeant Clark's intrepid actions, personal bravery and zealous devotion to duty exemplify the highest traditions of the military forces of the United States and reflect great credit upon himself, the Americal Division, and the United States Army. [71]
General Orders: Headquarters, U.S. Army Forces in the South Pacific Area, General Orders No. 39 (1943)
Action Date: 25-Oct-42
Service: Army
Rank: Sergeant
Company: Company M
Regiment: 164th Infantry regiment
Division: Americal Division

---

[69]http://en.wikipedia.org/wiki/164th_Infantry_Regiment_%28United_States%29
[70]http://creativecommons.org/licenses/by-nc-sa/2.0/deed.en (picture of 164th on Negro Island)
[71]http://militarytimes.com/citations-medals-awards/recipient.php?recipientid=30534

The Distinguished Service Cross is a military medal
Awarded by the United States Army [72]

Eligibility: Distinguishes himself by extraordinary heroism not justifying the Medal of Honor while in an action against an enemy of the United States.

Awarded for: Extraordinary heroism not justifying the Medal of Honor; and the act or acts of heroism must have been so notable and have involved risk of life so extraordinary as to set the individual apart from his or her comrades.

First awarded: 01/02/18

Total awarded: 13,400

Next (higher): Medal of Honor

Equivalent:
Navy-Marine Corps	(Navy Cross)
Air Force	(Air Force Cross)
Coast Guard	(Navy Cross)

Next (lower): Distinguished Service Medals: Defense, Army, Navy, Air Force, Coast Guard

---

[72]http://en.wikipedia.org/wiki/Distinguished_Service_Cross_%28United_States%29

LETTER 24

Pvt Martin Paulson   Postage: 8 cents Airmail
Co A 88 Inf Tng Bn   Mar 30, 1944 3:30 PM
Camp Roberts, Calif   Camp Roberts, Calif

Mrs. A. Furford
Rt 1 Box 352
Kent, Wash.

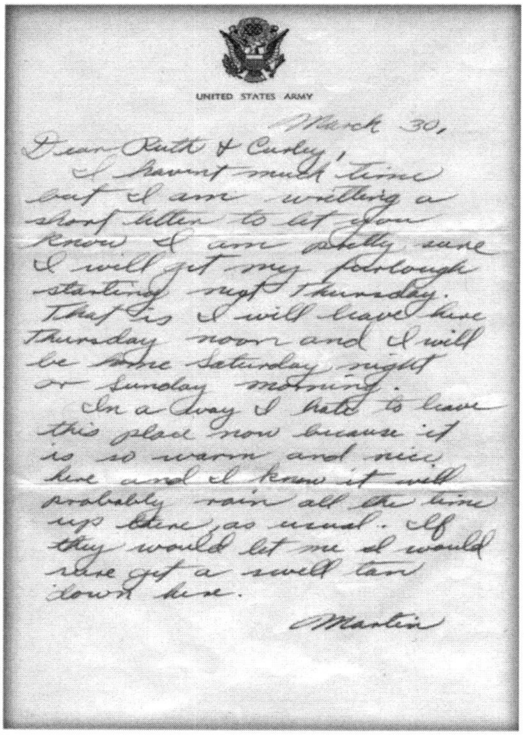

March 30,

Dear Ruth & Curly,
    I havent much time but I am writing a short letter to let you know I am pretty sure I will get my furloough starting next Thursday. That is I will leave here Thursday noon and I will be home Saturday night.
    In a way I hate to leave this place now because it is so warm and nice here and I know it will probably rain all the time up there as usual. If they would let me I would sure get a swell tan down here.

Martin

MARTIN GOT HIS FURLOUGH!

We will not hear from Martin again until April 20! The following pictures were taken while he was on furlough. Martin looks very happy to be home with family!

Pvt. Martin Paulson enjoying a day on Lake Tapps, Washington 1944

Standing: Martin with his Dad, Adolf Paulson Sitting: sister Ruth (George on lap), sister Karen, sister Myrtle

Standing: Ruth, Martin Sitting: Myrtle, Karen

Martin with sister, Ruth (and Myrtle's dog Snuffy)

SOUTH PACIFIC
&
NEW CALEDONIA

One of the transports identified as heading to New Caledonia.

LETTER 25

Note the return address:
Albert V. McGee
Co H – 5 BN 2 REGT
AGF REPL DEPOT #2
FORT ORD, CAL

Postage: Free
April 30, 1944 12 - M
Fort Ord, Calif

Mrs A. Furford
Rt 1, Box 352
Kent, Wash

Dear Ruth,   *April 28*

I am not supposed to write this letter because I am on shipping orders and I think I am headed for a port of embarkation. I havent been asigned to any outfit yet so will probably go into some outfit over in Australia or some place and take at least 6 months training with them before I ever get into anything. It will most likely be a month or more before I get on a boat so if you dont hear from me for awhile dont be surprised.

I am still in heavy weapons and I found out that I had a real good record from Roberts so I will probably stay in them. I am sure glad they didnt stick me in a rifle outfit.

By the way you ought to see my hair cut. They finally (really) gave me a real GI haircut. One thing I dont have to comb my hair every morning now.

I dont think I will be able to write to anyone else so would you tell them for me.

I broke my watch the other day so I am going to try and send it to you to keep for me. I also took off my crossed rifles off my blouse and am sending it to you. You said you wanted one.

Talk about silly regulations. I am sure glad I am leaving this place. I eaven had to get a special pass to wear that overseas cap that I wore most of the time at home before I could wear it. If I can find the slip I will send it to you. That is just one example.

Well I guess I had better close and try to find a way to mail this letter. Tell everyone that I will write as soon as I can.

Love Martin

All previous letters had been signed simply "Martin." By signing *"Love, Martin,"* it speaks volumes of Martin's emotions. He tries hard to reassure family,

Sign at entrance to Fort Ord

but in the process you can almost feel his concern of events to come. This letter was mailed from Fort Ord, California.

Fort Ord is near Monterey Bay in Monterey County, California, approximately 80 miles south of San Francisco. In 1917, land was purchased just north of the city of Monterey for use as an artillery training field for the Army. The area was known as the Gigling Reservation, U.S. Field Artillery Area, Presidio of Monterey and Gigling Field Artillery Range. In 1933, the artillery field became Camp Ord, named in honor of Maj. Gen. Edward Ord, a Union Army leader during the American Civil War who also served in the Second Seminole War and Indian Wars.

In 1941, *Camp Ord* became *Fort Ord*. For the next thirty years, the fort was the Army's primary facility for basic training. Fort Ord was also a staging area for units departing for war, and at one time had 50,000 troops on the installation.[73]

Fort Ord Army Post - in use 1917-1994

Martin says he is sending his sister, Ruth, his *crossed rifles* as she had said she would like to have one. This U.S. Army branch insignia represents each individual service member's specific field of service. In this case: *The Infantry.* Each soldier (both enlisted personnel and officers) wear

---

[73]http://en.wikipedia.org/wiki/Fort_Ord

their branch insignia badge on his or her formal uniform. Enlisted soldiers wear the branch insignia on the left coat lapel. Martin mentioned he was removing it from his 'blouse.' The uniform in the picture at right is the Army 4-pocket "blouse."

DID YOU NOTE THE RETURN ADDRESS? It is not Martin's return address. *Albert V. McGee* is the person Martin handed his letter to in hopes it would get mailed since he was being shipped out (and they were under orders not to tell anyone).

Albert & Celia "Pie" were married June 1948 (picture from their grave stone)

Albert Vernon McGee
PFC US ARMY   WORLD WAR II
Sep 28, 1924 - Mar 20, 2001

Albert V. McGee's military enlistment records stated:
- ✓ he was from Oklahoma;
- ✓ his enlistment date Aug 2, 1943 in Sacramento, California;
- ✓ his residence at that time as San Joaquin, California;
- ✓ and his terms of enlistment were…

"for the duration of the War or other emergency, plus six months, subject to the discretion of the President or otherwise according to law."

It also stated he was single, had 4 years of high school, and that he was *"selected"* (drafted).

The 1940 Census lists: Thomas J. McGee (Head of household) age 40; May F McGee (wife) age 34; Hubert L McGee (son) age 18; **Albert V. McGee (son) age 15**; and Ruthell McGee (daughter) age 13 of Tuskahoma, Pushmataha County, Oklahoma.

Albert would have been 18 years of age when he was drafted in 1943. He passed in 2001 and was interned at a cemetery in Clayton, Oklahoma. Online cemetery records show Albert as 76 years of age at the time of his death. Along with wife Celia "Pie", he had a son, Tommy Joe; a daughter, Carolyn Sue; and grandchildren Jackey, Valerie & Christy.

The lady who answered the phone at the cemetery was amazed as her husband was a relative of Albert's! At the time of this writing, Celia "Pie" is in a nursing home and their children and extended family live in the area of Clayton, Oklahoma. The information of what Albert did for Martin *(mailing a letter for a fellow soldier being shipped overseas*) was passed on to his family. When Martin was told that Albert's family had been located, he was surprised as he did not know the soldier's name to whom he had handed the letter, or if the letter had been mailed!

Was Celia's nickname "Pie" because she made wonderful pies?! The family did not know. They had not thought to ask her as they had always known her as "Pie," not Celia.

Co A 88th Infantry Training Battalion Graduation,
February 1944
Pvt Martin Paulson is in 3rd row from bottom
(second standing row) 5th from left

LETTER 26

WAR & NAVY
DEPARTMENTS
V-MAIL SERVICE
OFFICIAL BUSINESS

Mrs. A. Furford
Rt 1 Box 352
Kent, Wash

From: Martin Paulson Pvt
Co. 26 APO 15258
% P.M. San Francisco Cal.

Postage: Penalty for private use
to avoid payment of postage, $300
June 5, 1944 6 PM
US Postal Service NO 2

Dear Ruth,

There isnt very much I can write about. I cant tell you where I am going because in the first place I dont know and in the second place the censor would give me my letter back if I did tell you. All I can say is that I am at sea and as soon as we land I will write and let you know where I am.

There isnt much entertainment on a troop transport and I am sure getting tired of being crowded around. They have boxing matches and music for entertainment, and then there are always lots of gambling which so far I have managed to keep out of.

Thats all I have room to write. Would you send those pictures to me as soon as you can if you haven't already.

Love   Martin

When interviewing Martin, he said he didn't know what there would be to write about as all the letters were censored. This short censored letter contains abundant history!

V-MAIL

V-mail, short for *Victory Mail*, is a *hybrid mail* process used during WWII in America as the primary and secure method to correspond with soldiers stationed abroad. To reduce the logistics of transferring an original letter across the military postal system, a V-mail letter would be...

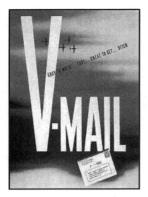

WWII poster promoting the use of V-mail

- censored,
- copied to film,
- and printed back to paper upon arrival at its destination.

Staying in touch with family and friends stationed overseas was just as important in WWII as it is in current military undertakings. Therefore, it is important mailings be

- fast,
- free,
- and difficult for the enemy to intercept.

Victory mail (V-Mail) played the same role over 70 years ago that email, face book, & Twitter play today in keeping lines of communication open between loved ones. V-mail correspondence was written on small letter sheets, 7" by 9 1/8" that would go through mail censors before being photographed and transported as thumbnail-sized images in negative microfilm. Upon arrival to their destination, the negatives would be blown up to 60% their original size 4 ¼" by 5 3/16" and printed.

According to the National Postal Museum, "*V-mail ensured that thousands of tons of shipping space could be reserved for war materials. The 37 mail bags required to carry 150,000 one-page letters could be replaced by a single mail sack. The weight of that same amount of mail was reduced dramatically from 2,575 pounds to a mere 45 pounds.* This saved considerable weight and bulk in a time in which both were hard to manage in a combat zone. [74]

In addition to postal censorship, V-mail also deterred espionage communications by foiling the use of invisible ink, microdots, and micro-printing, none of which would be reproduced in a photocopy. V-Mail could be purchased by civilians also [none of Ruth's letters were by V-Mail]. They would obtain the standard, pre-printed form from the local post office or five and dime store on request. The form contained:

Poster displaying Sheaffer Pen Company's V-Mail canister writing kit

- ✓ space for a letter of about 100 to 300 words,
- ✓ the address of the serviceman or woman to whom the letter was to be delivered,
- ✓ the address of the sender,
- ✓ and a circular area for the censor's stamp of approval.

---

[74]http://en.wikipedia.org/wiki/V-mail

Once the message was written, the form was to be folded and sealed. It then made its way to a processing center where the form was re-opened and fed through a machine that photographed the letters on 16mm film. A continuous roll of this film (100 feet long by 16mm wide) could hold up to 1700 messages and, with the metal container it was housed in, weighed 5.5 oz. A sack of mail holding the same number of regular letters would have weighed 50 lbs. When the V-Mail reached the destination, it was sent to a local processing facility that reversed the process, printing photographs of the letters to be sent to the intended recipient in a three inch by four inch envelope [See Martin's letter for example]. [75]

WWII
V-Mail poster

The letter Martin sent *before* shipping out was dated April 28 (sent April 30). His V-Mail letter is dated May 21, and the photo copy of that letter was sent June 5 from San Francisco. His family received the regular letter a month after the V-mail letter so they did not know he shipped out! Can you imagine getting this V-Mail from a ship and not knowing where your loved one was heading? However, since Martin was shipped from Fort Ord, it would have been reasonable to believe he was heading to the South Pacific battle fields.

Troop sea transport has a history of its own. The following is Martin's memories of his experience:

Converted WWI Freighter
Note how crowded!

"Our ship was the WORST ship in the Navy! It was the SS General Tyler. It was an Army/Marine transport. It was built in WWI as a freighter and was converted in WWII as a transport. It had shacks on the deck for toilets, no air conditioning, and no fresh water except for drinking. Had to use salt water for washing and showering. And it was SO CROWDED. You could barely move. We would build up scum on our skin because of the salty sea water. When we crossed the equator a strong rain shower came. I ran and got soap and went on deck and scrubbed and scrubbed, but couldn't get all the scum off. I had a neighbor who was a Marine and as we were sharing stories about our experiences, he said the ship he was shipped out on was the 'worst' transport ship. I told him it couldn't have been as the ship I was transported on was the worst! We laughed hard when we realized we were both on the same ship! Imagine that, to find all these years later that I had a neighbor who was on the same ship."

---

[75]http://www.armysignalocs.com/jokes/v_mail.htm

Men boarding transport ship during WWII

Research could not locate information on the SS General Tyler. The above photo may not be the actual ship, but it gives one a clear picture of the type of ship Martin described.

The records of ships used to carry troops to their theaters of operations were destroyed intentionally in 1951. According to *U. S. National Archives* records, in 1951 the Department of the Army destroyed all passenger lists, manifests, logs of vessels, and troop movement files of United States Army Transports for World War II. Sorry, but there was no word on why the records were destroyed. Thus, there is no longer an official record of who sailed on what ship. However, there is some very interesting historical information on transport ships.

Another Converted WWI Freighter

The U.S. Army had the largest fleet of vessels of any organization during WWII.

Though the following excerpt was before 1944, it is from an actual military report which gives insight into some Army transports issues.

WATER TRANSPORTATION- U.S. ARMY, 1939-1942, ASF.

According to Col. S. J. Chamberlin, G-4, ...in order to effect the considered movement it was found necessary to employ three vessels of the Mats on Lines (MATSONIA, MONTEREY, and MAUI), three vessels of the American President Lines (PRESIDENT GARFIELD, PRESIDENT TAYLOR, and PRESIDENT JOHNSON), together with six Army transports, and a number of chartered freighters to carry organizational impedimenta. The total movement involved about 1,043 officers and 19,422 enlisted men, with estimated organizational impedimenta of 110,000 tons. The vessels of both the Matson and the American President Lines had to be chartered and *hastily converted to carry troops* at an estimated total cost of $2,250,000.[76]

There were hundreds of U.S. Army Transport ships (U.S.A.T.),[77] and well over a thousand SS ships (Steam Ships). There is not one complete list of ships used for transport in WWII. All maritime commercial cargo and passenger *type* vessels were under strict control of War Shipping Administration (WSA) under

---

[76] http://cgsc.cdmhost.com/cdm/ref/collection/p4013coll8/id/2245
[77]http://www.ask.com/wiki/List_of_ships_of_the_United_States_Army

Executive Order No. 9054. Exempted from WSA control were combatants, vessels owned by Army or Navy and coastal and inland vessels.[78]

War Shipping Administration Established by President Franklin Delano Roosevelt <u>Executive Order No. 9054</u>. February 7, 1942

BY VIRTUE of the authority vested in me by the Constitution and statutes of the United States, including the First War Powers Act, 1941, approved December 18, 1941, as President of the United States and Commander in Chief of the Army and Navy, and in order to assure the most effective utilization of the shipping of the United States for the successful prosecution of the war, it is hereby ordered:

1. There is established within the Office for Emergency Management of the Executive Office of the President a War Shipping Administration under the direction of an Administrator who shall be appointed by and responsible to the President.
2. The Administrator shall perform the following functions and duties:
    (a) Control the operation, purchase, charter, requisition and use of all ocean vessels under the flag or control of the United States, except
    - ➤ combatant vessels of the Army, Navy, and Coast Guard;
    - ➤ fleet auxiliaries of the Navy;
    - ➤ and transports owned by the Army and Navy;
    - ➤ and vessels engaged in coast-wise, inter-coastal, and inland transportation...under the control of the Director of the Office of Defense Transportation.

Soldiers being entertained during transport

---

[78]http://www.usmm.org/fdr/wsalaw.html

LETTER 27

Pvt Martin Paulson
A.S.N. ------------
APO 15258
% PM San Francisco, Cal

Mrs. A. Furford
Rt 1 Box 352
Kent, Wash

Postage: 6 cents airmail
June 13, 1944 4:30 PM
U.S. ARMY APO502

Dear Ruth,   *June 1, 1944*

There still isnt anything that we are allowed to write about conserning where we are or what we are doing that the censors will pass. I suppose though that it wont hurt to write that we are in a safe place and there isnt anything around here to worry about.

I was sure glad to hear that we have finally opened a second front. We dont get many particulars about it though. I bet though that they must have really had a tough go to start with.

Our mail hasent been coming through very good so far. I guess it is mostly because we have been moveing around so much in the last few months. The only ones I have received from you are the two you sent to Fort Ord including the ones with the pictures. Thanks a lot for getting them developed for me. I wonder what was wrong with the ones that I took last and didnt come out? Were the negatives all black or could you see anything at all on them?

How is Ralph coming along? You haven't mentioned anything about him and I havent heard from him.

Thats about all I can think of to write now so I will have to sign off.

Love
Martin

Martin did not get all the pictures he had expected to receive. Most not received were from the week of Bivouac at Camp Roberts and may have been "censored." It sounds like he is very homesick and would really like to hear from family!

Family would have no idea where Martin had been shipped after reading his letter, but it must have been reassuring to know that he was in a safe place. He mentions hearing of a second front being opened and said, *"I bet though that they must have really had a tough go to start with"* ...as we know, D-Day was horrible. The following is a brief explanation of the issues of war leading up to the opening of the second front...

The second front refers to Stalin's wish for the Western Allies to open another front in Europe in 1942 against the Germans to take the pressure off the Russians on the Eastern Front [an invasion of France].

He wanted the Allies to invade mainland Europe as soon as possible to force the Germans to withdraw some of their troops from the Eastern Front. During this period of the war the Germans were pushing far into Southern Russia heading towards Stalingrad.

Roosevelt was keen and willing to launch an invasion in 1942 or 1943 but Churchill and the British did not think it

U.S. Army troops come ashore at Omaha Beach on D-Day, June 6, 1944

would be successful. The allies did not have any landing craft, they did not have air superiority, and the British Army was still under-prepared and equipped to face the German army in Europe again. While the British had a powerful naval and air force, more would still be needed. The American's were still in the process of putting an army together, their industrial might was only just beginning and they had no troops with any combat experience at all. Their navy was heavily involved in the Pacific and new units would be needed for the European Front. Their air force had old and outdated planes which would have been no match for the German air force which was still a powerful force at this stage of the war.

The British Command including Churchill were still haunted by the mass slaughter of the First World War, and as such wanted to ensure they had enough planes, tanks, men and ships to increase the chances of any invasion being successful. During 1942 and 1943 the allies were still a long way from this and a rift started between the Western allies on this issue. It was only with great reluctance that the British actually agreed to an invasion in 1944 in the end.[79]

The short answer: Russia wanted the Allies to invade Europe and put pressure on the Axis from another direction which would mean Germany would have to divide their forces as well as supplies. The landing at D-Day created the second front the Russians wanted. [80]

---

[79] http://answers.yahoo.com/activity?show=IKCxj9gHaa
[80] http://wiki.answers.com/Q/What_is_a_second_front_in_World_War_2

D-DAY: THE ALLIES COME ASHORE

Though originally scheduled for June 5, the landings in Normandy were postponed one day due to foul weather. On the night of June 5/6, the British 6th Airborne Division was dropped to the east of the landing beaches to secure the flank and destroy several bridges to prevent the Germans from bringing up reinforcements. The US 82nd and 101st Airborne Divisions were dropped to the west with the goal of capturing inland towns, opening routes from the beaches, and destroying artillery that could fire on the landings. Flying in from the west, the

Allied air-born troops parachute down into the Netherlands

American airborne drop went badly, with many of the units scattered and far from their intended drop zones. Rallying, many units were able to achieve their objectives as the divisions pulled themselves back together.

Beach Landings

The assault on the beaches began shortly after midnight with Allied bombers pounding German positions across Normandy. This was followed by a heavy naval bombardment. In the early morning hours, waves of troops began hitting the beaches. To the east, the British and Canadians came ashore on Gold, Juno, and Sword Beaches. After overcoming initial resistance, they were able to move inland, though only the Canadians were able to reach their D-Day objectives. On the American beaches to the west, the situation was very different. At Omaha Beach, US troops quickly became pinned down by heavy fire as the pre-invasion bombing had fallen inland and failed to destroy the German fortifications. After suffering 2,400 casualties, the most of any beach on D-Day, small groups of US soldiers were able to break through the defenses opening the way for successive waves. On Utah Beach, US troops suffered only 197 casualties (*the lightest of any beach*) when they were accidentally landed in the wrong spot. Quickly moving inland, they linked up with elements of the 101st Airborne and began moving towards their objectives.[81]

---

[81] http://militaryhistory.about.com/od/worldwarii/a/wwiieurdday.htm

In his letter Martin asks about Ralph (one of Arvid '*Curly*' Furford's brothers). Of the seven Furford brothers, four served in the Army during WWII (Leif, Erling, Ralph, & Stanley). Three served in Europe and one in the South Pacific. Since Martin had not heard from Ralph, he would of course want news. Leif Furford landed on the Normandy beaches with an artillery unit as part of the Second Front. Martin did not know Leif was part of this battle till later. Leif received a purple heart for shrapnel wounds. One of the brothers "*got shot in the butt.*" Current family members do not know which brother – Stanley?, and it is not known if he got a purple heart. All four brothers returned home after the War. Leif was never quite the same after returning home. I am sure today he would be diagnosed as having Post Traumatic Syndrome "PTS."

Mathias Furford and his children in order of birth -- Julius, Margaret, Leif, Lillian, Arvid, (Erling), Ralph, Harry, Stanley, Glady.
1962 - the day of Erling's Funeral

This generation of the Furford family have all passed. Mathias and his wife were immigrants from Norway. All the children are of Norwegian decent.

Stanley Furford
1943

Ralph Furford
1941

LETTER 28 & 29

Mrs. Ruth Furford
Rt 1 Box 352
Kent, Wash

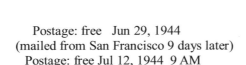

ARMY & NAVY DEPARTMENTS V-MAIL SERVICE OFFICIAL BUSINESS	Postage: free Jun 29, 1944 (mailed from San Francisco 9 days later) Postage: free Jul 12, 1944 9 AM (mailed from San Francisco 11 days later)	Pvt Martin Paulson APO 15258 % PM San Francisco, CA

Dear Ruth,   *June 21, 1944*

I hope my mail is getting to you better than my mail is coming in., I havent received a letter from you since the two you sent to Fort Ord and they were over a month old.

They havent been working us so very hard here. We took a little hike this morning and this after noon we are supposed to wash our clothes. My clothes are all clean so I have a little time off. The only trouble is there is never much to do except gamble and I have already lost all my money. That is all except most of my pay which I havent been paid yet.

Sunday I got a chance to go into town with another fellow. I cant say much about it except their towns are sure a lot different from ours. In fact I don't call it a town. We had a few drinks and then went back to camp. You can get whiskey for a dollar a shot and brandy for fifty cents. I a lot cheaper than I thought it would be.

Martin

Dear Ruth,   *July 1, 1944*

There still isnt very much I can write about. I have been taking it pretty easy since I left the states. That was up until a couple of days ago when they started putting me on some details that I really had to work on.

Would you do me a favor and send five dollars to Mrs. Ray Middleworth at Cedar City, Utah. I borrowed five dollars from Ray and then they split us up before I got a chance to pay him back. While you are at it would you send a money order for about twenty dollars to me. I have lots of money coming but they never get around to give it to me. I have only been paid thirty five dollars since I came back after my furlough. You cant spend much money over here but I get tired of being broke all the time.

I bet George is sure proud that he passed and is now in the second grade. It sure isnt taking him long to grow up. Seems like he should still be a baby.

Love Martin

Martin said, *"I was shipped to New Caledonia, an Island north of New Guinea. It was a French Colony and used as a prison camp. I walked by the Prison Camp and behind the prison camp was a Leprosy Colony! I was there 4-5 months."*

New Caledonia (*Nouvelle-Caledonia*), an overseas collectivity of France located in the sub-region of Melanesia, which makes the continental island group unique in the southwest Pacific. Austronesians from the west (*various populations in Southeast Asia and Oceania that speak languages of the Austronesian family*), now called Lapita, eventually moved into the area and intermingled with the Papuans, forming the diverse group of peoples we know today as Melanesians.

The Lapita were excellent sailors, and by 1500 BC had crossed over from Vanuatu to New Caledonia. They quickly spread to inhabit the islands of Fiji, Tonga, and Samoa as well, where they preceded the Polynesian arrival. For the next millennium the Lapita dominated the southwest Pacific waters with their navigation and trade. On land they were agricultural and very talented at making pottery.

In February 1942, with the assistance of Australia, the territory became an important Allied base. The first US

From Martin's photo album

Troops arriving in New Caledonia 1942

troops arrived March 1942 *[the 164ᵗʰ was part of the battle to take New Caledonia in 1942]*. Noumea *[the town Martin would visit on leave]* became the headquarters of the United States Navy and Army in the South Pacific. The fleet which turned back the Japanese navy in the battle of the Coral Sea in May 1942 was based at Noumea. It was here that the marines and soldiers who would capture dozens of islands embarked, and the ships and planes that supported them in battle refueled and refitted. As the war progressed, Noumea became less

Infantrymen and jeeps (14-ton 4x4truck) crossing a stream during training on New Caledonia, summer1942

strategically important as more forward bases were established, but it remained a large support base throughout the Pacific campaign. More than two million Allied servicemen and women served at Noumea during the war.

In 1946 New Caledonia became an overseas territory. By 1953 French citizenship had been granted to all New Caledonians, regardless of ethnicity. The population of New Caledonia changed radically in the decades following WWII. A nickel boom brought in workers form South East Asia and Polynesia. Then a strong movement for independence was led by native students who had studied in France and seen other Pacific islands such as Papua New Guinea and Fiji gain independence in the 1970's.

French penal colony from 1870 - 1913

The Caledonia penal colony was established in 1863. The first "shipped" common-law prisoners, arrived on May 9, 1864. **For 33 years**, 75 convoys brought about **21,000 convicts** sentenced to penal servitude (hard labor). These convicts have been instrumental in building the penal colony but also in banking up the bays of Noumea and in the construction of large buildings. After an eight-year sentence and another eight working the land, it was made available to the "free men" by the Penitentiary Administration to return to France, or to continue to work on the piece of land, which sometimes became their property.

For most prisoners, going to the penal colony was proposed as a way of

Prisoners at work at the Noumea penal colony in New Caledonia

"making amends." They **were selected based on their professional or artistic skills**. At the end of their sentence, *every effort was made so that the convicts would not return to their homeland*; the prison administration was ready though *to finance the trip of their extended family to come and settle in New Caledonia*.[82]

Very few of the freed convicts had the opportunity to get land concessions. The administration gave preference to convicts still undergoing their sentence because it had better control of them. Consequently most of the freed convicts were thrown on the colony roads without means of subsistence. Without money, without land which could feed them, they lived a poor nomadic life trying to find work with the farmers and miners. Consequently the freed convicts left few descendants.

In 1884, Seven Thousand prisoners were in New Caledonia compared to the settlement of 11,000 Europeans ...one third of them being from penal origin. In 1897, at the end of transportation there were 1,700 penal settlers in New Caledonia. Comparing this figure with the total of 22,000 deportees sent to this place shows how the penal colonization scheme was a failure. [83]

"Would you do me a favor and send five dollars to Mrs. Ray Middleworth at Cedar City, Utah. I borrowed five dollars from Ray and then they split us up before I got a chance to pay him back."

Martin's namesake. His grandfather, Martin Paulson 1890

Sending the five dollars attests to the wonderful character instilled in Martin. It was later learned that Ray was killed in action. Martin did not know the details of where or how.

[82]http://en.visitnewcaledonia.com/zoom/penal-colony-prison
[83]http://www.croixdusud.info/hist_eng/hist_bagne_eng.php

LEPROSY

The *Journal of the American Medical Association,* March 22nd, 1890, says: *L'eprosy is reported to have found its way to New Caledonia, the French penal colony, and already there are hundreds of cases among the natives and convicts. "*

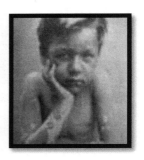

Though it was not until 1883 that the first cases of true leprosy among the aborigines of New Caledonia were observed, more or less legendary accounts of earlier appearances of the disease are current among them. Thus a Chinaman, covered with hideous sores, is said to have arrived in 1866 or 1867, and to have lived for several years with a native tribe, several of whom afterward developed a disease of the same nature. Whatever may be the true history of the importation of leprosy, there can be little doubt that it was imported, and at the present time, according to M Legrand, it exists everywhere in New Caledonia, and has acquired a foothold in the great majority of the native tribes. Europeans

Child inflicted with leprosy

have also suffered. The course of the disease appears to be more rapid than elsewhere, a fact which M. Legrand attributes to the habit which the natives have of scarifying the maculae (a discolored spot or area on the skin that is not elevated above the surface and is characteristic of certain conditions, such as smallpox, purpura, or roseola) and the tubercles (a round nodule, small eminence, or warty outgrowth found on bones or skin, or, in cases of tuberculosis, in the lungs), often to a considerable depth, with pieces of glass, and to their ruthless use of caustics. M. Legrand considers that these barbarous therapeutics, together with tattooing and burning with moxas, which seems to be their fashion of expressing affliction at the loss of relatives, have much to do with the spread of the disease. He explains the ravages made by the disease in virgin soil like New Caledonia by the fact that the people, not being aware of the danger, take no precautions against it."—*Archives de Médecine Navale, February, 1891* [84]

Dr. Armauer Hansen of Norway was the first to see the leprosy germ under a microscope. This was 1873, and Hansen's discovery was revolutionary. The evidence was clear for all the world: leprosy is caused by a germ (*Mycobacterium leprae*). It was not hereditary, a curse, or from sin. Because of Dr. Hansen's work, leprosy is also called Hansen's Disease. [85]

The organism infects the skin because it thrives at temperatures slightly lower than that found inside the human body. It also has an affinity for nerve cells, which is why leprosy is characterized

---

[84] http://www.whale.to/v/tebb/tebb1.html#NEW%20CALEDONIA

[85] http://www.bilkent.edu.tr/~bilheal/aykonu/ay2007/ocak07/leprosy.htm

by loss of feeling on the skin surface. *M. leprae* is the only mycobacterium known to infect nervous tissue.

Although there remains some uncertainty about the mode of transmission of leprosy, most researchers agree that it is spread from person to person in respiratory droplets or nasal discharge. *M. leprae* may survive outside a human host for a period of hours or even days. Only the lepromatous form of the disease is thought to be infectious.

While human-to-human respiratory transmission is thought to be the likely cause of most infections, exposure to insect vectors, infected soil, and animal reservoirs may also be possible modes of transmission. Most people are immune to leprosy. In endemic areas, sub-clinical levels of the disease are common, but only in a select few cases will the infection progress to clinical disease levels. [86]

GLOBAL SITUATION ON LEPROSY

Prevalence at beginning of 2006, and trends in new case detection 2003-2005, and 2010, excluding Europe *[registered prevalence is the national total of chronic cases]*.

Region	Registered Leprosy cases (per 10,000 pop.)	New case detection during the year			
	Start of 2006	2003	2004	2005	2010
Africa	40,830 (0.56)	47,006	46,918	42,814	25,345
Americas	32,904 (0.39)	52,435	52,662	41,780	37,740
South-East Asia	133,422 (0.81)	405,147	298,603	201,635	156,254
Eastern Mediterranean	4,024 (0.09)	3,940	3,392	3,133	4,080
Western Pacific	8,646 (0.05)	6,190	6,216	7,137	5,055
Totals	219,826	514,718	407,791	296,499	228,474

During WWII leprosy was not only prevalent in the South Pacific, but worldwide. For practical purposes, leprosy may be considered a disease of the tropics and subtropics. Because of the lack of knowledge about the mode of spread of the disease and because there were no effective vaccines or chemical prophylactics during WWII, there was not much that the Preventive Medicine Service (Office of the Surgeon General) could do to provide protection against leprosy for troops and other military personnel. Dependence for protection had to be placed almost entirely upon recognition of the disease when it occurred and upon avoidance of contact.

---

[86] http://www.stanford.edu/group/parasites/ParaSites2005/Leprosy/history.htm

The Preventive Medicine Service recognized that leprosy, because of its long latency and low incidence of adult infection, could not be a disease of military significance insofar as loss of manpower during World War II was concerned. It was recognized also that the area of exposure was vastly extended and that the number of possible contacts was increased by large multiples by the placing of thousands of U.S. soldiers among populations where incidence of leprosy was high, particularly in the Pacific regions. The late consequences of acquisition of leprosy during the war by soldiers exposed in the course of their service were also matters of grave concern. A balanced program designed to stimulate awareness of the disease and at the same time to support reasonable precautionary measures was adopted.

Preliminary data for the Army indicate that 26 cases of leprosy occurred during the period 1942-1945. Of these, 13 were in the United States and 13 overseas. Among 45 patients in whom the first signs of the disease were observed either during *or subsequent* to Army service, it is known that 7 had prior contact with leprosy within the family, a factor which certainly should be given priority in determining the probable source of the disease.

During World War II, significant progress was made in the therapy of leprosy. Particularly important was the discovery that prolonged treatment with sulfones (*any of various organic sulfur compounds having a sulfonyl group attached to two carbon atoms, especially such a compound formerly used as a drug to treat leprosy or tuberculosis*) gives favorable results in a large proportion of cases.[87]

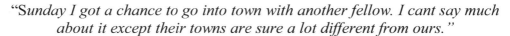

"Sunday I got a chance to go into town with another fellow. I cant say much about it except their towns are sure a lot different from ours."

Noumea, New Caledonia - circa late 1943-1944
Photo by E.A. Bradford, Sydney

---

[87]http://history.amedd.army.mil/booksdocs/wwii/communicablediseasesV5/chapter4.htm

LETTER 30

Pvt Martin Paulson
APO 15258
% PM San Francisco, Cal

Mr. A. Furford
Rt. 1 Box 352
Kent, Wash.

Postage: Free
U.S.Postal Service No. 2
Jul 12, 1944   9 AM

Dear Curly,

I intended to write to you sooner, but I have been having too much time off and too many card games around here. The boys insist on having me show them the finer points of pinocle playing. The trouble is we play pay day and there isnt any pay days.

How is the drinking situation lining up now days. I bet you got about four quarts lined up in the cooler just waiting for the fourth right now. Well maybe you have been sampling one. I sure wish I had a couple. They charge us a dollar a drink for it over here and then they never gives us a pass to town so we can get it. Drink a few for me, will you.

How is the Army situation getting along with you. If I remember right your number was due about this fall. But by that time the war will probably be over. If you do think you are going in take the Sea Bees and you wont be sorry. You should get a pretty good rating in them.

Martin

This letter was written to "Curly" (Ruth's husband, Arvid). There is no date on the letter, but Martin refers to July 4th (*note that it was stamped in San Francisco on July 12th*). It was not uncommon for families to make their own home brewed beer, wine, etc., for holiday celebrations. Even today at age 94, Martin enjoys a cold glass of beer. The author remembers her mother making a large batch of "Root-beer" that went very wrong (*too much yeast?*) and bottles started bursting! Her mother was devastated, but the children loved the explosions! The corrected batch was delicious!!

The card game of *pinochle* was played by both adults and children alike. With no TV or electronics in those days' kids, adults, friends, and families (*even groups of strangers*) would gather around tables and play board games and card games for hours. It was a wonderful time as there was food, drink, conversation and an all-around good fun time for all. Children would be at their tables, and adults at theirs...or all at the same table. Wonderful memories!! For those who are not familiar with the game of pinochle...

Type: Trick-taking
Players: 4 in partnerships or 3 individually, variants exist for 2-6 or 8 players
Skill(s) required: Strategy, Social Skills, Team Work, and Card Counting
Cards: 48 (double 24 card deck) or 80 (quadruple 20 card deck)
Play: Clockwise
Card rank (highest to lowest): A, 10, K, Q, J, 9,
Playing time: 1 to 5 hours

GAME VARIATIONS
(The following are short definitions of the game variations)

Two-handed Pinochle: Two-handed Pinochle is the original Pinochle game.
Three-handed Pinochle: In Three-handed pinochle each player plays for himself. The dealer deals 15 cards to each player and three cards to the widow—a separate pile in the middle.
Four-handed Pinochle: Four-handed Pinochle, or partnership Pinochle is played with two teams consisting of two players each. Partners are seated opposite from each other. Each player is dealt 12 cards.
Five-handed and larger Pinochle: Games with five hands or more typically modify partnership Pinochle in a variety of ways. They are generally played with 1 1/2 or doubled decks.
Double-deck Pinochle: Today "Double Deck" pinochle is a popular form of the game, exclusively played by the National Pinochle Association, the American Pinochle Association, the Cambridge Pinochle Association, and is played for the "World Series of Pinochle". Double-Deck Pinochle is played with 2 Pinochle decks, minus the nines. This makes for an 80 card deck. [88]

---

[88] http://en.wikipedia.org/wiki/Pinochle

LETTER 31

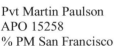

Pvt Martin Paulson	Postage: 6 cents airmail	Mrs. A Furford
APO 15258	US ARMY APO 502	Rt 1 Box 352
% PM San Francisco	Jul 16, 1944 4:30 PM	Kent, Wash

Dear Ruth,   *July 13, 1944*

What did you mean when you said Karen and Sharon were staying with you? Are they up there for a visit or are they there permanently?

I bet Sharon does have a lot of fun getting out in the open and playing with George. It should be good for her too to get out in the fresh air. It is hard to realize that she is big enough to run away up to the service station though.

Would you ask Curly why he spends so much time trying to polish up that old piece of junk that he keeps in that shed in back of your house. You know you cant make a rusty tin can look good and with his crate its the same principal. He hasent anything to start with.

Have you heard any news about any of the guys from the Harbor. There must have been some of them in the invasion of France. I havent heard anything from the Harbor about whether anyone has been wounded and I have been wondering about it.

I dont believe I ever mentioned anything about the food we get over here. I know for sure I'm not losing weight on it. It is all been canned or dehidrated or both. Eaven the butter comes in cans. We had fresh eggs for breakfast this morning and boy did they taste good. I imagine they were cold storage eggs, but I never tasted fresh eggs in the states that tasted as good. When I get back if I ever see a can of corned beef or spam I will lose my appetite. I used to like corned beef pretty well, but when I started getting it eaven for breakfast it didnt take long to get tired of it.

Well that is about all I can think of to write about now that the censors will pass.

Love,   Martin

123

Martin asks about Karen (his younger sister) and Sharon (Karen's daughter). Imagine being away from home so long and not getting letters regularly, then hearing your little sister and niece are staying at big sisters house with no

mention of the husband. Karen's husband was a Deputy Sheriff. Martin was probably wondering if something had happened to Karen's husband, but Karen was just there for a visit. Back then, if you traveled a distance you usually stayed a few days or longer.

Just down the road about half a block from where Ruth & Arvid lived in Kent, Washington was a Service Station/General Store. It sounds like from Martin's letter that Sharon may have wondered off...

Karen Bauder & daughter Sharon 1943

Sharon Bauder & cousin George Furford 1944

"It is hard to realize that she is big enough to run away up to the service station though."

George said as a young boy he would walk by the Service Station to the school which was half a mile away to see a friend, and that there were a couple horses in a field between the house and the service station. What little girl wouldn't want to go see the horses! She may have wandered down that way after walking there with the grownups or seeing her cousin George walk that way.

Martin mentions Curly spending time on an old piece of junk. In our interview, Martin said Curly had a real Junker of a car before he later bought a newer Buick.

He goes on to ask if there had been any news about any of the guys from the Harbor as...

"There must have been some of them in the invasion of France."

As mentioned before, Curly had four brothers serving in the war and at least one, Leif, was part of the invasion of France. The invasion Martin was referring to would be the Battle of Normandy which began June 6, 1944. Martin's letter is dated July 13, 1944. Martin did not know at the time that Leif Furford was one of the men who landed with the Artillery beach landings.

ANNOUNCEMENT
(by *The Associated Press*)

A dramatic 10-second interval preceded the official announcement today that the invasion had begun.

Over a trans-Atlantic radio-telephone hookup direct from supreme headquarters, allied expeditionary force, to all major press services, and broadcasting networks in the United States came the voice of Col. R. Ernest Dupuy, Gen. Eisenhower's public relations officer.

"This is supreme headquarters, allied expeditionary force," Dupuy said. *"The text of communique No. 1 will be released to the press and radio of the United States in 10 seconds."*

Then the seconds were counted off — one, two, three… and finally ten.

"Under the command of General Eisenhower," slowly read Col. Dupuy, *"allied naval forces supported by strong air forces began landing allied armies this morning on the northern coast of France."* [89]

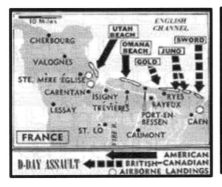

Beach Landings

Tank landing ships unloading supplies on Omaha Beach, building up for the breakout from Normandy

Operation Overlord was the code name for the *Battle of Normandy,* the operation that launched the invasion of German-occupied Western Europe during World War II by the Allied forces. The operation commenced on June 6, 1944 with the Normandy landings (*Operation Neptune*, commonly known as **D-Day**). A 12,000-plane airborne assault preceded an amphibious assault involving almost 7,000 vessels. Nearly 160,000 troops crossed the English Channel on June 6; more than three million troops were in France by the end of August.

Allied land forces that saw combat in Normandy on D-Day itself came from Canada, the United Kingdom, and the United States. Free French Forces and Poland also participated in the battle after the assault phase, and there were also minor contingents from Belgium, Greece, the Netherlands, and Norway. Other

---

[89]http://yesteryearsnews.wordpress.com/2011/06/06/

Allied nations participated in the naval and air forces.

Once the beachheads were secured, a three-week military buildup occurred on the beaches before Operation Cobra, the operation to break out from the

Aerial bombings

Normandy beachhead, began. The battle for Normandy continued for more than two months, with campaigns to expand the foothold on France, and concluded with the closing of the *Falaise pocket* on August 24, the *Liberation of Paris* on August 25, and the *German retreat* across the Seine which was completed on August 30, 1944.[90]

The cost of the Normandy campaign was high for both sides. From D-Day to August 21, the Allies landed 2,052,299 men in *northern France*. There were around 209,672 Allied casualties from June 6 to the end of August, around 10% of the forces landed in *France*. The casualties break down to:

36,976   killed
153,475   wounded
19,221   missing

Split between the Army-Groups, the Anglo-Canadian Army-Group suffered:

16,138   killed
58,594   wounded
<u>9,093   missing</u>
83,825   casualties

The American Army-Group suffered:

20,838   killed,
94,881   wounded
<u>10,128   missing</u>
125,847   casualties

French civilians placing flowers on the body of a dead American soldier, 1944

To these casualties it should be added that 4,101 aircraft were lost and 16,714 airmen were killed or missing in direct connection to Operation Overlord. Thus total Allied casualties rises to 226,386 men.[91]

---

[90]http://en.wikipedia.org/wiki/Operation_Overlord
[91]http://en.wikipedia.org/wiki/Operation_Overlord#Allies

Mess in the field, Camp Roberts, Calif. (during training)

Martin says, *"I dont believe I ever mentioned anything about the food we get over here. I know for sure I'm not losing weight on it. It is all been canned or dehidrated or both. Eaven the butter comes in cans. We had fresh eggs for breakfast this morning and boy did they taste good. I imagine they were cold storage eggs, but I never tasted fresh eggs in the states that tasted as good. When I get back if I ever see a can of corned beef or spam I will lose my appetite. I used to like corned beef pretty well, but when I started getting it eaven for breakfast it didnt take long to get tired of it."*

Martin has made it plain what he thinks of eating the same thing continuously. Especially corned beef and Spam. Camp Roberts Infantry Training Center knew the troops would be eating a lot of rations and prepared them for this reality. Military rations were covered earlier, but for those who would like to do a thorough study, the best information on the history of military rations can be researched at:

http://www.qmfound.com/army_rations_historical_background.htm
US Army Quartermaster Foundation
Fort Lee, Virginia
Army Operational Rations - Historical Background

(This report is an excellent historical overview of Operational Ration development from the Revolutionary War to the end of World War II. Focuses on World War II development and fielding of the C, D, K, 5-in-1, and 10-in-1 rations.)

Below are excerpts from an article *by Bruce Heydt*. Bruce Heydt is a former editor of American Heritage magazine. This article originally appeared in the June 2006 issue of *America in WWII*.

SPAM AGAIN
By Bruce Heydt

It was the grub GI's loved to grumble about—not because it wasn't tasty, but because it was always there, sometimes three times a day.

The uncensored military slang for creamed chipped beef on toast.
*POS: **P**oop **O**n a **S**hingle [troops also called it SOS – '**S****t **O**n a **S**hingle']*

1940's SPAM poster (baked bean SPAM which)

SPAM: Say that word to a WWII veteran, and you're in for a true gut reaction. My own memories of Spam and the frequency with which it appeared on my plate are only a faint shadow of what the so-called "miracle meat" brings to mind for those who ate it seemingly three times a day for the length of their military service. For many, it must have seemed as though there were no food other than this ubiquitous, gelatinous, pink, canned concoction.

In fact, the Hormel Company had celebrated Spam's birth not long before the war, in the mid-1930s. It was developed not in response to a prophetic vision of the need for a non-perishable, easily transported military ration—nor, as some may still think, as a practical joke played by someone in the US War Department—but in response to the vision of one man, Jay Hormel. President of the meat packing company that shared his family name, Hormel had already introduced canned ham to the American consumer. Now, looking for a way to turn previously discarded pork shoulder meat into a marketable product, he hit upon the idea for an inexpensive canned luncheon treat that fit the budget of Depression-era housewives and had a much longer shelf life than other meats.

When America entered the war in 1941 and began shipping fighting men overseas, military officials bought large quantities of Spam for the same reason housewives bought it—it was cheap, easily transportable, had a long shelf life—and yes, it was fairly nutritious. But Spam was not the only canned meat to go to war. According to Wyman, the army initially bought 10 different varieties of canned meat to feed the troops. That number grew to 60 by the war's end. These products found their way into K and B rations (field and communal rations, respectively), where Hormel's pork shoulder ended up cheek-to-jowl with its competitors' canned pig ears, noses, and tongues. Soon, the troops were eating these dubious delicacies as often as three times a day. To fed-up servicemen, it was all Spam.

Hormel made a doomed attempt to point out the misconception. But to disgruntled troops who'd had more canned meat than they could stomach, the effort only fanned the flames of discontent.

Ironically, by war's end Spam had become one of the great unifying forces among American GIs. Whether they served in Italy, France, North Africa, Asia, or the Pacific, they had shared the danger of combat and the ever-present threat of more Spam. Spam became, in a sense, a common enemy. Jokes about Spam drew strangers together. Cartoonists such as Sergeant George Baker, creator of the popular Sad Sack cartoon, lampooned Spam. Satirists took aim at Spam, too.

The armies of America's allies moved on Spam, too. Along with tanks and destroyers, the list of wartime products that America provided to Allied nations through the Lend-Lease program included Spam. On the whole, the British and Russians took more kindly to the omnipresent

Sergeant Arnold Bourdreau eating canned corned beef in Italy in 1945

canned meat than GIs did. A veteran rifleman of the US 4th Infantry Division remembers how he and his mates were complaining about army food during the Normandy campaign in 1944 when two visiting Brits, without a word, lifted a slab of meat from the Americans' mess, dropped it in the dirt, and then picked it up and swallowed it. The message was clear: You pampered Yanks have nothing to complain about; this is a treat compared to what we get.

Certainly, citizens of war-ravaged nations felt the bite of wartime shortages more than Americans did, so they tended to tolerate, even appreciate Spam. Wyman spotlights a pair of particularly notable advocates. Margaret Thatcher, who would later become Britain's prime minister, remembered that on Boxing Day (a public holiday the day after Christmas) in 1943, "We had friends in and…we opened a tin of Spam luncheon meat. We had some lettuce and tomatoes and peaches, so it was Spam and salad." Thatcher even went so far as to call Spam "a war-time delicacy." And Soviet leader Nikita Khruschev, best remembered in the United States for threatening to "crush America under our feet," conceded that the Soviets had been in critical condition after German armies overran their best agricultural regions. "Without Spam," he reasoned, "we wouldn't have been able to feed our army."

Sentiments of this kind elicited mostly sneers from Americans in uniform. Trying to put a positive spin on Spam, Hormel circulated an advertisement depicting a letter purportedly from a former Hormel salesman now serving in the Pacific. The letter read, "Boy! You never fully realize how delicious and good Spam really is until you taste it out here in the bottom of a fox-hole. All the boys out here think Spam is the best meat product in the world." The ad brought howls of derision from GIs.

By war's end, the military had bought, shipped, and served roughly 150 million pounds of Spam. How much of it was actually eaten will never be known. Rumor has it that soldiers sometimes used it to grease gun barrels, but I've not found a veteran who attested to having done so.

Perhaps the most even-handed assessment of Spam and its role in the US war effort came from a man who, not coincidentally, may have been the war's greatest diplomat. In a letter written to a retired Hormel executive after the war, Dwight D. Eisenhower, the supreme Allied commander who had so masterfully coaxed effective command relationships out of hot-spirited generals such as George Patton and Great Britain's Bernard Montgomery, graciously declared, "During World War II, of course, I ate my share of Spam along with millions of other soldiers. I'll even confess to a few unkind remarks about it— uttered during the strain of battle, you understand. But as former Commander-in-Chief, I believe I can still officially forgive you your only sin: sending us so much of it." [92]

Martin Paulson 1947

---

[92]   Photo credits: National Archives; courtesy of Hormel Foods Corporation;

LETTER 32

Pvt Martin Paulson
APO 15258
% PM San Francisco, Cal

Mrs. A. Furford
Rt 1 Box 352
Kent, Wash.

Postage: 6 cents airmail
July 23, 1944 2:30 PM
US ARMY APO 502

Dear Ruth,   July 21, 1944

I have been pretty busy lately and havent had time to do much writing. To write letters we just about have to do it in the day time because we havent any lights in our tent. We can go down to the Red Cross but it is so crowded that you can hardly get a place to write.

I saw a show the other night that I have wanted to see for a long time. Guadicanal Diary. I have heard so much about it that I guess I expected too much. It was a good show allright but nothing like I expected it to be.

The other day I got to see a T3 or Staff Sergeant doing some pipe welding and I got a few pointers from him. It was a easy job right out in the open on two inch pipe. When he got finished I looked the weld over and I am telling you I never seen a worse weld on pipe. A friend of mine asked me what I thought of the weld so I told him if it even held water it would be a miracle. In the army a T3 is supposed to be able to do any type of welding. Well this guy sure made a liar out of me. He got some paint and painted the weld and filled all the holes with paint. After the paint dried he tried it out again and it still leaked. He didn't give up though. He reached in his tool box and got out a roll of tape and really fixed it so it wouldnt leak. One thing you will have to admit is that he is sure resourceful anyway.

I can just picture George watching the older boys diving in the water and having a lot of fun doing it. And then George trying the same thing. He always liked to do the things bigger kids would do.

Well I guess that is about all I can think of to write now so I guess I will have to quit. From what we hear the war is sure going our way now. Maybe I will be home for Christmas. I cant hardly believe I will but it has sure started to break fast and it might break faster.

Love   Martin

THE RED CROSS: Upon researching their role in New Caledonia during WWII, it was interesting to learn that the Red Cross provided across the globe more than 104,000 nurses, prepared 27 million packages for American and allied

WWII Poster

prisoners of war, and shipped over 300,000 tons of supplies overseas. They provided entertainment when possible and tried to provide a place where military personnel could gather...to write letters, etc. At the military's request, the Red Cross also initiated a national blood program that collected 13.3 million pints of blood for use by the armed forces.

New Caledonia became home to seven Station and two General hospitals because the climate was mild and the island was malaria free. More nurses served on New Caledonia and remained there longer than on any other Pacific island except for Australia and Hawaii. The first nurses to see the island were those of the 9th and 109th Station Hospitals and the 52nd Evacuation Hospital, who arrived in New Caledonia in March 1942. Both the hospitals and the nurses' quarters were prefabricated buildings with electricity and running water.

The hospitals on New Caledonia received malaria patients from Guadalcanal, the Solomon Islands, and the New Hebrides. More than 50 percent of admissions for disease between 1942 and 1944 were malaria patients. Battle casualties arriving from New Guinea, New Britain, Guadalcanal, and Saipan were predominantly abdominal cases, but chest wounds were also common. [93]

Nurse Harriet Styer takes a break from her duties outside her tent. Many physicians and nurses from the Pennsylvania Hospital served in WWII, in particular as part of the 52nd Evacuation Hospital in New Caledonia (Pacific Theater).

801st Medical Air Evacuation Squadron

We were the first *flight nurse squadron* to go to the Pacific, landing in New Caledonia in February 1943. We enjoyed the temperature and flowers, which are equally beautiful there all year, but conditions were very primitive. The river behind our tents was our washing machine, and we hung clothes to dry from trees. There were twenty-four nurses, and

---

[93] *http://www.redcross.org/about-us/history*

millions of mosquitoes, all living in one tent. One night during the first week, the tent blew down during a **typhoon,** and our foot lockers almost floated away.

C-47s [acting as medical evacuation planes] flew to the front with cargo and ammunition, and the nurses rode on top of the cargo. We often had troops going to the forward areas, which was sad for us. They would get into long discussions, feeling that they would probably never come back. The worst part is, some of them didn't.[94]

Martin mentions seeing the movie "Guadalcanal Diary," a 1943 war film about a war correspondent who takes you through the preparations, landing and

1943 film poster

initial campaign on Guadalcanal during WWII, concentrating on the personal lives of those involved. It was directed by *Lewis Seiler* and based on the book of the same name by Richard Tregaskis. The film recounts the fight of the United States Marines in the Battle of Guadalcanal, which occurred only a year before the movie's release. While the film had notable battle scenes, its primary

focus was on the characters and back stories of the Marines. Martin expected to see more of the battle and less of the background stories of the men.

The reader would have enjoyed the look on Martin's face as he talked about the T3 Staff Sergeant who messed up on the welding job. Remember, Martin was a Master Welder at the Seattle/Tacoma Ship Yards prior to being drafted. It was hard for Martin (a Private) not to correct the T3 Staff Sergeant on his welding job.

"He reached in his tool box and got out a roll of tape and really fixed it
so it wouldnt leak. One thing you will have to admit is that he is sure
resourceful anyway."

The rank insignias for the U.S. Army in World War II were modified on January 8th, 1942 with the addition of the ranks of Technician 3rd Class (T/3), Technician 4th Class (T/4) and Technician 5th Class (T/5). On September 4th, 1942 a "T" was added to the standard chevron designs for these new grades.

---

[94] *http://www.history.army.mil/books/wwii/72-14/72-14.HTM*

A T/5 was properly addressed as a "corporal," while T/4 and T/3s were referred to as "sergeants." Although they wore chevrons similar to corporals and sergeants, technicians had *no command authority* or *duties,* and *could not issue orders* to regular sergeants, corporals or privates. The technician grades were deleted in 1948, and the enlisted ranks were further restructured in 1955. In 1951 the pay grades were reversed and changed to the system that is used in today's modern Army.

WWII RANKS WERE AS FOLLOWS:

<u>Enlisted (non-commissioned):</u>
E-7 (Grade 7): Private (no insignia)
E-6: (Grade 6): Private First Class
E-5: (Grade 5): Corporal
E-5: (Grade 5): Technician 5th Class
E-4: (Grade 4): Sergeant
E-4: (Grade 4): Technician 4th Class
E-3: (Grade 3): Staff Sergeant
E-3: (Grade 3): Technician 3rd Class
E-2: (Grade 2): Technical Sergeant
E-1: (Grade 1): Master Sergeant
E-1: (Grade 1): First Sergeant

<u>Officers (commissioned):</u>
O-1: Second Lieutenant (gold)
O-2: First Lieutenant
O-3: Captain
O-4: Major
O-5: Lieutenant Colonel (gold)
O-6: Colonel
O-7: Brigadier General
O-8: Major General
O-9: Lieutenant General
O-10: General

There is an interesting story behind Martin's comment on George watching the older boys and jumping into the water. George (now 76 yrs. of age) recalls the incident of watching the boys jumping into the water and wanting to have the same fun. They were at Lake Meridian in Washington State which had a large dock/walkway out over the lake. George (7 ½ yrs. old) ran past where the boys were and jumped in! His father (Curly) ran and jumped in after him (clothes and all) and rescued him as he had not yet learned to swim. George saw that the boys were standing up and thought he would be able to stand up, but where he jumped in there was no bottom!

George with Dad (Curly) the day of the event.

LETTER 33

WAR & NAVY
DEPARTMENTS
V-MAIL SERVICE
OFFICIAL BUSINESS

Pvt Martin Paulson
APO 15258
% PM San Francisco, Cal

Mr. A. Furford
Rt 1, Box 352
Kent, Wash

Postage: free
US POSTAL SERVICE NO 2
Jul 30, 1944 2:30 PM

Dear Curly,

I sure have some swell inspiring music to listen to while I write this letter. The guys in a tent a little ways from mine are really putting out some cowboy music that would put Gene Autry to shame. I dont mind the way the Southerners talk, and I have gotten used to them calling the afternoon evening, but I still dont like their music.

You know I have just about come around to believe that the old timers on this is------[Martin left name off as he knew it would be censored] *are right when they say that natives arent dark. They have just got a darn good suntan. Its getting so every time we see a white woman it doesn't matter how bad she looks she still look like a queen. Maybe its a good thing they dont let us out on passes. Next time you get a bottle take a couple of drinks for me will you.*

Martin

Martin grew up in a community of people who migrated to the United States from Norway, and was surrounded by music from their homeland as well as being introduced to the current music of the day. **Music in the 1940s** was mainly built around **jazz and big band** styles. Artists like **Rosemary Clooney, Count Basie, and Artie Shaw** helped to define the musical era with their unique brand of entertaining crowds through their music. Bing Crosby and Frank Sinatra were a couple of the best-selling male pop artists of the 1940's. Pure jazz began to become more popular, along with the blues. Some of the most notable Jazz artists of the

1940s include Ella Fitzgerald, Billie Holiday, Louis Armstrong and Nat King Cole.

Throughout the 1930s and 1940s, cowboy songs, or Western music, became widely popular through the romanticizing of the cowboys and idealized depictions of the west in Hollywood film. In the post-war period, country music was called "folk" in the trades, and "hillbilly" within the industry. In 1944, The Billboard replaced the term *"hillbilly"* with *"folk songs and blues*," and switched to *"country"* or *"country and Western*" in 1949. Though Martin may have enjoyed

Gene Autry movies, etc., his choice of music was not 'cowboy' music but more towards bands, movie tracks, classical.

Other trends: In 1941 Les Paul designs and builds the first solid-body electric guitar, and in 1942 Bing Crosby recorded and released *"White Christmas"* which became the best-selling single record of all time with estimated sales in excess of 50 million copies worldwide.

GENE AUTRY (Orvon Grover Autry) was an American performer who gained fame as a singing cowboy on the radio, in movies, and on television for more than three decades beginning in the early 1930s. From 1934 to 1953, Autry appeared in 93 films and 91 episodes of *The Gene Autry Show* television series. During the 1930s and 1940s, he personified the straight-shooting hero—honest, brave, and true—and profoundly touched the lives of millions of Americans. His singing cowboy movies were the first vehicle to carry country music to a national audience. In addition to his signature song, *"Back in the Saddle Again,"* Autry is still remembered for his Christmas holiday songs, "Here Comes Santa Claus" (which he wrote), *"Frosty the Snowman,"* and his biggest hit, *"Rudolph the Red-Nosed Reindeer."*

The following is a history of JAPANESE OCCUPATIONS and THE IMPORTANCE OF THE ISLANDS TO THE ALLIED FORCES. It gives us a better understanding of the role our soldiers endured during WWII.

THE ISLANDS – There were several French territories in the South Pacific. One of the most important was the relatively large island group of New Caledonia. The group consists of the main island of New Caledonia which is actually one of the larger in the Pacific Ocean. The archipelago (Island chain) also includes the Iles

Loyaute (larger islands of the French territory of New Caledonia) and many small, sparsely populated islands and atolls (ring-shaped coral reef including a coral rim that encircles a lagoon partially or completely). The major islands are not volcanic in origin, but rather broke off from what is now Australia. It is located south of Guadalcanal and 680 miles northeast of Sydney, Australia. The island was not a typical South Pacific island. It had important nickel and chromium mines and much of the output was exported to

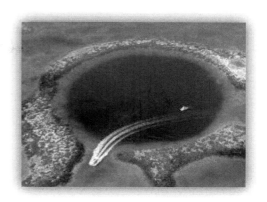

An 'atoll' in the South Pacific

Japan before the War. About 1,300 Japanese nationals worked the mines. When World War II began in Europe (1939), the Japanese increased their orders, apparently anticipating that supplies might be cut off.

JAPANESE OFFENSIVE (DECEMBER 1941 - JUNE 1942) – The Japanese strike on Pearl Harbor immobilized the American Pacific fleet. Pearl Harbor was in actuality a blessing in disguise. If the American battle fleet had sailed out to meet the Japanese on the high seas, the losses would have probably been astronomically higher. At any case, the American fleet was immobilized. And it was the only powerful military force in the Pacific capable of resisting the Japanese. What followed was a series of Japanese offensives which defeated the Allies time after time. Most shocking of all was the fall of Singapore (February 1942). It was thought to be an impregnable British fortress. The Japanese seized their primary goal, the oil fields of the Dutch East Indies (March 1942). The Americans in the Philippines held out a little longer (April 1942). The Japanese rapidly moved through the DEI (Dutch East Indies) although the number of islands slowed them somewhat. The Japanese then moved on New Guinea and succeeded in seizing almost all of the island.

DEI: The Japanese Empire occupied Indonesia, known then as the *Dutch East Indies*, during *World War II* from March 1942 until after the end of War in 1945.

BATTLE OF THE CORAL SEA (MAY 4-8, 1942) – The Japanese dispatched a naval task force to mount an amphibious landing to seize Port Moresby (in order to consolidate their position in the South Pacific and provide a springboard for attacking the Allies in Australia). Alerted by American code breakers, Admiral Nimitz ordered two carriers to the Coral Sea to intercept the Japanese. They did so, sinking a light carrier. The Japanese troop transports turned back. The first important reversal suffered by the Japanese in the War. In the ensuing naval action the U.S. Navy lost their ship the *Lexington,* and *Yorktown* was seriously damaged, but they succeeded in putting two Japanese fleet carriers out of action. The American carriers thus prevented the completion of that conquest by seizing Port Moresby (April 1942).

*Port Moresby,
New Guinea 1944*

Luckily for the French, they were located just outside the area the Japanese managed to seize. The United States had just enough naval power to prevent the Japanese from reaching the French islands.

FS OPERATION *(Operation FS was the name of the Imperial Japanese plan to invade and occupy Fiji, Samoa, and New Caledonia in the south Pacific during the Pacific conflict of World War II)*

*Early hospital, located at the Advance Base,
Port Moresby, Papua,
August 1942*

New Caledonia islands were added to the Japanese objectives, both because of the mines and the strategic location. The islands could play a very important role in severing the sea lanes between Australia and the United States. The Japanese offensive to seize the islands were part of the FS Operation and included the seizure of Fiji and the Samoa Islands. Cut off from America and with its Army in North Africa, the Japanese believed that Australia would be forced to surrender. The American carrier action in the Coral Sea forced the Japanese to postpone FS. Rather they decided to first destroy the American carriers at Midway. Then they would return south and complete the conquest of Port Moresby and the islands northeast of Australia. The Japanese did not think that they had sufficient land forces to invade Australia. Most of the Japanese Army was still based in China. They did think that they could seize Port Moresby and the islands and thus force Australia to come to terms.

Battle of Midway

MIDWAY (JUNE 1942) – Admiral Yamamoto decided that despite the fact that two fleet carriers had been put out of action in the Coral Sea, that the remaining four fleet carriers would be sufficient for the Midway operation, especially as Japanese naval intelligence reported that two American carriers had been sunk in the Coral Sea. The Japanese carriers at Pearl Harbor had failed to strike a death blow to the Pacific fleet because the carriers were not there. Yamamoto saw Midway as perhaps his last chance to decisively defeat the United States by providing a base for attacking Hawaii, and force an end to the War. On June 4, 1942, US aircraft flying from the ships USS Enterprise, USS Hornet, and USS *Yorktown* attacked and sunk four Japanese carriers forcing Yamamoto to withdrawal. The Battle of Midway marked the turning point of World War II in the Pacific.

THE SOUTH PACIFIC – The Japanese FS Operation, however, required Japanese naval dominance and Midway (June 1942) had significantly altered the balance of naval forces. To replace the missing carriers, the Japanese decided to build air bases in the southern Solomons which could help disrupt the sea lanes and support possible invasions. This set up the Solomons Campaign.

Located in the eastern province of the island of New Britain, Rabaul is perhaps best known for when Japanese soldiers stashed grenades and artillery in small caves near the shoreline. It was in fact the WWII headquarters for the Japanese fleet in the Pacific.

SOLOMON CAMPAIGN – New Caledonia played a major role in the Solomons campaign. Noumea and the southern tip of the island, became the principal American base for the naval operations that were fought to protect the Marines who seized Guadalcanal (August 1942). Noumea proved to have just enough facilities to keep *Enterprise* patched up after it became the single operational American carrier. After the Americans began moving up the Solomon Islands toward Rabaul (the main base of Japanese military and naval activity in the South Pacific), *New Caledonia became a remote, but important rear area of the War.*

United States Army soldiers hunt Japanese infiltrators on Bougainville March 1944

Allied success in the Solomon Islands campaign prevented the Japanese from cutting Australia and New Zealand off from the U.S. Operation Cartwheel — the Allied grand strategy for the Solomons and New Guinea campaigns — launched on June 30, 1943, isolated and neutralized Rabaul and destroyed much of Japan's sea and air supremacy. This opened the way for Allied forces to recapture the Philippines and cut off Japan from its crucial resource areas in the Netherlands East Indies.

The Solomons campaign *culminated in the often bitter fighting of the Bougainville Campaign*, which continued until the end of the war. The Allied campaign (Bougainville), which had two distinct phases, began on November 1, 1943 and ended on August 21, 1945, with the surrender of the Japanese. Before the war, Bougainville had been administered as part of the Australian Territory of

New Guinea, even though, geographically, Bougainville is part of the Solomon Islands chain. As a result, the campaign is referred to as part of both the New Guinea and the Solomon Islands campaigns.

In March–April 1942, the Japanese landed on Bougainville as part of their advance into the South Pacific. At the time, there was only a small Australian garrison on the island which consisted of about 20

Amphibian tractor passing men who stopped to rest. The advance on foot progressed at a rate of 100 yds. an hour.

soldiers from the 1st Independent Company and some coast watchers. Shortly after the Japanese arrived, the bulk of the Australian force was evacuated by the Allies, although some of the coast watchers remained behind to provide intelligence. Once secured, the Japanese began constructing a number of airfields across the island. These bases allowed the Japanese to conduct operations in the southern Solomon Islands and to attack the Allied lines of communication between the United States, Australia and the Southwest Pacific Area.[95]

---

[95]http://histclo.com/essay/war/ww2/cou/island/pac/w2pi-nc.html

LETTER 34

Mrs. A. Furford
Rt 1 Box 352
Kent, Wash

Pvt Martin Paulson   US Army A.P.O. 502   Postage: 6 cents
APO 15258   July 31, 1944 4:00 pm   US POSTAGE VIA AIR MAIL
% PM San Francisco, Cal

Dear Ruth,   *July 28*

I got today off. I worked last night and when you work nights you get the day befor and the day after off. That is all the time we get off as we work seven days a week here. When we go out on details they always pick a few of us to go on KP and help serve a meal to the rest of the guys at diner time. This is usually the easiest job so everyone trys to get it. Well last night I was fast enough and lucky enough to get it so I didn't have to work very hard. It seems funny I suppose to you after all you have heard about KP in the Army to hear of guys trying to get it.

Something over here seems to agree with me. Maybe its because of all the sleep we get. There isn't any lights in our tents so about the only thing to do when it gets dark is go to bed. Well anyway I have gained about ten pounds over here. I weigh one ninety now. Maybe the chow has some calories in it but it sure doesnt taste like it. On the other hand maybe that is what makes it taste so bad.

I started this letter yesterday and didnt have time to finish it so I will finish it today. I am off again today with another night detail tonight.

There is a fellow in our tent you ought to meet. Right now he is trying to talk another guy out of a flashlight he got ahold of. He doesnt want to sell it but I will bet ten to one that he gets it befor he is through. I was only half right. He just got half ownership in it now.

Well anyway this guy is really a card. He is always telling stories, joking and making inventions of some kind. He can keep you laughing for hours. If he wanted to he could talk you out of your eye teeth.

Yesterday I got a chance to buy a twelve fifty shafer pen for six fifty at the PX. I spent all my money that I had left from my last pay for it so I will probably have to sell it. I can always get my money out of it.

                                           Love   Martin

Private Charles Parker was named outstanding K.P. in Mess Hall #2 Knoxville, Tenn. Photo used in the Sept. 18, 1943 edition of the Tyndall Target.

Martin sounds very upbeat in this letter. He describes being eager to get KP to serve meals to his fellow troops. When speaking to other Veterans, each has stories to tell of KP duty. KP is an acronym for *Kitchen Patrol* or *Kitchen Policing*. KP duties can include any tedious chore in the military mess at an installation or in the field, such as food preparation [although not cooking], or the more obvious dish washing and pot scrubbing, sweeping and mopping floors, wiping tables, serving food on the chow line, or anything else the kitchen staff sees fit to assign to its KP crew.

KP duty can be particularly onerous because it is on top of all regular duties at institutional kitchens, as institutional kitchens often open before and close after regular duty hours and generate large volumes of unpleasant food wastes. The image of enlisted soldiers peeling potatoes in an installation's kitchen was once associated with the popular culture image of KP duty due to its frequent appearance in mid-twentieth century movies and comic strips about life in the service for Americans. Irving Berlin's 1918 *"Yip Yip Yaphank"* musical revue contains the song "*Kitchen Police (Poor Little Me)*."

When Martin served in the Pacific, there were no "institutional kitchens" (big kitchens in buildings). Soldiers were pulled to serve KP duties in place of doing

Detail work. It was just another job to the men and as Martin alludes too, *"easier than pulling Detail."* He said people form ideas of KP as being negative from watching movies. In movies about military life

KP duty would usually be assigned as some type of punishment.

KP duty is not seen much in today's military as civilian contracting companies have now taken over many kitchen duties. [96]

---

[96]http://en.wikipedia.org/wiki/KP_duty

Song: Kitchen Police *(Poor Little Me)*
Composer & Lyricist: Irving Berlin

[Verse:]
There's dirty work to be done in the army
And it's not much fun
It's the kind of work that's done
Without the aid of a gun
The boys who work with the cooks in the kitchen
Holler out for peace
For they have to do the dirty work
And they're called the Kitchen Police

[Refrain:]
Poor little me
I'm a K.P.
I scrub the mess hall
Upon bended knee
Against my wishes
I wash the dishes
To make this wide world safe for Democracy

Yip Yip Yaphank

...is the name of the musical revue composed and produced by Irving Berlin in 1918 *(the year Martin Paulson was born!)* while he was a recruit during World War I in the United States Army at Camp Upton in Yaphank, New York.

Martin's humor shows in telling of the fellow trying to *'pull one over'* on another soldier, but then he turns around and decides to earn a few extra bucks in selling his new Sheaffer pen!

THE ROLE OF THE SHEAFFER PEN DURING WWII

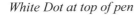

White Dot at top of pen

White Dot above clip on the cap

In 1929 on the Sheaffer ads, the white dot brand on the top of the pen cap was changed to show the dot was moved to a place just above the clip on the cap. In the 1930s, the Lifetime guarantee and the White Dot were trumpeted in many ads or featured as a tag line.

The US military had some influence on the White Dot as well. In the 1940s, the US military made it a requirement that pens sit flush with the top of the shirt pocket, probably to make the appearance of the uniform neater or so the pocket flap could be buttoned over the pen. This was a real problem for Sheaffer, as their streamlined pens had the clips mounted to the front of the cap. The result was that the pen was sticking its head out of the top of the pocket, which would make it unacceptable for use by military personnel. Sheaffer was faced with retooling the pen or losing sales.

Sheaffer 1943 advertisement detail emphasizing the Lifetime Point guarantee

In the early 1940s, the Lifetime guarantee was being advertised as unconditional "for the life of the first user." Once World War II was fully underway, Sheaffer changed the guarantee to only cover the nib. This change led to the eventual separation of the White Dot from the Lifetime guarantee.

When the Triumph line was introduced in 1942 the Crest models followed suit with many of the design improvements. A significant change was the move of the cap threads from the end of the section nearest the nib to a metal ring near the back of the section, a design that was more reliable. The new Crest had the traditional open nib replaced by the new Triumph wrap around nib. By 1943 the peaked cap gave way to a more rounded design, which style carried forward in all subsequent Crest models through 1959.[97]

2012 For Sale Ad: *Sheaffer Triumph Crest c.1943 – Most Triumph nibs were fine or extra fine, this one is a true broad medium and hard to find. This is an example of an iconic American pen which works well and writes beautifully. This 1943 Sheaffer pen is priced to sell today at $120.00!*

This advertisement for the *Sheaffer Pen Company's V-mail kit* appeared on the inside cover of Life magazine on May 24, 1943. The ad includes an image of the kit, as well as a description of its use. It was not unusual for print ads of the early to mid-twentieth century to include a large amount of text describing Voyager. In this ad, the company instructs consumers on the use of this new product, including directions for when to buy it for their loved ones going off to war. Images on the ad show the kit container as well as the items it contains. A small insert illustration shows a woman buying the kit and addressing it for mailing. Pen care instructions were placed in the tube. The last paragraph states: **Your pen is one of your most personal possessions**.

---

[97]http://penhero.com/PenGallery/Sheaffer/SheafferWhiteDot.htm

V-Mail service, was used in the U.S. from June 15, 1942 through April 1, 1945. Unlike regular mail, which traveled by ship and could take up to a month to reach its destination, V-Mail traveled by air and cut down transport time to 12 days or less. *Sheaffer advertised to civilians.* The military had their own V-mail to reduce the logistics of transferring an original letter across the military postal system. As discussed in previous letter, military V-mail letter would be censored, copied to film, and printed back to paper upon arrival at its destination.

ARMY DETAILS: When Martin was asked about doing 'DETAIL' work, he talks of detail as *"being told what to do and doing it!"*

"We did all kinds of things – anything that came up – like fueling airplanes, and going to supply warehouses where we loaded and unloaded supplies that would then be sent to troops fighting in various areas."

New Caledonia was once a French penal colony, and many of the local people were descendants of those original prisoners. The people spoke French and had very little contact with the U.S. Servicemen stationed on the island. The island was safe and the soldiers were kept busy until they were called to go forward, or as Martin said, *"We didn't do much training in New Caledonia and got bored easily. There wasn't much to do in town, either, so we enjoyed doing detail as it kept us busy, or we would be bored out of our skins."*

Cargo ship docked at New Caledonia

145

LETTER 35

Pvt Martin Paulson	Mrs. A. Furford	Postage: 6 cents airmail
APO 1558	RT 1 Box 352	US ARMY APO 502
% PM San Francisco, Cal	Kent, Wash	Aug 8, 1944 4:00 PM

Dear Ruth   *August 5*

I got your letter today with the money and pictures in it and I am answering right away to let you know and thank you for sending them. That money is sure coming in handy. I have only been paid twenty five dollars since I left the States and I have been over seas three months now. Some of the fellows signed the payroll the other day but I didn't so it is hard to tell when I will get any money. One thing about it when they do pay me I will sure be rich. They owe me plenty already.

The only time we can get ice cream over here is when we go to town. So far I have never been alowed or had a pass to get into town.

I just got a new job yesterday. I am now a sniper. I go around sniping cigarett buts and keeping our area clean. It isnt such a good job, but it is a lot better than some of the jobs I have been getting. At least I dont have to go out and work nights.

Both George and Sharon seem to have grown a lot in those pictures you sent. By the way was Curly thinking about his income tax or something when you took that picture of him. He sure got a big frown, but that picture of you is about one of the best ones I ever seen. It must have been a strong sun though because all of you are looking down.

What is Curly going to do with two cars. Is he going to use one for work and one for Sunday or is he going to sell the Buick while he can get a big price out of the old pile of junk. If he sold it now he should get about eighteen hundred for it but if he waits until after the war it will drop at least five or six hundred. Tell Curly that he has finally shown a little wisdom and better judgment by finally buying a good make of car.

It will sure feel funy for me, I bet, when I get back and try to sleep in a bed and have a pillow and sheets again.

Well that is about all I can think of now so I guess I will have to close.

Love   Martin

Note Martin's new job as *sniper* [sniping cigarette butts]... he still has that same humor! Ruth must have asked Martin if he had eaten any ice cream. Martin loved ice cream! He had mentioned previously about getting all the ice cream he wanted when at Camp Roberts which tasted *almost as good as what he got at home.* Nothing like mentioning ice cream to make one miss home!

"It will sure feel funny for me, I bet, when I get back and try to sleep in a bed and have a pillow and sheets again."

The pictures Martin received were taken at the time young George tried to be like the big boys and *jumped into the lake!* Sharon is his sister Carnie's (Karen) daughter. Sharon was staying with Aunt Ruth and Uncle Arvid (Curly) at the time. We can see the *'looking down'* on Ruth's face, and *'Curly's big frown'* which Martin referred too... *from strong sunny day?*

George Furford, Ruth Furford, Sharon Bauder

Ruth 'Paulson' Furford

George Furford, Arvid (Curly) Furford, Sharon Bauder

Martin asks what Curly is going to do with two cars. He spoke about the piece of junk Curly had in a previous letter. Below is a picture of the new Buick *[the old car was also a Buick].* This is a 1942 Buick purchased by Curly & Ruth in July 1944 (car companies stopped making cars in 1942 to focus on making items for the war effort). The 1942 Buick was one of the best cars the company produced, and did not begin producing new models until 1946. It was interesting to hear Martin speak of the pricing which Curly would get for the old Buick in 1944. Curly did eventually sell this Buick after the war (1946) to purchase a Cranberry Bog which provided a living for his family.

LETTER 36

Pvt Martin Paulson
APO 15258
% PM San Francisco, Cal

Postage: 6 cents airmail
US ARMY APO 502
Aug 26, 1944 4:30 PM

Mrs. A. Furford
Rt 1 Box 352
Kent, Wash

Dear Ruth,   *August 21*

It sure seemed funny to hear that you were buying school clothes for George again. This summer sure sliped by fast. It seems like it has been a long time since I was home but then again it doesnt seem so long I have been over four months now. Twenty more and I should be up for rotation. The way the war is going I should get home sooner than that though. I hope.

I got those pictures you sent the other day. There were sure good but why dont you send or take more of yourself. I also got that money order. I wrote to you before about receiving it but in case that the other letter gets lost you will know I got it.

By the way you should see the wonderful watch I bought the other day. A fellow went broke in a crap game so he sold me his watch and dice for $10. It isnt an expensive watch but it is a Swiss make and keeps good time. I guess that is main thing anyway.

Boy when I get home I will be able to eat anything and like it. I take that back. Anything but mutton and I never liked it. I can eaven eat powdered eggs and enjoy them now. You know how bad cold storage eggs taste to you. Well we have had them a couple of times and boy do they taste good now. If you want to you can buy eggs over hear for thirty five cents each. A chicken cost eight dollars.

Well that is about all I can think of that I can write so I guess I will have to stop.

Love   Martin

PS By the way none of your mail has ever been censored. They only spot out a letter once in awhile to censor. I have never received one yet that was opened.

Martin received a money order from Ruth. In our interview he gave this reason for not getting his pay:

"You had to be signed to a company to be paid. While in Caledonia I was waiting as a 'replacement guy' to be assigned to a company, and that didn't happen until they knew where I would be needed. I didn't get paid the whole four months I was in New Caledonia."

The pictures Martin referred to were the pictures he received in the last letter. The camera that took the pictures originally belonged to Martin's dad, Adolph Paulson. It was then passed down to daughter Ruth, then to Ruth's son, George, and will eventually be passed to Ruth's grandson, David. All pictures of Martin as a child included in this book were taken by this camera, a No. 2C Autographic Kodak Jr. patented in U.S.A. Jan 18, 1910 and Jan 7, 1913 (as stated on the "Kodak Ball Bearing Shutter").

This camera is now over 90 years old!

SWISS WATCHES AVAILABLE IN THE EARLY 1940'S

WRISTWATCH: In the early 1900s, the wristwatch, originally called a *Wristlet*, was reserved for women and considered more of a passing fad than a serious timepiece. Men, *who carried pocket watches*, were quoted as saying they would *"sooner wear a skirt as wear a wristwatch."* This changed in World War I, when soldiers on the battlefield found pocket watches to be impractical and *attached their watches to their wrist by a cupped leather strap*. It is also believed that Girard-Perregaux, equipped the German Imperial Navy with wristwatches in a similar fashion as early as the 1880s, to be used while synchronizing naval attacks and firing artillery .

The pin-lever escapement (called the Roskopf movement after its inventor, Georges Frederic Roskopf), which is a cheaper version of the fully levered movement, was manufactured in huge quantities by many Swiss manufacturers as well as *Timex*, until it was replaced by quartz movements.

MUTTON: Martin makes it very clear he does not like mutton. Mutton was a staple in most households in the era of WWI and WWII as sheep were abundant. As a young girl, the author remembers large flocks of sheep being herded past the family farm as they were brought down from high hill pastures to lower pastures each fall. This was in Washington State in the mid 1940's.

 **Lamb**, **hogget**, and **mutton** (UK, New Zealand and Australia) are the meat of domestic sheep (species *Ovis Aries*). The meat of a sheep in its first year is *lamb*; that of a juvenile sheep older than one year is *hogget*; and the meat of an adult sheep is *mutton*. [98]

Older sheep produce a richer flavor, but it can be tough if not cooked properly. The best way to cook any cut of mutton is very long and slow. In the process of winning the war in the Pacific, American troops were fed mutton from Australia. That meat was said to be so foul that the troops came home with a permanent aversion to eating anything like it ever again. The following excerpts from an article by Ken Root mirrors this comment....

I don't know if you have ever had an uncle or father who railed against this product, but in our house when the WWII generation gathered, they could talk about it for hours. Maybe it was one of the things they could talk about, and maybe it shifted their anger and disgust to what the military fed them away from the fighting and death they faced every day. No matter, most never knowingly ate any meat from sheep or goats again...

I admit I'm light on market research, but the increase in lamb and goat consumption today seems to be based on two factors. First, the WWII generation is no longer making decisions on buying. If you were 18 years old in 1941, you are now 87 years old. That is not the most active consumer segment. Secondly, we've increased our immigration from countries where lamb and goat are staple foods...

You'll notice that I have not used the term "mutton" in this article except to describe what our veterans ate in WWII. The taste and smell of this meat can be bad, especially in conditions of wartime. I don't have any animosity toward them--only admiration for their sacrifice for our freedom. What I want to recognize is that a bad experience can stay with us for a lifetime, and our reaction within a culture can cause others to dislike something without ever trying it.

[Ken Root is an independent agricultural journalist. He was named the 2009 Farm Broadcaster of the Year and was the 2008 winner of the Oscar in Agriculture.]

---

[98]http://en.wikipedia.org/wiki/Lamb_and_mutton

LETTER 37

Pvt Martin Paulson
APO 15258
% PM San Francisco, Cal

Mr. A. Furford
Rt 1 Box 352
Kent, Wash.

Postage: 6 cents airmail
US ARMY APO 502
Aug 26, 1944 4:30 PM

Dear Curly   *August 24*

I got your letter the other day and I am answering almost right away. I was glad to hear the Army isnt interested in you, but dont bank to much on your ear. You cant hardly tell what the Army will do. I had talked to a lot of fellows that are over here that thought they would never pass the physical to eaven get in the Army.

Do you know what screwed means in New Zealand? It means to get paid. When a girl is knocked up she is tired, and f******g is some kind of stew or something. They sure use a lot of words for different meanings than we do, don't they.

I am sure meeting a lot of fellows that used to work down in the yard, but I never run into anyone from Elma. There are a lot of them over here somewhere but I never run into them. Maybe some of them are eaven on this island.

I bet no one can eaven talk to Happy anymore since he got his new job. I bet he thinks he owns the whole place. I bet Bert sure got mad when he heard about it. Do you remember what he used to say about the yard when he was welding. I bet that the yard is really a cut throat place now. How do you even manage to hold your job with all the guys bucking?

Well that is about all I can think of to write. There wouldn't be a heck of a lot to write about if I could write everything, because nothing much happens around here. When I do get a chance though I will have a lot to write about my opinion of a lot of things including this place.

Martin

Man to man letter! The tone of the letter is very different than when writing to his sister! The ear problem Martin was referring to is that Curly had a broken ear drum. Curly never did get called up to serve. Part of that may have been due to the fact he was a welder at the ship yards and the military considered this job as serving the country. Remember, the military had held back Martin's draft due to him being a 'master welder' and part of the reason Martin didn't get called to serve until he was 25 years of age. Curly felt he should have served, but Ruth was always happy he did not. It must have been hard for Curly with four brothers already serving.

As mentioned earlier, four of the seven brothers in Curly's family served during WWII (Leif, Erling, Rolf 'Ralph', & Stanley). It is said that the oldest brother, Julius, did not serve as he was too old. He would have been 31 yrs. old in 1939 when the war first began, and 37 yrs. old in 1945 at wars end. It is not known why brother, Harry, did not serve. He would have been 21 yrs. old in 1944.

Bert &Myrtle
Rae 1937

Curly had lived in the Elma Washington area for several years and had asked Martin if he ran across any of the men from that area. Martin tried to get information if he could.

'Happy' was a neighbor and friend who worked at the Bremerton Naval Yards and had most likely received a promotion. Bert (Harvey) is the husband of Martin's older sister, Myrtle (Harvey & Myrtle Rea). Curly had attained Foreman by this time at the ship yards and "bucking" meant that men would try to get his job for a better paying position. Remember, as men were called to serve in the military, jobs would become available and men would try hard to get these positions. Bremerton Ship Yard jobs paid very well and were highly sought after. [99]

Aerial Photo of the Bremerton Naval Shipyard at Bremerton, Washington in 1940 during construction of Dry Dock No. 5. Visible (among other ships) are eight battleships and the aircraft carrier USS Enterprise.

---

[99]This is a file from the Wikimedia Commons. Commons is a freely licensed media file repository.

LETTER 38 & LETTER 39

Pvt Martin Paulson
APO 15258
% PM San Francisco

Postage: Free
US Postal Service No 2
Aug 29, 1944 9 AM

Mrs. A Furford
Rt 1 Box 352
Kent, Wash.

Dear Ruth,   *August 22, 1944*

Say Ruth do you think you could get my Boulava watch fixed and send it to me. If I remember right the only thing wrong was it didnt have a stem and if you can would you send it air mail. You remember me telling about getting a watch over here. Well the other day I broke it and it cant be fixed over here. It isn't a very good watch so I wont send it home unless I get something else to send with it.

Do they ever censor anything in my letters? I have been wondering and no one has even mentioned that they had.

Did Sylvin ever get to come home on a furlough? When I was home they expected him to be coming hone anytime and I have been wondering if he had.

Thats about all I can think of today. It would be hard to think of things to write about over here eaven if we could write everything.

Love Martin

Pvt Martin Paulson
APO 15258
% PM San Francisco

Postage: Free
US Postal Service No 2
Sept 7, 1944   1 PM

Mrs. A Furford
Rt 1 Box 352
Kent, Wash

Dear Ruth,   *Sept 1, 1944*

As usual there isnt very much to write about, but I guess I had better let you know that I am still kicking.

By the time you get this George will be back in school and will be seven years old wont he? Time sure flies doesnt it?

By the way did I ever tell you about these South Sea Island natives. Well about the best way to describe them is that they are just about opposite from what they look like in the shows. Another thing that the movies are not right about is the bamboo trees. They are sure nice and cool on a warm day, but I will guarantee that you will keep warm fighting the mosquitoes.

The last few days we have been playing football, and so am I sore now. Every time I get up I can hardly move. If I had my way I would lay in bed all day, but you know how these Sergeants are. I really dont believe some of them are really human. You really appreciate a good one when you find them.

Love Martin

When researching Bulova watches during WWII, the author came across this interesting story:

WATCH RETURNED TO OWNER AFTER 67 YEARS IN OCEAN, STILL WORKING

The last time Teddy Bacon saw his expensive gold watch it was sinking down into the harbour in Gibraltar. That was in 1941, and the watch had slipped off his wrist when Lieutenant Bacon threw a line to shore from his ship, HMS Repulse. After two divers failed to find his lost treasure, the young officer gave up on ever seeing it again. But 67 years later, it turned up on his doormat – still ticking.

The Bulova Automatic, wrapped in a brown paper bag, did not seem at all the worse for wear after decades on the ocean floor. The timepiece had been discovered by workers dredging the harbour in 2007, who scooped it up with other debris in their machine. Because the deputy harbourmaster in 1941 had made a log with a description of the watch and its approximate location, staff knew who it belonged to. So they posted it back to the address Lieutenant Bacon had left for them on a scrap of paper all those years ago.

After being redirected from his many former homes it eventually landed on the doormat of his house in Tarvin, Cheshire. 'To say I was stunned could be considered a major understatement,' said Mr. Bacon, a widower and father of four who is almost 90.

'It truly was a miracle that I had been reunited with that watch after a lifetime. Now I wear it every day and it keeps perfect time, even after all those years in the water. It is absolutely excellent and I consider it a long-lost friend.'

Lieutenant Bacon bought the watch in the Azores for 55 dollars on his way to Singapore as part of a fleet sent to counter the Japanese invasion, and was wearing it in Gibraltar. He said:

'I was showing one of the sailors how to throw a line to shore and I remember, as clear as day, seeing the watch sail off my wrist and disappear into the water. 'I was pretty annoyed about it and two divers attached to the flotilla went down to have a

look for it but could not see it. So I went to the deputy harbourmaster and left a full description, location and probable depth of around 40ft and left it at that. Obviously I didn't expect to see it again.'

He continued on to Singapore where he narrowly escaped with his life when Repulse was sunk during an attack by Japanese planes. Teddy Bacon was on HMS Repulse when he lost his watch. After the war Mr. Bacon continued his nautical career with his family's shipping brokerage and is now enjoying his retirement.[100]

In the year 1941 the Bulova Watch Company Board of Directors adopted a resolution to manufacture products for national defense at actual cost. Throughout World War II, having perfected the skill of creating precision timepieces, Arde Bulova, Joseph's son, worked with the U.S. government to produce military watches, specialized timepieces, aircraft instruments, critical torpedo mechanisms, and fuses. Then in 1945, the Joseph Bulova School of Watchmaking opened its doors to help disabled veterans learn watchmaking skills.

Martin asked Curly if "Sylvin" [hometown fellow] got home on furlough. (Martin does not remember if Sylvin made it home on furlough, but did say Sylvin served in the Navy and was sent home after he got jungle rot in his eyes.)

Bamboo Trees

[100]http://weirdnewsfiles.com/weird-news/weird-world-news/watch-returned-to-owner-after-67-years-on-seabed-still-working/

LETTER 40

Mrs. A. Furford
Rt1, box 352
Kent, Wash.

Pvt Martin Paulson
APO 15258
% PM San Francisco, Cal

Postage 6 cents airmail
US ARMY APO 502
Sep 12, 1944 4:00 PM

Dear Ruth,   Sept. 10

The rest of the guys in the tent are 'fighting the Germans over in northern France' but I will still try to write a letter to you. You should listen to them. One guy will say one thing and everyone else will dissagree. One thing there is never a quiet moment while we are in the tent.

Last night I had KP. I went to work at six oclock in the eavening and we peeled spuds until midnight. Some fun. I was never so tired of anything as I was of that after a couple of hours. These potatoes werent like the ones they have in the states. They were just a group of bumps. I am sure glad most of, or practically all of our spuds comes in cans dehidrated. I know now why they always make pictures of KP's surrounded with spuds.

Well it looks like we are going to move again. Dont ask me why but every time we set up a camp and get settled they move us. It might only be a few hundred yards. This is the seventh time I have had to pack my bag and move since I landed here. The trouble is some times we eaven have to take our tents down and take them with us and then put them up at the next place. I had a little good luck yesterday and got to sign the pay roll for fifty bucks. Its been so long since I have had that much money at one time I dont think I will be responsible for my self. I will probably go around buying every thing I see. One thing I have made up my mind to do is keep out of all the poker and crap games.

Every thing we see do or have anything to do with over here is GI and boy am I getting tired of it. When I get back and I see one thing GI it will be too much. If you buy anything that isnt GI though you can be sure you will really be gipped.

That's all I have time for now.   Love Martin

Any information the troops received regarding war activities from around the world was sketchy at best. Most of the news the men received was from their officers or other soldiers who returned from the fronts. News in printed material like newspapers would have been received well after the fact. New Caledonia, where Martin was stationed, was a "replacement" facility where many soldiers from the front were sent to recuperate at one of the medical stations on the island, or just to rest up to be sent out again where needed. These soldiers would have come with valuable information of what was happening on the different fronts. What the soldiers had heard would most certainly be events and issues that would create *opinionated discussions*.

It is important to understand WWII war events within the "Western Front." Martin was serving in *The Pacific Front* which dealt with the war against Japan. The *Western Front* dealt with the war against Germany.

THE WESTERN FRONT JUNE-SEPTEMBER 1944

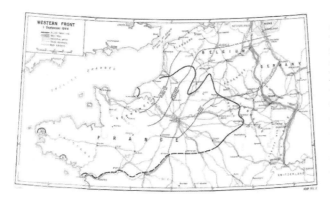

The Western Front of the European Theatre of WWII encompassed Denmark, Norway, Luxembourg, Belgium, the Netherlands, France, and West Germany. The Western Front was marked by two phases of large-scale ground combat operations. The *first phase* saw the surrender of the Low Countries and France during May–June of 1940, and consisted of an air war between Germany and Britain that climaxed during the Battle of Britain. The *second phase* consisted of large-scale ground combat, which began in June 1944 with the Allied landings in Normandy and continued until the defeat of Germany in May 1945.

Although the majority of German military deaths occurred on the Eastern Front (Europe against Soviet Union, Poland & Norway), German losses on the Western Front were almost irreplaceable, because most of Germany's resources were being allocated to the Eastern Front. This meant that, while losses there could be replaced to some extent, very little replacements or reinforcements were being sent to the west to stop the advance of the Western Allies. The Normandy landings (which heralded the beginning of the second phase of the Western Front – *and would be the center of topic by the soldiers in Martin's tent*) was a tremendous psychological blow to the German military and its leaders, who had feared a repetition of the two-front war of WW I.

NORMANDY, FRANCE

Hedgerow Country, Normandy WWII

Hedgerow Country, Normandy WWII

On 6 June 1944, the Allies began *Operation Overlord* (also known as "D-Day") – the long-awaited liberation of France. The deception plans, *Operation Fortitude* and *Operation Bodyguard*, had the Germans convinced that the invasion would occur at the Pas-de-Calais, while the real target was Normandy. Following two months of slow fighting in hedgerow country (terrain of mixed woodland and pasture, with fields and winding country lanes sunken between narrow low ridges and banks surmounted by tall thick hedgerows that break the wind but also limit visibility), *Operation Cobra* allowed the Americans to break out at the western end of the lodgment. Soon after, the Allies were racing across France. They encircled around 200,000 Germans in the Falaise pocket (see def. below). As had so often happened on the Eastern Front. Hitler refused to allow a strategic withdrawal until it was too late. Approximately 150,000 Germans were able to escape from the Falaise pocket, but they left behind most of their irreplaceable equipment and 50,000 Germans were killed or taken prisoner.

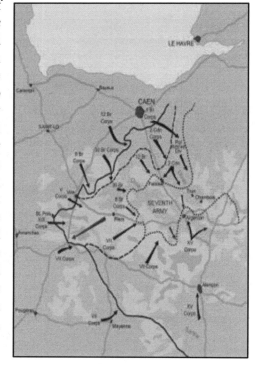

Falaise Pocket - Part of Operation Overlord

Falaise Pocket: The battle of the Falaise Pocket, fought during WWII from 12–21 August 1944, was the decisive engagement of the Battle of Normandy. Taking its name from the pocket around the town of Falaise within which Army Group B, consisting of the German Seventh and Fifth Panzer Armies became encircled by the advancing Western Allies.

The Allies had been arguing about whether to advance on a broad-front or a narrow-front from before D-Day. If the British had broken out of the Normandy bridge-head around Caen when they launched *Operation Goodwood* and pushed along the coast, facts on the ground might have turned the argument in favor of a narrow front.

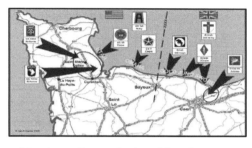

21st Army Group Outline Plan Operation Overlord 6 June 1944

However, as the breakout took place during *Operation Cobra* at the western end of the bridge-head, the *21st Army Group* that included the British and Canadian forces swung east through Belgium, the Netherlands, and Northern Germany, while the *U.S. Twelfth Army Group* advanced to their south via eastern France, Luxembourg and the Ruhr Area, rapidly fanning out into a broad front. As this was the strategy favored by supreme Allied commander Eisenhower and most of the rest of the American high command, it became the strategy which was adopted.

12th Army Group Plan August 8, 1944

LIBERATION OF FRANCE

On August 15, 1944, the Allies launched Operation Dragoon – the invasion of Southern France between Toulon and Cames. The U.S. Seventh Army and French First Army making up US 6th Army Group rapidly consolidated this beachhead and liberated southern France in two weeks, and advanced north up the Rhone valley. Their advance only slowed down as they encountered regrouped and entrenched German troops in the Vosges Mountains.

Allied advance from Paris to the Rhine

The Germans in France were now faced by three powerful Allied army groups: *in the north* British 21st Army Group commanded by Field Marshal Sir Bernard Montgomery, *in the middle* the American 12th Army Group commanded by General Omar Bradley, *and to the South* the US 6th Army Group commanded by Lieutenant General Jacob L. Devers. By mid-September, the 6th Army Group, advancing from the south, came into contact with Bradley's formations advancing from the west and overall control of Devers' force passed from AFHQ *[Allied Force Headquarters]* in the Mediterranean so that all three army groups came under the central command of General Dwight D. Eisenhower at SHAEF *[Supreme Headquarters, Allied Expeditionary Forces]*.

Under the onslaught in both the North and South of France, the German Army fell back. On 19 August, 1944, the French Resistance (FFI) organized a general uprising and the liberation of Paris took place on August 25, 1944, when general Dietrich von Cholitz accepted the French ultimatum and surrendered to general Philippe Leclerc de Hauteclocque, commander of the Free French 2nd Armored Division, ignoring orders from Hitler that Paris should be held to the last and to destroy the city.

RED BALL MILITARY TRANSPORT takes its name from the famous WWII truck supply route, the Red Ball Express that originated in Normandy in the fall of 1944.

The liberation of northern France and the Benelux countries was of special significance for the inhabitants of London and the south east of England, because it denied the Germans launch zones for their mobile V-1 and V-2 *Vergeltungswaffen* (reprisal weapons).

As the Allies advanced across France, their supply lines stretched to the breaking point. The Red Ball Express, the allied trucking effort, was simply unable to transport enough supplies from the port facilities in Normandy all the way to the front lines (as Germans destroyed all bridges), which by September, were close to the German border.

Major German units in the French southwest that had not been committed in Normandy withdrew, either eastwards towards Alsace (sometimes directly across the US 6th Army's advance) or into the ports with the intention of denying them to the Allies. These latter groups were not thought worth much effort and were left "to rot," with the exception of Bordeaux, which was liberated in May

US soldiers cross the Rhine River in assault boats

1945 by French forces under General Edgard de Larminat (Operation *Venerable*).

Fighting on the Western front seemed to stabilize, and the Allied advance stalled in front of the Siegfried Line (*Westwall*) and the southern reaches of the Rhine. Starting in early September, the Americans began slow and bloody fighting through the Hürtgen Forest (*Passchendaele with tree bursts*"— Hemingway) to breach the Line.

The port of Antwerp was liberated on September 4, 1944, by British 11th

Armored Division. However, it lay at the end of the long Scheldt Estuary, and so it could not be used until its approaches were clear of heavily fortified German positions. The campaign to clear the Scheldt Estuary was a decisive victory for the First Canadian Army and the Allies, as it allowed greatly improved delivery of supplies directly from the port of Antwerp, which was far closer to the front than the beaches of Normandy.[101]

Battle of Hürtgen Forest, US infantry take cover in the woods.

Martin peeled potatoes from 6pm to midnight – 6 hours!

He said, *"I was never so tired of anything as I was of that after a couple of hours. These potatoes werent like the ones they have in the states. They were just a group of bumps. I am sure glad most of, or practically all of our spuds comes in cans dehidrated. I know*

now why they always make pictures of KP's surrounded with spuds."

Martin said they were moving again, for the seventh time! It was very frustrating as they would just get settled and familiar with the area and would have to get up and move again - tents and all. He said he was sure it was to *"keep them active, familiar with duties, keep them from being bored, and that they 'had their reasons,' but it seemed senseless at the time."*

Please note that Martin got to sign the pay roll for fifty bucks. This is very

---

[101]http://en.wikipedia.org/wiki/Falaise_pocket

important because as we learned earlier, a soldier had to be assigned to a company to get paid. This means that Martin had been assigned to a company and would be sent out as a "replacement" soldier soon... and therefore was able to sign for pay.

The money he got was burning a hole in his pocket and he wanted to go on a buying spree. His comment, *"If you buy anything that isnt G.I. though you can be sure you will really be gipped."* As he stated in a previous letter, drinks were $1 which was very expensive. He said he wanted to purchase local items, but the locals and natives would try to get as much from the soldiers as they could. Also, due to malaria and leprosy soldiers were restricted from certain areas.

Picture from Martin's photo album of one of their camps

LETTER 41

Pvt Martin Paulson
APO 15258
% PM San Francisco

Mrs. A. Furford
Rt 1 Box 352
Kent, Wash.

Postage: 6 cents airmail
US ARMY POSTAL SERVICE
Sept 18, 1944   502

Dear Ruth,   Censored   Sept. 14

It looks like I might be pretty busy for the next few weeks so I probably wont have much time to write. They have finally started to give us some training. I ever go too much on what I say I am doing or going to do though because this is the army and anyone is a fool that tried to predict what he would be doing the next day.

One thing this trip over seas is doing for me is getting me a good sun tan. Every time I get on a detail in the day time, which is pretty often, I take off my shirt so I have the best suntan now that I ever have had.

By the way we moved again today and what do you think, I got into a tent with electricity in it. There is a catch though. We havent a light socket and globe and they are or seem to be pretty scarce over here. Five months without electricity and then when I could get it there has to be something like that to stop it. Just my luck.

You were wondering about what to send me for Christmas. Well there really isnt very much I need. And if you do send anything be sure it isnt very big. Everything I own I have to keep in my barracks bag, and when I move, which is pretty often, I have to carry it. You see my point I you.

A camera isnt any use over here at all. If you really want to get in trouble all you have to do is get out and take a few pictures or try to say something in a letter about where you are. I cant see why they are so strict, but then I'm not supposed to know anything anyway.

Its getting pretty late, nine o'clock, so I guess I will have to close. Nine is getting to be a late hour for me.   *Love   Martin*

It is evident Martin has received news that he will be pulling out as he wrote "*censored*" above the date of his letter. He now knows all the moving around and recent training was in preparation for what lies ahead. You can "feel" the tension in

163

this letter, and that he is also trying to cheer up his sister by saying something positive…

"One thing this trip over seas is doing for me is getting me a good sun tan. Every time I get on a detail in the day time, which is pretty often, I take off my shirt so I have the best suntan now that I ever have had."

Martin at right with his shirt off.
At 95, he still has that smile!

1944 Martin Paulson

Though it is only September his sister, Ruth, is asking Martin what he would like to receive for Christmas. She would have wanted to send him anything he wanted. Martin knew what lay ahead and tried gently to indicate it had to be something to fit into his barracks bag. She must have suggested a new camera as his comments were very clear and shows how negative he was feeling at the moment….

- If you really want to get in trouble all you have to do is get out and take a few pictures

Other negative comments…

- Five months without electricity and then when I could get it there has to be something like that to stop it (no light globe)
- or try to say something in a letter about where you are
- can't see why they are so strict,
- but then I'm not supposed to know anything anyway.
- Don't ever go too much on what I say I am doing or going to do though because this is the army and anyone is a fool that tried to predict what he would be doing the next day.

Listening to stories from soldiers whom had returned from action, then knowing you may soon see action, must have been very unsettling. In the previous letter Martin mentions moving around a lot and in this letter he said they were moving again. During the interview he said…

"They would get you up early in the morning, have you pack your bag and then you would go stand by the road…for hours. Then a truck would come pick you up and maybe drive ½ mile down the road and you would set up tents and create a whole new camp. We did that many times while on New Caledonia."

164

LETTER 42

Pvt Martin Paulson	Mrs. A Furford	Postage: 6 cents airmail
Co D 105th Inf APO 27	Rt. 1 Box 352	US ARMY POSTAL SERVICE APO
% PM San Francisco, Cal	Kent, Wash	Sept 27, 1944

Dear Ruth,   *September 24*

I just moved again and now I have a new APO number so I thought I would write right away and let you know. I am still in a safe place but all I can say about it is that I am still in the Pacific. These censors are driving me mad. I am not too sure what the censorship rules are here but I gather that they are pretty though.

The camp I am located in now is in a big coconut orchard. I could eat all of them I want to but I still dont like them.

The boat I came here on was almost a new boat and I thought boy heres where I enjoy myself. I finally came to the conclusion that it doesnt matter what kind of boat you get on you wont like it. They are always just to crowded.

This morning I got some beer and I drank three bottles. Believe it or not I felt it. When I get back to the states everyone will be drinking me under the table. It is sure funny how little it takes to make you feel it when you arnt used to drinking. Just writing about the beer made me thirsty so I had to open another bottle.

I had a real treat while I was on the boat though. I got a glass of milk. That was the first fresh milk I have had since I left the states. I also had fresh eggs this morning for breakfast so I am really doing all right.

I got a chance to see a lot of Jap weapons and things today. Rifles, and I eaven got to see a Jap sword. I have wanted to see one of them for a long time. You know every Jap officer caries a sword and it is handed down from generation to generation.

Well that is all I can think of right now so I will have to close.

Love, Martin

Note the new return address on the envelope. Martin mentions he has a new APO number, and what he *could not say* in the letter is that he has now become a replacement soldier to Company D, 105th Infantry, 27th Infantry Division, and 1st Battalion. The APO indicates the infantry division to which he was assigned.

The 27 Infantry Division had just completed one of the worst battles in the Pacific, the Battle of Saipan, and were being sent to the island of Espiritu Santo for a "rehabilitation period." There were 1,053 of the Division killed and 2,617 wounded of which more than half would never return to duty. On the way to Espiritu Santo from Saipan their ship picked up replacement soldiers in New Caledonia, one of which was Pvt. Martin A. Paulson. The following excerpt from a book written about the history of the 27th – THE 27TH INFANTRY DIVISION *in World War II*, by Captain Edmund G. Love, page 521 -- expresses the view of the battle worn soldiers regarding the Island of Espiritu Santo.

Whatever Espiritu Santo may have been to others, to the 27th Division it was a hellhole, ill-suited for rehabilitation and poorly chosen as a home for the troops fresh out of a great battle. Several circumstances combined to make the Division's stay there the worst single memory of the war. The physical aspects of the island were not the least of these conditions. Santo is a tropical island whose climate is hot and humid. Early in the war it had been one of the most important of all American bases in the Pacific, but even the intense activity of that earlier period had not served to transform the area from a malarial clearing on the edge of a vast and impenetrable jungle, populated by head hunters and pythons. The division was not even furnished any house facilities. As they arrived on the island, troops built their own camps in the great coconut plantations ten miles from the naval base. There was no place to go even if the men got a pass.

Japanese swords Martin brought back from Japan.
Photo courtesy of Barb Aue

WWII Japanese soldiers fought
relentlessly

Martin writes: *"The camp I am located in now is in a big coconut orchard. I could eat all of them I want to but I still dont like them."* Martin did not like coconut! In our interview, the look on his face made you laugh. He did say he loved to eat the shoots that grew out of the coconut that looked like celery stalks and were delicious. He loved the glass of milk! And the beer! He said he didn't drink much overseas and when he did, he felt the effects and got used to drinking beer warm and liking it warm.

Martin mentions seeing Japanese weapons aboard the ship he was on. These weapons included swords, some of which were Officers swords. He said most Japanese carried a sword.

Between WW1 and WW2 the Japanese military wanted to revive Samurai traditions to boost nationalism, morale and bravery and started issuing katana-style swords again. Some soldiers still had authentic Samurai swords in their family and carried them instead of the cheap copies that the army gave them. The purpose of the Samurai swords was to make the soldiers think they were Samurais and act like it *(die instead of surrender, unquestionable loyalty, etc.).* Swords held great symbolism and meaning for the soldiers.[102]

Japanese Samurai

One interesting WWII story regarding weapons is the capture on August 6, 1945 of the TACHIBANA MARU, a pre-war Japanese line and wartime troop transport masquerading as a hospital ship (contrary to international law) by two American destroyers from the 7th Fleet.

The following excerpts are from an article written by Don Moore. To read the full story please go to:

http://donmooreswartales.com/

CAPTURE OF THE TACHIBANA MARU

Harry Allcroft was aboard the destroyer that helped capture the TACHIBANA MARU 57 years ago. The 78-year old Port Charlotte man was a 2nd class motor machinist mate aboard the USS Conner, DD-582.

Early in the morning of Aug. 1, 1945, the 279-foot hospital ship smuggling 29 tons of weapons and ammunition and 1,663 Japanese soldiers bandaged to look like injured troops, was straddled by the Conner and the USS Charrette, DD-581, in the Banda Sea in the Southwest Pacific.

Weapons from the Tachibana Maru

---

[102]   http://en.wikipedia.org/wiki/Image:K...ldiers1877.jpg

"I was armed with a seven-shot automatic shotgun with buckshot. Some of the other guys had sub-machine guns," Allcroft said. "We'd practiced this boarding drill on the way to intercept the Japanese ship. We knew exactly where we were going once we got on board. I was headed for the engine room. When we got there, the Japanese engineers were milling around. Six of us pushed them away from the controls so they couldn't damage anything. We were all armed," he said. "We had 80 of our sailors, armed and aboard ship," Allcroft said. "We didn't' start opening the boxes aboard the Tachibana Maru until the prisoners were disposed of ashore. We didn't know what was in those boxes and neither did the prisoners who were sleeping on them."

Camp Roberts, Calif. bayonet training. From Martin's photo album

168

LETTER 43

V-Mail

Pvt Martin Paulson
Co D 105th Inf APO 27
% PM San Francisco, Cal

NAVY & ARMY
DEPARTMENTS
V-MAIL SERVICE
OFFICIAL BUSINESS
Postage: free
US POSTAL SERVICE NO.2
Oct 16, 1944

Mrs. A. Furford
Rt 1 Box 352
Kent, Wash.

Dear Ruth,   *October 16*

You will have to excuse the dihidrated mail because I am broke again and I am out of air mail envelopes. We are supposed to get paid in a week or so though.

Did you send my watch to my old A.P.O. or did you send it to the one I have now. The reason I ask is because I'm not getting the mail from the old APO yet. I will probably get a whole bunch one of these days though.

I sure do a lot of sweating over here. Eaven at night it is usually pretty warm. I bet I have sweat more over here than I did alltogether in the states. Its eaven warm on cloudy days.

I got in a checker game awhile ago and I got a lucky break and won the game. Boy was I surprised. It was the first game I have played since I dont know when and I think I will quit now with a good record.

We are going to get a case of coke tonight. I sure wish they would give us a quart of mixer to go with it. I will sure enjoy some after being so long without it. Will so long for now.

Martin

When Martin said, *"excuse the dihidrated mail,"* he is referring to V-Mail [Martin's letters are *transcribed as written* with his spelling of words - so that each letter is read as he wrote them].

In our interview, when asked if he received the watch mentioned in the letter, Martin said watches didn't last long in the dampness of the South Pacific and until he started buying the waterproof watches from the post exchange for $25, he would go through a watch in just a few weeks – and said he went through a LOT of them and does not remember any specific watch except the one his Dad gave him! When he was shipped back he said he bought, and brought back, a few of the waterproof watches as they were really good watches.

"I sure do a lot of sweating over here. Eaven at night it is usually pretty warm. I bet I have sweat more over here than I did alltogether in the states. Its eaven warm on cloudy days."

(Average Temperature: *93 degrees Fahrenheit with 95% humidity!*)

Espiritu Santo Beach

The Island of Espiritu Santo is part of Vanuatu, an island nation located in the South Pacific Ocean. It is of volcanic origin east of northern Australia, 310 miles northeast of New Caledonia, west of Fiji, and southeast of the Solomon Islands near New Guinea. The Vanuatu island archipelago [group of islands] consists of approximately 82 relatively small islands with about 800 miles north to south distance between the outermost islands.[103] Espiritu Santo is home to Vanuatu's four highest peaks: Mt Tabwemasana, Mt Kotamtam, Mt Tawalaala and Santo Peak, each over 5,000 feet. The western side of the island is rugged mountainous terrain whereas the

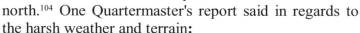

southern and eastern edges of the island are vast and flat, ideal for plantations and grazing cattle. As the largest island of Vanuatu, Santo has a great expanse of original rainforest and is home to a diverse range of colorful butterflies, tropical birds and beautiful orchids. Subtropical conditions in the south and tropical conditions in the north.[104] One Quartermaster's report said in regards to the harsh weather and terrain:

Vanuatu Island Nation

[103]http://en.wikipedia.org/wiki/Espiritu_Santo
[104]http://www.espiritusantotourism.com/climateandgeography.html

Perhaps more than anything else, environmental factors worked against Quartermaster efforts in the Pacific. Excessive heat and humidity, mold and mildew, long exposure to tropical sunlight, drenching rain storms, and the ravages of insects all had a debilitating influence on supplies. [105]

During WWII the island was used by Allied forces as a military supply & support base, naval harbor, and airfield. It was only the advent of WWII that had any real impact on the people and landscape of the island.

During the course of the war, over 100,000 allied troops and support staff was stationed here. Amid the thick jungle there are remnants of crashed B17 bombers, deserted Dakotas and Quonset huts. Many of the buildings in

ID check at the entrance to the base during WWII

the only town, Luganville, are old Quonset huts, with fences of upright Marsden matting rusting away under a deluge of decorative vines. As the war raged on further north, Santo was safe and relatively comfortable except for the heat, humidity, flies and disease-carrying mosquitos.

Evacuation of the doomed S.S. President Coolidge

---

[105]http://www.qmfound.com/qmcpacific.htm

The ship SS President Coolidge has interesting ties to Espiritu Santo. She was originally built as a luxury liner providing trans-pacific passage and commercial service. Passengers had a luxurious experience on the ship with spacious staterooms and lounges, swimming pools, a barbers shop, beauty salon, and soda fountain.

Another view of the evacuation of the doomed S.S. President Coolidge

In early 1942, the SS President Coolidge began her days servicing the South West Pacific as a troop carrier. She was never intended to see any action. On October 6, she set sail from her home port of San Francisco, California for New Caledonia and Espiritu Santo. Espiritu Santo and the harbor was heavily protected by mines. Information about safe entry into the harbor had been accidentally omitted from the Coolidge's sailing orders and upon her approach to Santo on October 26, 1942, the Coolidge, fearing Japanese submarines and unaware of the mine fields, attempted to enter the harbor through the largest and most obvious channel. A friendly mine struck the ship at the engine room and moments later, a second mine hit her near the stern. The captain, knowing that he was going to lose the ship, ran her aground and ordered troops to abandon ship. Not believing the ship would sink, troops were told to leave all of their belongings behind under the impression that they would conduct salvage operations over the next few days. Over the course of the next 90 minutes, she listed too heavily on her side, sank, and slid down the slope into the channel. She now rests on her port side with her bow at a depth of 65 feet and her stern at 230 feet. [106]

Today, Espiritu Santo is a diver's paradise as after the war all leftover equipment was bulldozed into the sea, and the USS Coolidge is an archeological

---

[106]http://www.wreckstorainforest.com/santo.html

divers dream. After the war, it was determined it would be too costly to ship the equipment back and reason for leaving it behind. One tourist company had this to say about the dives:

> The ship is so big that even if you dived it ten times in different locations, you would still only view a part of it. As most of the dives are over 98 feet, decompression stops are necessary. These stops are made on the coral garden where you can see a colorful array of hard corals and fish life. *Max Depth*: 65-230ft. [107]

Checkers is a board game played by all ages and easy to pack up and take with you, and it appears Martin was very successful at the game. The object of Checkers is to capture all of your opponent's pieces by jumping your pieces over them or to corner your opponent so that he or she cannot move any pieces. Books were written on the game in Spain as early as the mid-1500s. Through the years the game has retained its popularity.

Genre(s)	Board game/Abstract strategy game
Players	2
Age range	5 years and up
Setup time	10-60 seconds
Random chance	None
Skill(s) required	Strategy, Tactics

---

[107]http://www.diveadventures.com/pages/destinations/Vanuatu/santo.htm

LETTER 44

Pvt Martin Paulson
Co D 105th Infantry APO 27
% PM San Francisco, Cal

Mrs. A. Furford
Rt 1, Box 352
Kent, Wash.

Postage: 6 cents airmail
US ARMY POSTAL SERVICE
Oct 18, 1944

Dear Ruth,   October 15

I will probably be pretty busy for the next few days so I guess I had better write to you while I have the chance. What I am doing isnt so important or anything but you know how it is. I cant say anything about what I am doing. If I write anything wrong anymore they say they will return the letter and make us write it over.

I think I am going to get paid in a few days in full and I dont think it is a false alarm this time. You know they have only paid me seventy bucks since I was home on furlough and that isnt very much if you ask me. They say you dont need any money over seas when you are getting shipped out but when you get over here you still have to pay for every thing you get.

I was on a hike the other day and I picked some bananas and carried them in with me. I got them in my barracks bag now and put them under my bunk. You know you have to pick them green and keep them in a dark warm place to ripen them. They get some things that grow on trees like apples and they look like table green squash over here. It sure worried me what they were until I finally found out they were Cocoa beans. They cut them open and take out the beans which are inside of them. One thing about being in the army is that I am getting a chance to see a lot of strange things.

You know it will sure taste funny now to drink cold beer. Our beer is always warm. I might not eaven like cold beer again but I dont think there is much chance for that. I can remember the time though when I wouldnt drink beer if it was warm though.

Every time I go on a hike I am really on the tail end of the collum. I am in D Company which is the last company in the battalion and I am in the third platoon which is the last platoon in the company. Some of the other guys at the front could be taking a shower by the time I get in.

Well that is about all I can think of right now.   *Love, Martin*

174

Note that Martin wrote this letter in the middle of October saying he was going to be busy the next few days, but couldn't say what he was doing. According to historical records on the 27th Infantry Division, General Griner received word in the middle of October that the 27th would be employed in the coming invasion of Okinawa. From that time forward, all emphasis was placed on training and preparation for the coming operation. Physical conditioning was again emphasized, but specialized training was also taken up. [108] In our interview, Martin was asked about the training. He said the best part was that they wanted everyone to learn to swim so they got to swim in a lagoon that was beautiful and the water wonderful! He knew how to swim so he got to swim all he wanted. There was also firing range practice and a lot of bayonet drills *as they needed to be very skilled in close contact fighting with the Japs."* Martin became sullen and pulled into himself when talking about the bayonet drills.

Military pay: According to Army policy, a soldier had to be assigned to a Company before pay could be issued. It was one policy they realized was a hardship to many soldiers as they still had to pay for personal items. The policy was rectified in later years. However, it did not help the men at this time. With the exception of a couple small paychecks, Martin had not been paid since being on furlough nearly a year earlier!

COCOA TREE: a small (13–26 ft. tall) evergreen tree native to the deep tropical region of America. Its seeds are used to make cocoa powder and chocolate

Banana Tree

In our interview, Martin said they took hikes every morning and he would be in the last group. On one of the first hikes he said he saw a bunch of bananas on a tree and decided that when he got back he would get them, but when he went to get them someone had beaten him to them. So the next time he was out and saw some, he picked a bunch right then and put them in his pack! He said once they ripened they were the best bananas he had ever eaten. He broke into a big smile and you could see he was back there eating those bananas!

Then he mentions the cocoa beans. In the interview he said they would lay the cocoa beans out in the sun and there would be *"big fat ugly women – I guess I shouldn't say that, but they were – would sit in the center and sort the beans."*

---

[108]The 27th Infantry Division - In World War II, by Captain Edmund G. Love, Washington Infantry Journal Press. Also from research at National Archives, College Park, MD

175

One of the staples of Army rations are the specially made chocolate bars that contain nutrients to sustain soldiers in battle. The U.S. government recognized chocolate's role in the Allied Armed Forces and allocated valuable shipping space for the importation of cocoa beans. Today, the U.S. Army D-rations include three 4-ounce chocolate bars. Chocolate has even been taken into space as part of the diet of U.S. astronauts.

Raw cocoa beans

Young Cocoa Tree

Martin on outing with family at one of the lakes in Washington State.

Rakel (mother), Carnie (Karen), Myrtle, Ruth & Martin Paulson

LETTER 45

Pvt Martin Paulson   Postage: 6 cents airmail   Mrs. A. Furford
Co D 105th Infaf APO 27   US ARMY POSTAL SERVICE APO   Rt 1   Box352
% PM San Francisco, Cal   Oct 26, 1944   Kent, Wash.

Dear Ruth   *October 24,*

I am really running out of things to write about. About the only thing we do is train and I cant say anything about what kind we are taking or anything so there you are. I have told you about everything about the island also.

If George ever gives you any trouble about taking his vitamins you can tell him that we have to take them. We get three vitamin pills a day. Sometimes I think they are trying to run this army on pills.

I am sure glad you finally got a chance to send my watch. Did you get my new APO number in time to send it to it. It really doesn't make a heck of a lot of difference but I will get it sooner if you put my new APO on it.

By the way if you havent heard from Stanley or anything yet check up with the Red Cross. They will trace him down and find out why he doesnt write. A lot of times when you are fighting you dont get a chance to write and you dont feel like it when you do have time. If anything had happened you would have been notified by now.

I guess I must have forgotten to tell you about my finger but it has healed up now. One night I got ambitious enough to stand in line a hour and got a couple of beers. When I got back to the tent I used my belt buckle to open it because I didn't have an opener. Well I came down on the cap taking the whole top of the bottle off and following up with bringing my finger down on the top of the broken bottle. Believe me I am careful how I open them now.

Did you ever hear of Papaia. They grow on trees and taste something like cantalope. They are sure good. Another thing I just found out is grass skirts arent made of grass. They are made of the inside bark off a tree called hau. Well thats all I can think of now.

Love, Martin

This picture represents an aspect of the training the 27th received while in the jungles of Espiritu Santo.

Martin's comment, *"If George ever gives you any trouble about taking his vitamins you can tell him that we have to take them. We get three vitamin pills a day. Sometimes I think they are trying to run this army on pills"* ... makes us ask what the medical polices were regarding our soldiers in WWII? Research unveiled some interesting information.

SOLDIER STANDING IN A CAMOUFLAGED FOXHOLE during an infantry training problem in jungle warfare

Wounded American and Australian soldiers waiting to be evacuated. Natives often acted as litter bearers for causalities.

MEDICAL DEPARTMENT
UNITED STATES ARMY
IN WORLD WAR II
ORGANIZATION AND ADMINISTRATION
IN WORLD WAR II

Prepared and published under the direction of
Lieutenant General Leonard D. Heaton
The Surgeon General, United States Army

Editor in Chief
Colonel John Boyd Coates, Jr., MC, USA

Editor for Organization and Administration
Charles M. Wiltse, PhD D., Litt. D.

OFFICE OF THE SURGEON GENERAL
DEPARTMENT OF THE ARMY
WASHINGTON, D.C., 1963

by
Blance B. Armfield, M.A.

http://history.amedd.army.mil/booksdocs/wwii/orgadmin/org_admin_wwii_chpt9.htm
(for the complete study, please go to the above internet address. Below are excerpts from the
South Pacific Area study)

SOUTH PACIFIC AREA
(Excerpts from the original report)

FIELD HOSPITAL - Two of the tents were used for surgery, the other two for Wards. Foxholes were dug in the side of the hill for protection at night.

The creation of the Army command which administered medical service for Army troops throughout the South Pacific Area took place in mid-1942. During the early months of the year, Army troops, as well as Marine and Navy units, had moved into the islands of the southern Pacific; the chief Army elements were the Americal Division in New Caledonia and the 37th Division in the Fijis, smaller troop elements being scattered over a number of other islands and atolls. Until the end of the year, with the exception of the work of a few station and general hospitals, medical service was largely furnished by the units that had come in with

SHIPS LOADING at the harbor, Noumea, New Caledonia, 12 February 1943. During the tactical offensive of the U.S. forces throughout 1943, New Caledonia remained a stepping stone in the supply line to the forces fighting up the Solomon-New Guinea ladder.

troops. It became standard policy to decentralize responsibility to local commands, each island tended to become medically independent.

One of the most difficult problems encountered was the establishment and supervision of a, satisfactory system of inspecting foods for Army troops. The usual system prevailed among local commands on the various islands, where foods were inspected when they were received at island ports and at various stages of distribution and preparation for troop consumption. A more serious problem arose in connection with inspection of foods at the point of origin, mainly New Zealand. From mid-1942 to the close of 1945, millions of pounds of dairy products and fresh vegetables and fruits, as well as canned foods, were bought monthly in New Zealand for consumption by Army, Navy, and Marine Corps troops on the scattered islands

By the end of 1943, 49 Army Medical Department officers, including malariologists, sanitary engineers, entomologists, and parasitologists, and 264 enlisted men were working on malaria control. The headquarters of the organization was first located at Efate, then at Espiritu Santo after April 1943, and finally moved to the headquarters of the Commander, South Pacific Area, on New Caledonia in February 1944. With the addition of about a dozen malarious islands to the command, the South Pacific Malaria and Insect Control Organization eventually directed a large network of Navy, Army, Marine, and Allied personnel in antimalaria (*to prevent or cure malaria*) work among a troop population of more than 200,000. Later, it had responsibilities for control of other epidemic diseases as well, including two other mosquito borne diseases-filariasis (*considered globally as a neglected tropical disease, is a parasitic disease caused by microscopic, thread-like worms*), which appeared in epidemic form on several of the eastern bases in 1943 , and dengue fever (*a virus-caused disease with high fever that is spread by mosquitoes*) which reached epidemic proportions on New Caledonia early in 1943- as well as the mite borne scrub typhus (*a form of typhus transmitted by some species of trombiculid mites "chiggers" which are found in areas of heavy scrub vegetation*). The mosquito was unquestionably the outstanding disease vector in the South Pacific islands.

An Anopheles stephensi mosquito shortly after obtaining blood from a human (the droplet of blood is expelled as a surplus). This mosquito is a vector of malaria, and mosquito control is an effective way of reducing its incidence.

The responsibilities of the island malariologist were of broad scope: The initiation of malaria surveys, the preparation of directives for protective measures to be enforced by unit commanders among troops, and measures taken in collaboration with colonial authorities or native chiefs to reduce the threats of transmission of malaria from natives to troops. In order to prevent transmission from infected natives, camps were located at some distance from native villages, or if necessary, the villages were moved. Another task of the island malariologist was the inspection of departing ships and planes for the presence of mosquitoes; some areas- New Zealand, New Caledonia, Fiji, and Samoa- were nonmalarious, and disinfestation of ships and planes was undertaken to prevent transmission of malaria vectors to uninfested islands. The island malariologist- as well as the island entomologist, the parasitologist, and the engineer- also had the job of training troop personnel assigned to malaria control work.

The malaria control carried out in Army tactical units was done exclusively by personnel of the Army Medical Department; that is, the programs of the Army and Navy were separate at this level. For the Army division the control group consisted of a malariologist, responsible to the division Surgeon, and one malaria survey and one malaria control unit. Whenever the division went into a new combat area, its antimalaria group carried out control work until the base organization was in working order; thereafter the antimalaria work of the division was closely integrated with that of the base. The number of units and their assignments varied with the terrain and climate of the island bases and were modified within the base or the Army unit in accordance with change of season, shifts in the tactical situation, and so forth. During periods of combat or movements of units, emphasis shifted from environmental control of malaria to the mass taking of Atabrine (quinacrine hydrochloride), then the drug of choice for suppression of malaria.

A steady decline in malaria rates took place in the South Pacific Area, beginning in mid-1943 and continuing in 1944 and 1945, interrupted only by sporadic rises whenever troops went on maneuvers or entered uncontrolled areas. While some problems arose in the South Pacific Area wherever local command relationships were not well defined, Army and Navy forces attained a high degree of cooperation in their joint program in the South Pacific.[109]

IMMUNIZATION TO PROTECT THE US ARMED FORCES

U.S. Army nurse instructs Army medics on the proper method of giving an injection, Queensland, Australia, 1942. (DA photograph)

For over 230 years, the military health-care system has immunized troops to protect them personally and to help them accomplish their missions. Military researchers have invented, developed, and improved vaccines and immunization delivery methods against more than 20 diseases. The immunization program of the US Department of Defense is broad ranging, protecting the forces from a variety of pathogenic threats. Because of both direct and indirect benefits, most US military immunizations are required, rather than voluntary. [110]

World War II, 1941–1945
Required Vaccines

Vaccines (specific type)
Influenza (whole virus inactivated),
Smallpox (live),
Tetanus (toxoid),
Typhoid (whole cell),
Paratyphoid A and B (whole cell)

Antibodies
Therapeutic diptheriaanitoxin,
gas gangrene antitoxin,
tetanus antitoxin.
Immune globulin (measles prophylaxis)

---

[109] **http://history.amedd.army.mil/booksdocs/wwii/orgadmin/org_admin_wwii_chpt9.htm**

[110] http://epirev.oxfordjournals.org/content/28/1/3.full

Stanley Furford
1943

It was so like Martin to reassure his sister and family and direct them to the Red Cross who were a valuable resource in locating soldiers as they kept records of all wounded and killed in action. Stanley is one of Arvid (Curly) Furford's younger brothers who served in the Army on the European Front. Stanley saw heavy fighting and had difficulty adjusting after the war, never married, and died young at the age of 45.

Reading about Martin injuring his finger while opening a beer bottle brought smiles. He reminisced during our interview on his drinking while serving in the war. He said, *"It sounds like I drank a lot, but in truth I didn't drink that much because we couldn't get passes and you had to stand in line too long in camp! But once you got a bottle of beer, even though it was warm, it sure tasted good! And it surprised me how a couple of bottles would hit you. Though I liked beer, my favorite drink when I could get it was whiskey. Beer cost .50 cents, and a shot of whiskey cost $1! but I would pay the dollar. And I never opened another bottle without a bottle opener!"*

Leaf of a papaya tree

Martin asks,
"Did you ever hear of Papaia. They grow on trees and taste something like cantalope. They are sure good."

Papaia? (PAPAYA)!

Papaya Fruit

The papaya is a large, tree-like plant, with a single stem growing from 16 to 33 ft. tall, with spirally arranged leaves confined to the top of the trunk. The lower trunk is conspicuously scarred where leaves and fruit were borne. The leaves are large, 20–28" in diameter,

Papaya Trees

deeply palamately lobed (*consisting of leaflets or lobes radiating from the base of the leaf*), with seven lobes. Unusually for such large plants, the trees are dioecious (*species having distinct male and female organisms*). The flowers are similar in shape to the flowers of the Plumeria (*named in honor of the seventeenth-century French botanist Charles Plumier*), but are much smaller and wax-like. They appear on the axils of the leaves,

Papaya Blossom

maturing into large fruit 5.9–18" long and 3.9–12" in diameter. The fruit is ripe when it feels soft (as soft as a ripe avocado or a bit softer) and its skin has attained an amber to orange hue.

HAU TREE

Hibiscus tiliaceus is a species of flowering tree in the mallow family, Malvaceae (*flowering plants containing over 200 genera with close to 2,300 species*), that is native to the Old World tropics. **Hau** (Hawaiian). It has been used in a variety of applications, such as sea craft construction, firewood, and wood carvings. Its tough bark can be made into durable rope, for sealing cracks in boats, and was used to make grass skirts in the South Pacific. The bark and roots may be boiled to make a cooling tea to cool fevers, and its young leafy shoots may be eaten as vegetables.

The Hau plants normally looks like a twisting mess of curved branches and 5 pedaled flowers

Picture from Martin's photo album of native woman making grass skirts (hanging in background) 1944

ESPIRITU SANTO
ISLAND

Martin often spoke of the lagoons on
Espiritu Santo as being wonderful to swim
in. At the time he was on the island, he said
it was a wall of jungle!

LETTER 46

Pvt Martin Paulson	*Mrs. A. Furford*	*Postage: 6 cents airmail*
Co. D 105th Inf APO 27	*Rt 1 Box 352*	*US ARMY POSTAL SERVICE APO*
% PM San Francisco, Cal	*Kent, Wash.*	*Nov. 3, 1944*

Dear Ruth,   *September 1,*

Well I got paid the other day so I am sending you that money I have been saying I would send as soon as they paid me. There are two money orders one for one hundred dollars and one for fifty. By the way would you take some money out of it to buy some Christmas presents with. Then would you buy everyone in the family a present for me. There isnt anything over here that I could buy except grass skirts and beads made out of shells and I dont think they are so hot. Pay at least a couple for all the presents and I will eaven have to have you buy something for yourself. I hate to put you to all the trouble though because I know how hard it is to pick presents.

Did you know that Dad sent me a watch for Christmas? It is a waterproof shockproof job. I really think he must have paid quite a bit for it and is really too good to have over here. If it is waterproof though I guess it will be allright. Do you know it came clear over here in only fifteen days. That is really a record for a package. There is a fellow on this island from Bishop Museum and he found a tribe of natives back in the jungle that are really primitive. In fact he said they are the most primitive tribe he knows about. He was the first white man that has ever been in their village. They had these round grass huts you see in the movies and had the old stew pot out in the middle to cook meat in. You know the kind you always see pictures of explorers being cooked in.

I have been playing a little bridge lately. I always thought I could pick up a game if I didn't know it in a short time but bridge is different. There are so much that you have to remember to do when you are betting that it really mixes me up.

Well that's all I can think of now. Write and let me know when you get the money would you.

                                      Love   Martin

Did you notice the date of the letter and the postage date? I think Martin was thinking of other things! I am sure he meant November 1. The pay and what he asks Ruth to take out for Christmas gifts is amazing! The following pages from the 1944 Sears Christmas Catalog show prices for that year which the reader will thoroughly enjoy, and the older folk will enjoy the walk down memory lane!

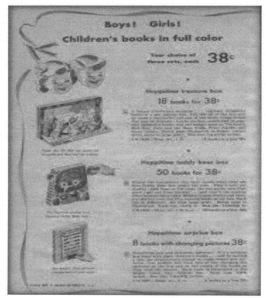

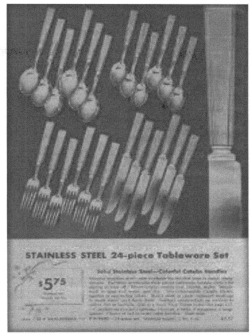

WATCHES: Martin had received a watch from his dad for Christmas. He could not remember what the brand was, but said it got him started on buying army waterproof watches. Again, he stressed that with the strenuous training and wet humid weather, watches did not last long. WWII watch company history of the war effort is quite interesting.

ELGIN – It was during the Second World War that all civilian work was stopped and Elgin made military watches, chronometers for the U.S. Navy, fuses for artillery shells, altimeters and instruments for aircraft and sapphire bearings used in the aiming of cannon. The Elgin Company was awarded ten Army-Navy "E" awards, for fulfilling contracts ahead of schedule. [111]

Elgin WW II military canteen case wristwatch with massive canteen style screw down crown protector for secure water resistance

Bulova vintage Army Watch

BULOVA – In 1941 Bulova airs the first television commercial: a simple picture of a clock and a map of the United States, with a voice-over proclaiming, "America runs on Bulova time." 1941 also marks the year that the Bulova Board of Directors adopts a resolution to manufacture products for national defense at actual cost. Throughout World War II, having perfected the skill of creating precision timepieces, Arde Bulova, Joseph's son, works with the U.S. government to produce military watches, specialized timepieces, aircraft instruments, critical torpedo mechanisms and fuses. In 1945 the Joseph Bulova School of Watchmaking opens its doors to help disabled veterans learn watchmaking skills. Bulova has been an official timekeeper for NASA and Air Force One pilots. [112]

OMEGA – has always been driven by its pioneering spirit: six lunar landings; the first divers' watch; the world's only certified marine chronometer wristwatch. No watch company in the world holds more records for accuracy. OMEGA is also a world leader in sports timekeeping. They are proud of this legacy and of the commitment to innovation which led to the launch of the exclusive OMEGA Co-Axial calibres. On account of its precision and reliability, OMEGA's Speedmaster watch was chosen by NASA as its official chronometer in 1965 and 4 years later was the first watch to be worn on the moon, when, on 21 July 1969, Neil Armstrong made his giant leap for mankind. [113] Go to their Internet Site: *www.omegawatches.com/* for a space age web experience!

1944 Vintage OMEGA stainless steel U.S. Army watch

WATERBURY CLOCK COMPANY/TIMEX – Though the company had fallen on hard times during the Great Depression it still had the manufacturing capability to make large numbers of timing devices. In 1930, a license agreement was reached with Walt Disney,

---

[111]http://www.thewatchguy.com/pages/elgin.html
[112]http://www.thewatchguy.com/pages/bulova.html
[113]http://www.omegawatches.com/spirit/history

1933 vintage Mickey Mouse Watch

resulting in the production of the famous Mickey Mouse watches and clocks under the Ingersoll brand name. The new Mickey Mouse timepieces were introduced to the public at the Chicago World's Fair in June 1933. Two Norwegian immigrants to the United States, shipbuilder Thomas Olsen and engineer Joakim Lehmkuh – both of whom fled Norway after the German invasion of their country in 1940--founded Timex Inc. in 1941. They purchased the nearly bankrupt Waterbury Clock Company, seeking to aid the allied war effort by producing bomb and artillery fuses that utilized clockwork mechanisms. In August 1943, the Army-Navy 'E' Award for excellence was awarded by the United States Under-Secretary of War to Waterbury Clock Company for the "Anglo-American fuse."[114]

WWII Poster

BELL & ROSS – When researching watch companies and their role in WWII, the poster at right was found, but historical information was difficult to find. If you go to their Internet Web Site – www.bellross.com/ – there you will see an inventive web page showing their vintage watches.

It is amazing what "gems" are uncovered in Martin's letters. In this letter he mentions a man from Bishop Museum whom said he found a tribe of natives back in the jungle that were really primitive, and said he was the first white man that has ever been in their village. The Bishop Museum still exists today!

Bishop Museum

BISHOP MUSEUM: The Bernice Pauahi Bishop Museum, designated the Hawaii State Museum of Natural and Cultural History, is a museum of history and science in the historic Kalihi district of Honolulu on the Hawaiian island of O'ahu. Over the past 120 years, the Museum's world renowned scientists have acquired 24.7 million items telling the full story of Hawaii and the Pacific. These items include over 1.3 million cultural artifacts representing Native Hawaiian, Pacific Island, and Hawaii immigrant life deriving from the museum's rich legacy of research in Hawaii and the Pacific. The museum directed me to Barbara E. Dunn, Administrative Director of the Hawaiian Historical Society, who took time to research and directed me to the book "Keneti: South Seas Adventures of Kenneth Emory," by Bob Krauss, Univ. of Hawaii Press, 1988.

---

[114]http://en.wikipedia.org/wiki/Timex_Group_USA

Kenneth Emory was on Espiritu Santo from September 13, 1944 to October 28, 1944. It is worth giving a little historical background as it is packed with information, not only on the island, but also on the natives of which Martin talks about a lot when speaking about his time in the Pacific South Sea islands. It is History of World War II one does not hear about, but should be told, and relates to Martin's letters and experiences.

Kenneth was a pioneer anthropologist of the Pacific, sailed with Jack London, worked with Margaret Mead, and encouraged a youthful Jacques Cousteau. He spoke three Polynesian dialects. Natives of South Sea Islands took him into their homes and called him "Keneti." A book was written about Kenneth Emory and his life in the South Seas.[115] This includes his time with Bishop Museum, the military, and his time on Espiritu Santo Island. The most important moments of his adventurous life were spent in tropical valleys and arid atolls (Islands) so remote most people still don't know how to reach them. He found lost Polynesian temples, collected the last scraps of ancient Polynesian mythology, and revolutionized modern archeology in the Pacific by finding clues to the past in the ground.

Kenneth lived in Hawaii and after the bombing of Pearl Harbor, residents were very fearful of invasion by the Japanese. He joined the Businessman's Training Corps that drilled on weekends and patrolled their neighborhoods at night to enforce the blackout. As the war continued, Kenneth said he might have tried to enlist but his eyes didn't pass muster. Besides, somebody had to stay and take care of the museum.

On Wednesday, October 14, 1942, Kenneth was having dinner with a friend, Clark Ingraham, who was commissioned in the U.S. Navy. Ingraham worried about what would happen to his fliers if they were shot down over the Pacific. "Even if a man managed to reach a desert island, he would starve to death in a week. Nobody could stay alive on one of those miserable sand spits," Kenneth disagreed. He said Polynesians had been living on atolls for centuries and survived very well. Even uninhabited atolls provided food and water.

Kenneth teaching soldier how to husk a coconut during survival training [Emory family album]

Kenneth: Take the ubiquitous coconut palm. Each young nut contained nearly a pint of water so pure it could be used as plasma. The meat provided food, the shell utensils, and the husk fuel. The problem was that most young men in the service hadn't the foggiest notion how to go about husking a coconut. So they starved in the midst of plenty. All a person needed was a pointed stick. Plant the blunt end in the ground, bring the coconut down hard on the point, and twist. Once you got a strip of husk off, just keep ripping off strip after strip until the

---

[115] *Book...Keneti: South Seas Adventures of Kenneth Emory...by Bob Krauss pg.'s 295-302*

nut emerged. Crack it open on a rock and eat the meat. Better still, first punch out the eyes in one end and drink the water. That way, it wouldn't go to waste."

Kenneth explained that all of this could be done without even a pocket knife. The Polynesians didn't have iron until the white man arrived. He described the shellfish that grew in lagoons, a mainstay of the diet on inhabited atolls. It only had to be picked. Kernels of the stickery pandanus tree contained starch and sugar. Children ate it as candy. The thick leaves of pig weed that grew along the beaches made a juicy and nourishing salad when there was nothing else. Even an island without streams or springs had a store of rainwater in a lens riding below the ground surface and above sea level. Every native village had a well that tapped this source. The water was brackish but it kept people alive.

Stickery Pandanus tree

Ingraham listened in fascination and asked Kenneth if he would write down this information for his fliers. Kenneth did write down the information in a booklet call "Castaway's Baedeker to the South Seas" (Baedeker means 'guide book'). Ingraham took it to the Intelligence Center, Pacific Ocean Areas and found an enthusiastic reception. Immediately, officers on other aircraft carriers wanted copies. Kenneth began teaching classes around the information in this booklet which

Pig Weed

became very popular. Colonels, commanders, and captains in the U.S. Marines called to make appointments for survival demonstrations. Kenneth with friend, Hudson, set up a Jungle Training School in tropical Kahana Valley of Oahu where servicemen bound for the South Pacific could practice survival training. Admiral Nimitz praised the school in a nationwide radio broadcast.

An ambitious army colonel in charge of the Ranger & Combat School decided that the lectures fell under his jurisdiction and that Kenneth should be given an officer's commission in his command. Kenneth had no intention of surrendering his freedom to military bureaucracy. However, wartime inflation had sent prices skyrocketing in Honolulu and Kenneth could no longer support his family on the museum salary.

Kenneth Emory (center) as a survival instructor teaching basket weaving to soldier [Emory family album]

Kenneth put his value at $500 a month (compare that to Martin's $54.00/mo.!) for an average of fifty hours work per week. This was rejected and countered at $385.75. Bishop Museum subsidized the difference and Kenneth, for the first time in his life, began to earn the magnificent sum of $6,000 per year. He lectured to fliers, chaplains, nurses, infantrymen, gunners, sailors, and WACs.

The classes continued at the same frantic pace into 1944 as U.S. Forces captured beachheads in the South Pacific. Kenneth received word September 13, 1944 that he would be leaving in two days for Espiritu Santo, the northernmost island in the New Hebrides chain, located below the equator (where he would set up advance base Jungle Training School and advise on how to handle the natives).

Upon arrival to Espiritu Santo, Kenneth saw his first wild parakeets flying among the coconut palms. As he strolled into the forest early the next morning he saw ground pigeons and swallows saying they filled the air with music just before dawn. Espiritu had become an international military outpost, the staging area for General Douglas MacArthur's re-invasion of the Philippines which was already underway. At Espiritu Santo the British occupied the coast, Americans had a large base inland, and the French claimed general jurisdiction. Nobody had bothered to ask the natives for permission to camp, Kenneth said.

Tridacna Shell:
A menacing peril of pearl diving is the giant clam whose shell measures two or three feet in diameter.

At the moment that didn't concern him, however. He set out after breakfast to look around. He saw papayas, coconut palms, big breadfruit trees (but no fruit), a Polynesian chestnut in fruit, two kinds of limes, wild pumpkin and tomato and, on the beach large Tridacna shells. Freshwater ran luxuriously out of the forest onto the beach. They had time to get acquainted with a Melanesian boy and two women before lunch.

Breadfruit Tree

At 1 pm the colonel and major escorted Kenneth and Hudson along a trail hacked through the jungle three-quarters of a mile inland to the training area. Kenneth saw rattan as well as water vine for the first time, and bamboo containing water up to one-third of every joint. Mountain apple grew in profusion around the camp area. Nobody with any sense could starve on islands so richly endowed.

Kenneth supervised the construction of a thatched village and the survival training went ahead through September. The

Mountain Apple

camp was in the upland, cold and misty. There were plenty of army instructors now, so Kenneth spent a lot of his time adding to his store of information: Melanesian words, place names, and names for plants.

By October he had made contact with French planters and had found informants in the native villages. The ground ovens of the Melanesians on Espiritu Santo differed from those he had seen before. There they used small heated stones below and large stones on top of food wrapped in bird of paradise leaves called ravaro, and covered the whole not with dirt, but with more bird of paradise leaves. The natives fished with bow and arrow in the streams and also in the ocean. They used nets for fishing, too, and a snare with a bent handle with a loop on the end for small game, pig and chicken. Another method of catching wild pig was pitfalls. The natives assured him they could get all the pigs they wanted. Kenneth recorded the size of their fishnets and the materials they used to make the twine— heavy vae bark for the border rope and aro bark for the netting. The natives of the interior spoke a different language from those living along the coast. They did not understand one another.

Hillside of Lantana

On October 24 Kenneth led a small expedition into the interior. *"The Army was firing up there,"* he explained later. *"People were living in the place. We wanted to find out where they were living and warn our side where not to fire."* With an upland guide from the mission, the party pushed along a steep path through heavy forest hung, thick with vines. At almost forty-seven, Kenneth was by far the oldest in the group. But the others had not spent their lifetimes scrambling up cliffs, bulling through thorny lantana, and slogging over sharp-edged lava flows. He had no trouble keeping up except when he stopped to examine a new plant or watch a native in a tree shooting birds with a bow and arrow.

Lantana blossom & Thorns

Halfway up the mountain they found a small village of four or five houses thatched with palm leaves and floored with hard-packed dirt, with fireplaces in the center. The women did not appear until friendly relations were established. The people maintained no contact with the shore. They had chickens, pigs, and dogs, and fished in mountain streams. Kenneth discovered that they spoke basic Malaya, which he could understand. "We went all the way to the top of the island," he said later. "It was an all day trip to get up there, very steep."

Kenneth returned to Honolulu, Hawaii, on October 28, 1944

LETTER 47

Postcard: front & back

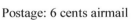

Pvt Martin Paulson
Co. D 105th Infantry APO 27
% PM San Francisco, Cal

Mrs. A. Furford
Rt. 1 Box 352
Kent, Wash

Postage: 6 cents airmail
US ARMY POSTAL SERVICE APO
Nov 11, 1944

Dear Ruth,   November 9,
    I sure got a big surprise this morning. Everyone that worked last Sunday got today off and I was one of them. Things like a day off in the middle of the week dont hardly ever happen in the army just because you had a detail on Sunday.

    I bet you cant guess what time we have to get up now. Four forty-five. We then take training until twelve thirty and then we are supposed to get the rest of the day off although I havent gotten one off yet.

    I got a few cards, Jap cards I mean, from a guy that picked them up on Saipan. I am sending one to you. All their cards seem to be trying to put over a idea or something. This one has the whole family out in the field working. Eaven the mother is out there nursing a small baby.

    Well I guess your father in law is still happy. I hear Rosevelt won the election again. He thinks Roosevelt is the only man for the Job doesnt he.

    Thanks a lot for the clippings. I sure enjoy finding out what some of the guys are doing. Maybe I will read about somebody near where I am sometimes. I hope.

    Well I cant think of anything else to write about now. I told you didnt I that I havent seen any white people here yet although there are supposed to be a few. Since there arnt any white people there arnt any places to go like towns. Well thats about all for now.

Love   Martin
PS. Did you get the money I sent.

Note: The postcard mentioned in the letter is shown above.

Each time Martin mentions going out on detail, he means any training detail, or doing any job that may have been assigned to him. The training on the island of Espiritu Santo was very intense in preparation for the upcoming landing on Okinawa. Though there were no towns to go to for "unwinding," Martin said the military would do their best to provide "moral boosting" things for the men like films and outdoor activities, and men would play cards, write letters, and play board games.

From Martin's comment it sounds as if he father-in-law liked Roosevelt. Below is information on the 32nd President of the Unities States who took the nation through The Great Depression and World War II.

Franklin Delano Roosevelt
Also known by his initials, FDR
Jan 30, 1882 – April 12, 1945)

Roosevelt signing the declaration of war against Japan, Dec 8, 1941.

Franklin Delano Roosevelt was the 32nd President of the United States (1933–1945) and a central figure in world events during the mid-20th century, leading the United States during a time of worldwide economic depression and total war. A dominant leader of the Democratic Party and the only American president elected to more than two terms. Energized by his personal victory over polio, FDR's unfailing optimism and activism contributed to a renewal of the national spirit. He worked closely with Winston Churchill and Joseph Stalin in leading the Allies against Germany and Japan in World War II, and restoring prosperity to the nation's economy.

As World War II loomed after 1938 with the Japanese invasion of China and the aggression of Nazi Germany, FDR gave strong diplomatic and financial support to China and Great Britain, while remaining officially neutral. His goal was to make America the "Arsenal of Democracy" which would supply munitions to the Allies. In March 1941, Roosevelt, with Congressional approval, provided Lend-Lease aid to the countries fighting against Nazi Germany with Britain. With very strong national support, he made war on Japan and Germany after the Japanese attack on Pearl Harbor on December 7, 1941, calling it a "date which will live in infamy." He supervised the mobilization of the U.S. economy to support the Allied war effort. As an active military leader, Roosevelt implemented an overall war strategy on two fronts that

Roosevelt signing the declaration of war against Germany, Dec 11, 1941

ended in the defeat of the Axis Powers and the development of the world's first atom bomb. Unemployment dropped to 2%, relief programs largely ended, and the industrial economy grew rapidly to new heights as millions of people moved to new jobs in war centers, and 16 million men and 300,000 women were drafted or volunteered for military service.

FOURTH TERM PRESIDENT: In a relatively close 1944 election, Roosevelt and Truman won 53% of the vote and carried 36 states. The President campaigned in favor of a strong United Nations, so his victory symbolized support for the nation's future participation in the international community.

Due to the President's health and the ongoing state of war, the President's fourth inauguration was held on the White House lawn. Reflecting on Roosevelt's presidency, "which brought the United States through the Great Depression and World War II to a prosperous future," said FDR's biographer Jean Edward Smith in 2007.

"He lifted himself from a wheelchair to lift the nation from its knees." [116]

Franklin Roosevelt with Ruthie Bie and Fala
at Hilltop Cottage in Hyde Park, 1941
- Franklin D. Roosevelt Library

---

[116]http://en.wikipedia.org/wiki/Franklin_D._Roosevelt

LETTER 48

Pvt Martin Paulson
Co D 105th Inf APO 27
% PM San Francisco, Cal

Postage: 3 cents
US ARMY POSTAL SERVICE APO
Nov 14, 1944

Mr. & Mrs. A. Furford
Rt 1, Box 352
Kent, Wash

LETTER 49

Pvt Martin Paulson
CoD 105th Inf APO 27
% Pm San Francisco, Cal

Postage: 6 cents airmail
US ARMY POSTAL SERVICE
Nov 16, 1944

Mrs. A. Furford
Rt 1 Box 352
Kent, Wash

Dear Ruth,   *November 13,*

I got your letter last night and I am writing right away. I am sure sorry to hear that they are trying to frame Curly and if you need any of my money to beat them use it. It isnt doing me any good and I cant see where it will until at least after the war so if you need any of it use it. This letter will probl probably be to late though. Those guys that are framing Curly are the guys I would sure like to get out in front of me if we get into combat. We or I mean they are the ones we are fighting

197

for so they can keep on grafting all the money. Curly was on the four lane highway on that curve by the Red Pig wasnt he. I almost hit another car there once. He did the same thing this woman did, pulled right in front of me and I had to run clear off the road to miss him. Have they got any forged witnesses to try and prove he was going eighty. They were sure smart to keep him in jail until they could build up their case and you didnt eaven know where he was. Curly was going to take out liability. Did he ever do it or did he just have the regular accident insurance.

I am writing this this morning and I want it to get off right away, be sure to use all of my money that you want.   Love   Martin

The Christmas card speaks for itself, but in case you could not read the words...

૭

Once again the world recalls
That happy day of old
When Christ was born in Bethlehem,
As wise-men had foretold,
May all the tidings of good cheer
That fill this DAY of DAYS
Be bringing you deep, perfect peace
As joy in countless Ways!

ൟ

Where did Martin get the Christmas card, especially since there are no towns on the island of Espiritu Santo? Martin said he had taken a supply of cards with him, but said the Red Cross had them available for military personnel also.

This letter shows the depth of Martin's character and what "family" means to him as he didn't hesitate to give up all his money to help his sister and her husband. Even today, at age 95, those who know him speak of his kindness, love of family, and great character. When interviewing Martin, he would say he doesn't deserve all the fuss people make over him. His son, Marty (himself 60 yrs. of age), says he hopes he is half the person his Dad is when he gets old. He says his Dad sees only the

Arvid (Curly) Furford in his 1942 Buick

good in people and looks for the best out of each day!

Curly had been involved in an auto accident and the insurance company representing the woman was coming after him. One wants to laugh when Martin refers to them suggesting Curly was going 80 miles an hour. In 1944? What happened to Curly? Apparently, the policeman on the scene was the boyfriend of the girl in the other automobile! Ultimately, Curly was acquitted of any wrong doing, and they did not need to use Martin's money.

Though research could not find automobile speed for the 1942 Buick which Curly drove, research found a WWII domestic report that is very interesting..

A Controlled Materials Plan finally established an effective method of allocating critical commodities. The rubber shortage, caused by Japan's seizure of most of the world's rubber trees, was solved by building synthetic rubber plants and rationing gasoline. The rationing, which politicians feared people would reject, won popular acceptance after a distinguished panel led by the financier Bernard Baruch issued a report proving beyond doubt that there was no way to conserve rubber except by limiting automobile use. Consequently, in 1942 a national speed limit of 35 miles per hour was established, and most drivers were given a weekly limit of 3 gallons of gas.[117]

Then there is this interesting article regarding a change in speed limit in Utah:

'PATRIOTIC SPEED LIMIT' WAS 35 MPH
By Lynn Arave, Deseret News
Published: Tuesday, Feb. 17 2009 12:00 a.m. MST

The next time you feel confined or restrained by a 45 mph speed limit, you should be aware that more than 60 years ago the maximum speed limit anywhere in Utah was only 35 mph. On Oct. 28, 1942, a "Patriotic Speed Limit" of 35 mph was announced in an attempt to conserve gasoline and save on tires during World War II, according to the official history of the Utah Highway Patrol. Enforcement began on Nov. 10, 1942. Many cars were operating with unsafe tires because people were unable to buy new ones. The speed regulation resulted from a report following an engineering study of vehicle tires by the National Safety Council with the cooperation of the UHP and at the request of the Utah Highway Traffic Advisory Committee to the War Department. The study showed 46 percent of cars driven by war workers had at least one tire with the tread worn smooth; 23 percent with at least two tires worn smooth; and 11 percent with at least three. The study also indicated at least 40 percent of all the cars on Utah streets and highways had at least one smooth tire. Because all of Utah's 40 mph, 50 mph and 60 mph signs were reflectorized, all of them had to be replaced. The old signs were stored in anticipation that the speed limit would be raised following the war — and it was.

---

[117]http://www.answers.com/topic/world-war-ii-1939-45-domestic-course

Though no information could be found on the "Red Pig" (restaurant) where Curly's accident occurred, an interesting bit of WWII history emerged. And though it does not relate to the South Pacific, it is one of those small 'gems' of WWII history the reader may find of interest.

WESTWIND (Nicknamed: <u>Big Red Pig</u>,) was launched on March 31, 1943, commissioned September 1944. The Coast Guard contracted for five vessels of the class in November 1941 to fulfill the need to access military bases in Greenland that would be inaccessible during most of the year without the use of heavy icebreakers.

August 1964

Westwind was heavily armed for an icebreaker due to her design being crafted during World War II. Her main battery consisted of two twin-mount 5 inch deck guns. Her anti-aircraft weaponry consisted of three quad-mounted Bofors 40 mm anti-aircraft auto cannons and six Overlain 20 mm auto cannons. She also carried six K-gun depth charge projectors and a Hedgehog as anti-submarine weapons. After her return from Soviet service she received a single 5 inch 38 cal. mount forward and a helicopter deck aft. Sometime after 1966 she had the forward mount removed.[118]

CUTTER WESTWIND RETURNS FROM ARCTIC: The U.S. Coast Guard Cutter Westwind (WAGB-281), an icebreaker, approaches the Coast Guard LORAN Station at

Cape Atoll, Greenland. The station is located some 20 miles from Thule Air Force Base and 800 miles from the North Pole. The Westwind arrived in the area in July of 1945. Scenic fjords and rugged mountains loom in the background. [119]

Red Pig *in Artic seas*

[118]http://en.wikipedia.org/wiki/USCGC_Westwind_%28WAGB-281%29
[119]http://www.uscg.mil/history/webcutters/icebreaker_photo_index.asp

LETTER 50

Pvt Martin Paulson	Mrs. A Furford	Postage: 6 cents airmail
Co D 105th Inf APO 17	Rt 1 Box 352	US ARMYPOSTAL SERVICE APO
% PM San Francisco, Cal.	Kent, Wash	Nov 30, 1944

Dear Ruth,   *Nov. 38,*

Thanks a lot for the Christmas Package. I got it today and I opened it right away because if there was anything in there that would spoil it would do it pretty fast over here. You sure used good judgement in picking out things because the canned things are just what I like and want. We can get candy bars over here but if we ever want anything else to eat we cant get it in the eavenings. The watch also came over in good shape. I guess about the best idea will be to sell it to someone now though since Dad sent me one. I sure wish Dad had told you he was sending me one so you wouldnt have had to go to all the trouble with the old one of mine.

I have been expecting a letter from you telling how Curly came out in the trial although I cant quite expect to get it this soon. I was sure glad when I found out he was covered by liability insurance. He didnt have it when I left and I thought he might have been still putting off getting it. I sure hope he comes out all right.

Did you ever get that Jap postcard I sent to you. I sent one to Myrtle and she wrote that it wasnt in the envelope. I was sure they would go through the censor because lots of other guys have sent them and got them through. They have a little Jap writing and maybe that is the reason but I am sure what it says isnt any military secret or anything. We arnt supposed to write in any foreigne language so I guess that must be the reason.

How would you like a grass skirt? At first I didn't think you would want one but after thinking it over I thought you probably would at that. If you know of anyone else that wants one let me know. They are the only things we can buy over here. Grass skirts arn't really made out of grass. The natives peel the bark off a small tree they call Hau. They divide the bark and take the inside part and bleach it. They then paint it up or dye it or something anyway when it is finished it has a lot of different bright colors on it.

They have lifted the band so I hear on taking pictures so if I get a chance I will take a picture of one of these rough looking natives with bones in their noses, loin cloths and all. They dont seem to come out of the jungle very often lately though. At least I havent seen any tough looking ones lately.

I havent ever told you what I am doing befor because I havent been sure I would stay in it. I am in a mortar squad. It is what I would rather be in but I never had anything to do with it before so I havent been to sure I would make it. I am still not to sure so if you here that I am doing something else dont be surprised.

I was surprised the other day to get a Christmas box from Lillian and Ed. I havent their address so would you thank them for me. Also tell them I had just mentioned a couple of days befor I got the box that I would sure like some olives because I hadnt had one since I came over and you know how I like olives.

By the way we sure had a swell dinner for Thanksgiving. We had all we could eat including fresh turkey, which was really good. I ate so much that I couldnt eat all the ice cream they gave me. Our company went to a lot of extra trouble using paper plates and table cloths eaven napkins. All the other companies I saw had to eat out of their mess kits as usual.

Well I am about run down so I will have to close. How is George getting along now. You havent said much about him lately.   *Love Martin*

Lillian & Ed Lundgren

A great Thanksgiving meal, two Christmas boxes from home, and Ice Cream! Great morale boasters! His letter is very "chatty" of which I am sure Ruth enjoyed receiving. The second box with the olives was sent by Curly's sister and her husband, Lillian & Ed Lundgren. Martin said it was heaven receiving food he hadn't eaten since leaving home.

Martin couldn't remember receiving the watch or if he sold it. As he said before, he went through so many watches. When asked about the watch his father sent, he said he doubted it lasted as he had to buy so many watches because they wouldn't last long. But he did remember buying only waterproof watches after getting the one from his dad.

We know Ruth got the postcard (see Letter 47). Martin was surprised it was still around! He did not remember the picture on the postcard he sent to his sister Myrtle, and said the Army was really strong on telling them what they could and could not say in letters.

Martin said the band on taking pictures had been lifted...."*so I hear.*" To this day Martin talks about the natives and how primitive they were. He said they were not large people, in fact, most were very small. The ones that would come out of the jungle were fierce looking. In all the time he was on the islands where the primitive natives lived, he said it was hard to get a picture as they stayed to themselves in the jungle. He wanted to get a picture of one with the bone in the nose. Where he was, he said the bones were small and black so they were hard to see, but they all had bones in their noses. In researching, it was almost impossible to find pictures of early natives for the WWII time period.

South Pacific native

The island of Espiritu Santo was very remote and unsettled when Martin was there. Today it is full of banana plantations and is a wonderful tourist destination for the climate as well as for those interested in WWII weapons, machines, and ships that were left behind.

Martin asks Ruth if she would like a grass skirt. In 1944, travel across a state was a big event, so getting something from the South Sea Islands made by a native would be a big treat.

HOW ARE GRASS SKIRTS MADE?

Authentic Hau Tree grass skirt

Opihi Shell

In the old South Pacific Islands the natives would use the bark of the Hau tree to make authentic hula skirts. Hau grass is made from the wild hibiscus tree's inner fibers. Directions: using long cuttings approx. 4-5 feet, first roughly remove the outer bark, a length that doesn't have many branches as it will present knots in the fibers. Once prepped, immerse the branches in water for about 5-7 days. Ocean water is preferable to act as a natural wash. Remove the branches from the water and then gently remove the outer layer with a knife or other sharp object. Polynesians used the opihi shells or other limpets to remove the protective outer layers. Once cleaned, the fibers are hung to dry in the sun. Avoiding rain or moisture is preferable so mildew does not set in. A natural bleach may be used to dye the material after the drying process. A metal brush can be used to comb and shred the fibers into thinner strands.

Martin tells Ruth he has been training in a Mortar Squad. Ruth probably had no idea what a Mortar Squad was, or what he would be doing in a mortar squad.

Mortar firing 1944

Mortars lob small 'bombs' to distances ranging from a few hundred yards to a few miles. Mortar fire was extremely effective in breaking up incoming enemy infantry attacks. A three-mortar team could launch a hundred rounds or more in a five-minute period of intense fire. It would appear it is a safe job in combat since you are not in hand-to-hand combat with the enemy. However, this attitude ignores a key principle in warfare – first kill the enemy that is doing the most damage to your troops. In many cases, it was the mortar squad. The Japanese military records indicate that they hated the American mortar squad.

Take a look at a few things in the picture at right:

This public image is a work of a U.S. Army soldier or employee, taken or made as part of that person's official duties.

✓ Soldiers plugging their ears
✓ The two soldiers to left of the mortar are the loaders
✓ The soldier to the right of the mortar is the calibrator
✓ The radio man in the back who gave the calibrator the settings and reported results

Martin's job within the Mortar Squad was the role of the radio man. This will be his job going forward.

LETTER 51

Postage: free
US POSTAL SERVICE NO 2
DEC 10, 1944 8:30AM

This letter speaks for itself!

LETTER 52

PFC Martin Paulson	Mrs. A. Furford	Postage: 6 cents airmail
Co D 105th Inf APO 27	Rt 1 Box 352	US ARMY POSTAL SERICE APO
% PM San Francisco	Kent, Wash	DEC 11, 1944

Dear Ruth,   *Dec. 8*

Well, I bet you couldn't guess where I am now. I cut my foot a little on some coral the other day when I was swimming and it got infected. I went on sick call and they sent me to the hospital. It isnt anything serious or anything like that so I am kind of on a vacation. Nice soft bed to sleep on, meals brought right to my bed. Pretty soft or what.

I am sure glad Curly got out of the accident as easy as he did. When you first wrote about it it looked pretty bad for him but I guess they found it was harder to stick him than they thought it was.

No I dont get the Cronicle. The reason I havent sent for it is that papers come over third class and that takes a long time and they are usually in pretty bad shape if you get them. I would sure appreciate it if you keep sending the clippings like you have been because that is all I care to read about anyway.

By the way did you ever get that Jap post card I sent to you. I put one in a letter I sent to Myrtle and she didnt get hers. Let me know if you didnt get it and I will send another to you. Other fellows have sent them so I dont see why they took mine out. When they take something out they are supposed to give it back to you and they didnt eaven do that.

I almost forgot to tell you about my big promotion. I am now a full fledged PFC. Well at least it means four eighty a month more.

You know when I first came into the army I coudnt hardly sleep on the army bunks the first few nights. Now I have one here in the hospital and a feather bed never felt any better, is so comfortable that I slept all afternoon. Well that is all I can think of now so I guess I will sign off.

Love   Martin

Martin's memories of his hospital stay are of sleeping *between sheets* on a *soft bed* and being *well taken care of,* but he does not remember how the food was! He said he had thought about it many times and wonders why he can't remember the food...paying too much attention to the nurses, maybe? He does remember coral poisoning being very painful and surprised that you could get poisoning from coral.

South Pacific coral reef

Coral reefs are colonies of creatures with calcareous, or bony, exoskeletons that often feature sharp angles or ridges, so it's not uncommon for swimmers and divers to suffer lacerations after making contact with reefs. Once the skin has been broken, "coral poisoning," characterized by raised, itchy red welts that develop as capillaries become inflamed, can set in within minutes. In addition to minor side effects like localized pain and relatively low fever, coral poisoning may advance to ulcerative cellulitis and sloughing of the skin around the wound, which can take as long as three to six weeks to heal.

The newspaper clippings Martin received were of the war in other parts of the world. Today's generation may have a hard time understanding that you did not get instant news. Today's TV coverage of significant events is noted for its saturation of coverage as events unfold. Media through radio during WWII was very primitive by modern standards, but radio brought the war home to the American people in a way it had never done before and was rapidly improving to provide coverage across the nation. However, conditions in the South Pacific were far different than other parts of the world and radio had to be transmitted via ship to ship then to units on islands.

RADIO HISTORY: Throughout the 1930s, in spite of the Great Depression, electricity - and with it radio - was coming into most American homes. By 1939 a majority of housewives considered the radio to be more indispensable to their homes than the clothes iron or the refrigerator. Although most radio listening was music and entertainment in the form of comedies and dramas, the various radio networks developed news departments.

World War II began on Sept 1, 1939, when Nazi forces invaded Poland. The entire broadcast day of CBS affiliate WJSV, Washington DC, has been preserved, including coverage of the invasion. The internet site of *www.otrcat.com* has many of the complete radio broadcasts from WWII.[120] During World War II, America had ample reason to be proud of her fighting men and radio did all it could to show the folks back home the fine job they were doing.

The War Department created the Armed Forces Radio Service (AFRS). For the troops, the radio was a '*Touch of Home.*' Programs would be sent to overseas radio stations from the ARFS Hollywood studios. Sometimes shortwave transmission to the front-line stations was used when the program required immediacy, but the preferred method was by *phonographic disk*. Transcription to disk was a relatively expensive process, but it guaranteed quality and reliability that shortwave could not.

Command Performance (1942-49) was an early hit during World War Two. *Mail Call* (1942-49) was another early AFRS WWII radio show. Premiering in Aug 1942, the show drew its title from the military practice of gathering the troops when mail was delivered to the unit. The show also used A-list talent (working for free) and took the form of a love letter from the celebrities to the troops. *GI Journal* (1943-46) used the celebrities

Soldiers gathered around the radio

as the guest editors and staff for a weekly newspaper for the WWII troops. Comedy and Pin-up girl talent was featured with a healthy share of popular music.

Technology had improved in answer to the needs of the Military, and these

---

[120]http://www.otrcat.com/complete-broadcast-1939-nazi-invasion-of-poland-p-2139.html

improvements naturally made their way into the civilian market. Unfortunately for Radio, the electronic and manufacturing advances also made possible the rise of Television. Radio as the dominant entertainment medium was more a victim of post war prosperity than the superiority of TV. [121]

Martin asking Ruth if she got the postcard makes one ask the question... *how many letters crossed paths before a question asked in one letter got answered by another*? Mail from overseas went to a processing center for censorship and often in the case of V-Mail through various steps before reaching its destination. Mail from home was not censored regularly as news from home usually contained events that had already transpired and no threat to national security.

Private First Class Insignia

Promotion to Private First Class gave Martin $4.80 more a month, bringing his monthly pay to $58.80 a month! When asked if that was good pay, he said NO... *"I was getting really good pay at the ship yards. The Army didn't pay very much at all, but what was I going to spend money on while in the war? So it was OK, I guess. You still needed a little money to spend, but not much."*

As seen in the comparative chart below, the U.S. Army ranks during World War II were not abbreviated the same as they currently are today with all letters capitalized. Rather, in World War II only the first letter was capitalized followed by the rest of the abbreviated word in the lower case, and then a period to indicate it as being an abbreviation. In some cases, two or more letters were capitalized with a slash mark after the first letter to indicate there were more than one word in the full title of the rank.

Full Title	Current abbreviation	World War II abbreviation
Private	PVT	Pvt.
Private First Class	**PFC**	**Pfc.**
Corporal	CPL	Cpl.
Sergeant	SGT	Sgt.
Staff Sergeant	SSG	S/Sgt.
First Sergeant	1SG	F/Sgt.
Master Sergeant	MSG	M/Sgt

LETTER 53

Pfc Martin Paulson	Mr. A. Furford	Postage: 6 cents airmail
Co D 105th Inf. APO 27	Rt 1 Box 352	US ARMY POSTAL SERVICE APO
%PM San Francisco, Cal.	Kent, Wash.	Dec 18, 1944

Hello Curly,   *Dec. 17,*

I thought for awhile I might be writing to you in care of Pierce County jail but I guess I was wrong. I think those striped suits would look good on you.

Im still taking it easy up here in the hospital but it doesnt look like it will last much longer. I guess I will be out of here in a couple of days. Im getting tired of doing nothing and my luck is running very good in pocker so I guess I had better get out of here anyway. Ruth said that you werent feeling so good and was taking a rest. I bet you have been working every day seven days a week and that would be hard on anyone.

I am sure glad they didn't make a welder out of me here in the army and send me over here. I am sweating right now and all I am doing is sitting on the edge of the bed with a fan right in back of me with only a bottom part of a pair of pajamas on. This ward is also under some shady trees. You can just imagine how hot it would be to weld.

Back in camp we get up at four fourty-five now in the morning and then train until twelve thirty. We then get the rest of the day off if there isnt any details but there are always some of them. I have got quite a few afternoons off though.

I was sure glad to here that we took another island in the Phillippines. If we get control of them we can sure raise hell with the Japs shipping and everything in general.

Well Curly thats all I can think of now. Hope you are feeling better now and take a couple of drinks New Years for me.

                                                          Martin

It was thoughtful of Martin to write directly to Curly when learning Curly was not feeling well. He can relate to not feeling well with himself being in the

hospital. There were three hospitals on the island at this time with the naval hospital being the best established in Quonset huts. Pictures of the other two hospitals were not available. Compare the picture of the naval hospital on Espiritu Santo to the field hospital on Leyte Island.

Naval hospital station on Espiritu Santo Island

The Battle of Leyte in the Pacific campaign of World War II was the amphibious invasion of the Gulf of Leyte in the Philippines by American and Filipino guerrilla forces under the command of General Douglas McArthur, who fought against the Imperial Japanese Army in the

Philippines led by General Tomoyuki Yamashita from October 20– December 31, 1944. The operation code named King Two launched the Philippines campaign of 1944-45 for the recapture and liberation of the entire Philippine Archipelago [group of islands] and to end almost three years of Japanese occupation. This was also the first battle in which the Japanese used kamikaze pilots.

A scene at the 116th Station Hospital, Leyte Island, December 1944.

The Philippines were an important source of supplies, especially rubber, to Japan and also commanded the sea routes to Borneo and Sumatra by which petroleum was brought to Japan: holding on to the Philippines was vital. For the U.S., capturing the Philippines was

a key strategic step in isolating Imperial Japan's military holdings in China and the Pacific theater. It was also a personal matter for MacArthur. Two years previously he had left the Philippines vowing to return, and he insisted that it was a moral obligation of the U.S. to liberate it as soon as possible.

Leyte's population of over 900,000 people (mostly farmers and fishermen) could be expected to assist an American invasion, since

Gen. Douglas MacArthur and staff land at Palo Beach, Leyte, 20 October 1944.

many residents already supported the guerrilla struggle against the Japanese in the face of harsh repression. Japanese troop strength on Leyte was estimated by U.S. intelligence at 20,000.[122]

Allied forces:

United States	200,000
Philippine Commonwealth	3,189 guerillas
Australia	More than 94

Allied causalities:

Killed	5,534
Wounded	12,144

Axis:

Japan & Second Philippine Republic	55,000

Axis causalities:

Killed	49,000
Captured	389

---

[122]http://en.wikipedia.org/wiki/Battle_of_Leyte

LETTER 54

Pfc. Martin Paulson
Co. D 105th Inf. APO 27
% PM San Francisco, Cal

Mrs. A. Furford
Rt 1 Box 352
Kent, Wash.

Postage: 6 cents airmail
US POSTAGE SERVICE APO
Jan 2, 1945

Dear Ruth,   *Dec 30,*

I guess you have started to wonder if I was ever going to write. There really isnt much to write about any more. I have told you all about the island and I never do much. This is almost New Years but I guess it will be a pretty quiet one for us. We have a basketball game with the Navy tonight. We have a pretty good team but we havent had any practice to speak of and we havent played on a regular court so I imagine we will have a tough time.

That date wine loaf you sent me for Christmas sure was good. I didn't open it until Christmas. What I mean is I saved it until Christmas.

By the way Ruth any time anything comes up that I should give someone a present would you get one for me and give it to them. I sure would appreciate it and another thing be sure and take it out of my money. Do you ever get any chance to get ahold of any 127 film. If you do would you send me some. I took some pictures and I should get the prints back pretty soon now. If they are any good I will send them home to you. One thing I want to get is a picture of one of these natives. I mean a woman so you can see how they compare to Dorthy Lamour.

They just told me that I was going to school Monday and learn something about radios. I dont know what it is all about but I dont think it will amount to much. Maybe they will teach me how to use one of these Walki Talkies or something. There isnt much to that though because I can do that already. Dont get the idea now that I will be a radio man or anything like that. I really dont think it will amount to much.

I bet George has changed quite a bit since I left. Its sure hard to realize that he is almost through the second grade already. Hes big enough now to do a lot of little jobs like go to the store and get in the wood without much trouble.

I got a letter from Sweede. I guess he can only see out of one eye now and that one must not be too good. You remember he used to really be a good writer, now his writing is as bad as mine. Dont say anything about that though because it is only a guess.

Well that is all I can think of to write now. I broke the watch Dad sent me so I will put it in with a grass skirt and send it to you. I am also sending you a $80 money order with this letter. *Love Martin*

ARMY & NAVY were playing against each other in sports even in war time. What a wonderful way to unwind. Martin says they won this one! So the score at this time was Army won one, Navy won one.

Date Wine Loaf .... can be made with any Date Loaf recipe by substituting 2/3 of the water in the recipe with red wine. Sulfites are present in wine. Sulfites (preservative) are a group of chemical agents that prevent bacterial growth. Using red wine helps preserve bread and therefore, gives the loaf a better chance of arriving fresh. If you are planning to make and ship/send to a soldier or another person, it is important that the loaf cools completely. Then wrap in paper towel (to absorb any residual moisture that is in loaf during shipping) before putting into tin or package. If sending to tropical area, it is best to package in a tin container.

1	cup chopped dates
1/3	cup boiling water
2/3	cup boiling Red Wine
1	teaspoon baking soda
1	tablespoon butter
1	cup brown sugar
1	egg, beaten
1	cup chopped walnuts (optional, Martin loved the nuts!)
1/4	teaspoon vanilla essence
2	cups plain baking flour
1	teaspoon baking powder

1. Preheat oven to 350 degrees F. Lightly grease an 8x4 inch loaf pan.
2. Put dates, boiling water & wine, butter, and baking soda into a bowl and stir until butter is melted.
3. Set aside for one hour.
4. Beat sugar, egg, vanilla essence and walnuts into date mixture
5. Sift in flour and baking powder and stir until just combined.
6. Pour mixture into greased loaf pan
7. Bake for 45-50 minutes or until inserted skewer comes out clean
8. Leave in tin for about 10 minutes before turning out onto cooling rake.

Martin requests 127 film from Ruth...if she can find it. The 127 format in film was introduced by Kodak in 1912, along with the "Vest Pocket Kodak" folding camera.

1941 - Kodak marketed the versatile KODAK EKTRA Camera, with a shutter-speed range from 1/1000 to 1 second. Airgraph, or "V-Mail," was developed by Kodak as a system for microfilming letters to conserve shipping space during World War II. 1942 - KODACOLOR Film for prints, the world's first true color negative film was announced. Kodak's Rochester plants were awarded the U.S. Army-Navy "E" for high achievement in the production of equipment and films for the war effort.

A 1900 magazine advertisement for the popular BROWNIE camera. Note the cost: $1.00.

Dorothy Lamour (December 10, 1914 – September 22, 1996) was an American actress and singer. She is best remembered for appearing in the *"Road to"...* movies, a series of successful comedies starring Bing Crosby and Bob Hope. The *Road to...* films were popular during the 1940s. The last film in the series, *Road to Bali*, was released in 1952. Lamour was of French Louisianan, Spanish, and Irish descent.

When Martin spoke of Dorothy Lamour, he was being a little facetious in that the native women on the Islands he has been on were not at all like the native women you see in the movies. Kenneth Emory's life work (written about in previous letter) as an anthropologist in the Pacific South Seas studied mostly Polynesian natives (Hawaiian Islands). When asked to set up a jungle training school on the Island of Espiritu Santo, this observation was noted:

It is not clear whether the military command understood that his (Kenneth Emory) field of expertise lay in Polynesia while the inhabitants of the New Hebrides are Melanesians, a different race entirely. [Espiritu Santo is of the New Hebrides]

< Polynesian

Hebrides >

ᔕ Women ᔕ

Martin made light conversation regarding being trained on the Walkie Talkie, however, he was trained very thoroughly. Every rifle company had six Walkie Talkies; one for each of three rifle platoons, two for the weapons platoon, and one for the company CO (Company Commander).

The SCR-536 Radio was a hand held radio used by the United States during World War II. It was the first "Walkie

Radio Set SCR-536, the original Walkie Talkie in use on a beach during WWII

Talkie" and was very useful in that it was extremely portable. It incorporated five vacuum tubes in a waterproof case, was powered by a 1.5 volt BA-35 dry battery and a 103.5 volt BA-38 dry battery, and had an RF output power of 360 milliwatts. The battery life of the SCR-536 Radio was generally around a day of average use.

The SRC-536 is often considered the first of modern hand held, self-contained "handie talkie"two-way radios

It was also designed for short range two way communication and the radio was turned on simply by pulling out the antenna. It was the exact opposite process to turn off the Walkie Talkie. The range of the unit varied with terrain;

from a few hundred feet, to approximately one mile over land, and 3 miles over water. To talk, one must press a button on the radio. The unit operated in AM voice mode between 3.5 and 6.0 MHz frequency range and could operate in 50 different channels as well. It was carried among the first waves to hit Omaha Beach at Normandy in June 1944. By war's end, 130,000 of the units had been manufactured by Motorola.

Martin mentions getting a letter from Sweede. He lived in his neighborhood growing up so he knew him many years. Sweede Nichols served in the South Seas in the Seabees (a division of the Navy). He acquire "Jungle Rot," a common name for any disease acquired while in the extremely humid hot jungles. Soldiers could become infected with a fungus of which there were many types. If a soldier was susceptible to athlete's feet, he was sure to get terrible fungus of the feet from continuous moisture inside his boots. Sweede was unfortunate to get "jungle rot" in the eyes and lost sight in one eye, and a great loss of sight in the other. He eventually was discharged and sent home.

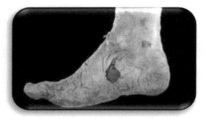

Example of a mild case of Trench Foot (Jungle Rot)

Soldier's feet were often in wet, muddy situations. Combine that with the warm tropical weather and conditions are ripe for Jungle Rot.

JUNGLE ROT: Tropical ulcer, Aden ulcer, Malabar ulcer, or tropical phagedena are the other names for jungle rot disease. It is essentially a lesion that occurs on the skin and can be caused by many different microorganisms such as mycobacteria. Jungle rot disease is common in tropical climes, and is often a result of continuous exposure of the feet and arms to damp, unsanitary conditions. Although the condition can affect any exposed part of the body, it is more common in the lower limbs. If neglected, it can extend through the muscles and tendons, and even reach the bones. The lesions can recur on the old abrasions or sores, which could have just begun as a mere scratch.

LETTER 55

Pfc. Martin Paulson
Co D 105th Inf APO 27
% PM San Francisco, Cal

Mrs. A. Furford
Rt 1 Box 352
Kent, Wash

Postage: 6 cents airmail
US ARMY POSTAL SERVICE APO
Jan 19, 1945

Dear Ruth   *Jan 16,*

Well Ruth I finally got a few pictures taken and developed and I am sending them to you. Would you have a couple of sets of Jumbo prints made of them and send one set to me and save one set for me. I have some more that I will have in a few days so maybe you had better hold these up a while and then send them all in together. I have a few pictures of natives as you will notice. These are the smaller natives they have here. Some of the natives live father inland and they are bigger and rougher looking. The woman with the grass skirts and the baby are Tongenese. I dont know if that is how you spell it but that is how it sounds. That is one of the few you see that arnt or isnt going to have a baby. It seems like everyone you usually see kind of stick out in front.

We just made a nine mile speed march this morning in two hours. It is sure hard on me or anyone in a hot climate like this. When I got in I could wring sweat out of my clothes although that happens quite often. I am eaven sweating right now writing this letter and it is about nine o'clock at night.

By the way if you can get any film for my camera would you send me some. The size is 127 if you dont remember.

That is all I can think of now. I will send those other negatives right away.

Love Martin

PS I am still trying to get close to a woman that is native to this island and get a picture of her but they never come out where you can get close to them.

Martin said a lot of film & pictures did not make it through the mail. Therefore, a lot of the pictures mentioned in this letter did not survive. Were they censored? Someone else want the pictures? Even in Kenneth Emory's book of the South Sea Islands, there were just a couple pictures of natives. It has been next to impossible through research to locate pictures of early natives from 1940-1945 which indicates the censorship of pictures must have been very rigorous.

Tonga located at right of Australia

Martin describes one native as Tonganese. The word references a person from Tonga. Tonga, is a sovereign state and an archipelago [group of islands] comprised of 176 islands scattered over 270,000 square miles of the southern Pacific Ocean. Fifty-two of these islands are inhabited. Tonga also became known as the *Friendly Islands* because of the friendly reception accorded to Captain James Cook on his first visit there in 1773. He happened to arrive at the time of the *'inasi'* festival [the yearly donation of the first fruits to the Tu'i Tonga - the islands' paramount chief], and so received an invitation to the festivities. According to the writer, *William Mariner*, the chiefs had wanted to kill Cook during the gathering, but could not agree on a plan.

Not much is known about Tonga before European contact because of the lack of a writing system. However, oral history has survived and been recorded

The haka is a traditional genre of Māori dance (Polynesian).
This picture dates from ca. 1845.

after the arrival of the Europeans. By the 12th century Tongans, and the Tongan paramount chief [the *Tu'i Tonga*] had a reputation across the central Pacific [from Niue, Samoa, Rotuna, Wallis & Futuna, New Caledonia to Tikopia], leading some historians to speak of a Tu'i Tonga Empire. In the 15th century and again in the 17th, civil war

Tāufa'āhau, King of Tonga (1845–1893)

erupted. Into this situation beginning in 1616, the first European explorers arrived. Humans have lived in Tonga for nearly 3,000 years. With the arrival of Western traders and missionaries in the 19th century, Tongan culture (especially in religion) changed so that today almost 98 percent of residents are Christian. The people have discarded some old beliefs and habits, and adopted others.[123]

---

[123]http://en.wikipedia.org/wiki/Culture_of_Tonga

You may have noticed in Martin's letters how he says he has nothing to write about (nothing he is allowed to write about), that once they finished for the day "he has nothing to do unless there are details to do ...of which there usually is some kind of detail." Research has revealed that while Martin was on the island of Espiritu Santo he was in intensive Jungle training. In this letter he mentions he made a nine mile speed march that morning in two hours. The terrain of the island does not allow for smooth trails! From what was learned during research, the army camp was inland...in the hills, and there was a lot going on Martin was not able to write about. From the book: THE 27TH INFANTRY DIVISION In World War II, by Captain Edmund G. Love, page 253, tells of the training which Martin could not speak about:

> In the month of October, 1944, General Griner received word that the 27th would be employed in the coming invasion of Okinawa. From that time forward all emphasis was placed on training and preparation for the coming operation... Jungle training centers were established and amphibious training was renewed... ...under the guidance of battle-tried troops (who fought in Saipan), all replacement troops who were newly inducted into the 27th, were indoctrinated in the principles of warfare against the Japanese. Night fighting, a new departure in the Pacific War, was emphasized. New doctrines of infantry-artillery-tank cooperation were taught. The training continued into the rainy months of January, February, and March 1945. The men marched along the jungle trails and sweated through the maneuvers in the almost unbearable jungle heat. Disease, the enemy of troops in tropical climates, began to take its toll. Here and there key figures began to disappear. Captain Renner of C Company, 106th Infantry, who had fought for eight days with a broken elbow, was hospitalized with a tropical skin disease. Other members of the Division were sent home because of infection or respiratory diseases.....

The following information and pictures are from tourism sites located on the Internet which gives the reader more insight on the Island of Espiritu Santo. The Island is now a favorite tourist spot, especially for WWII archeologists.

Vanuatu (the name of the group of islands) stretches over 683 miles in a north-south direction. Therefore, subtropical conditions in the south and tropical conditions in the north. The best time of year to visit Vanuatu is April/May to October, the "dry" season, when temperatures range from 64 to 82 degrees Fahrenheit. Light, casual clothing, plus a sweater for evenings usually suffice. November and December are warm but not unpleasantly so, generally. January to March is hot 78-93 degrees Fahrenheit with up to 90% humidity, often wet and prone to cyclones (Martin's letter is dated Jan 16). But being low season, it's also a good time of year to take advantage of travel deals. While you can expect slightly more rain over the wet months, tropical rain showers are relatively common, usually lasting for less than an hour.

Espiritu Santo is home to Vanuatu's four highest peaks: Mt Tabwemasana, Mt Kotamtam, Mt Tawalaala and Santo Peak, each over 5,000 feet. The western side of the island is rugged mountainous terrain whereas the southern and eastern edges of the island are vast and flat, ideal for plantations and grazing cattle. As the largest island of Vanuatu, Santo has a great expanse of original rainforest and is home to a diverse

Native boy with banana leaf umbrella

range of colorful butterflies, tropical birds and beautiful orchids. In the north lies Vanuatu's first National Park, Vathe Conservation Area.

Espiritu Santo Jungle Waterfall

Americans seeking a secure base for staging action in the Pacific during WWII selected Espiritu Santo. With the natural harbour of Segond Canal, it was the ideal location for a military base and the town of Luganville [as it is known today] was born. During the war, Luganville could accommodate up to 50,000 people and throughout the war years, over 500,000 military personnel were stationed there. In addition to building roads and erecting numerous Quonset huts, the Americans constructed 40 cinemas (not cinemas as we know them today as these were often outdoors or under tents), four military hospitals, and five airfields. When the war ended, the Americans left almost as quickly as they arrived and Espiritu Santo returned to a peaceful, quiet existence.

Espiritu Santo Lagoon

LETTER 56

Pfc. Martin Paulson
Co D 105th Inf APO 27
% PM San Francisco, Cal

Mrs. A. Furford
Rt. 1 Box 352
Kent, Was

Postage: 6 cents airmail
US ARMY POSTAL SERVICE APO
Jan 26, 1945

Dear Ruth,   *January 24,*

Well Ruth things are just about the same as ever around here. Just as dead as ever. You know this is the first place I have ever been where you dont need a pass to leave camp. They dont have to worry about awalls around here, there isn't any place to go. I sure wish we could be sent to New Zealand or Australia, but we couldnt get a break like that.

I finally got a grass skirt and sent it to you. I got one for Myrtle and Karen also and put them in the same box and sent them to Karen. I thought it would be easier for her to get it because she lives right in town and it was a pretty good sized box. I also put a couple of sets of a belt, wrist band, and necklace and one necklace made of shells in the package. You can decide with Myrtle & Karen and take one of them also.

The skirts are in three pieces. The skirt and then two things that look like little skirts that you put over the top of your chasis. It is made out of the inside part of bark from a tree call Hau. Most of the ones you get in Hawaii are made out of cellophane and come from the states. These skirts were made by natives. I would like to get something for George over here but the natives are too dumb on this island to make anything. Those belts and necklaces were imported from Somoa by the PX.

Well Ruth I cant think of anything else right now so I guess I will have to quit.

Love   Martin

PS. On those films I sent to you I think I mentioned it but if I didnt would you get jumbo prints.

221

AWALLS: an acronym used by the troops to mean someone who
"goes... climbs over the wall and runs away from the military."
The accurate acronym is AWOL (**A**bsence **W**ith**o**ut **L**eave).

Martin sounds like he wishes he were someplace other than where he is currently. As mentioned previously, troops were being put through strenuous marches on Jungle trails and being trained extensively on how to deal with the Japanese during battle. Martin wrote this letter at the end of January and as we have learned, Jan-Mar were the hottest months with high humidity and tropical rain storms. They were also having a lot of night training.

Martin said in his interview that training on the radio was completed during this time. He learned all about the Walkie Talkie and what codes and word phrases to use. With a big smile, he said the discouraging part is that they wouldn't let you take it apart and see how it really worked!

The picture of the two girls is from Martin's WWII photo album... but is not of his sisters. When asked who it was, Martin's face flushed a little and said, *"There were a couple of girls back home I sent grass skirts too."* It is a good illustration of the grass skirts he sent home. He said they loved all the "accessories" he sent along. The Natives made the colors used on the skirts from different plant & fruit juices.

For clarification, Martin could develop his film in the island's military "town" that sprung up while the military occupied the island. However, since they moved camp a lot, there were times he sent his film directly to Ruth. The 127 film made very small pictures. The Jumbo prints he requested Ruth to make from the negatives were about 3"x4" (this black/white photo is from a 3"x4" enlargement).

The author deeply regrets not having read Martin's letters in earlier years as Ruth (the author's mother-in-law) would have been a great source of information like finding out if pictures and film were received and sent as mentioned in the letters. Sadly, at the time of writing, 95 year old Martin is the only living family member of his generation.

Research discovered that even undeveloped film was "censored" with some negatives on the undeveloped rolls being blackened out. It was feared that pictures of natives and certain land marks, if intercepted, could lead the enemy to their location. Martin also learned the shutter on his camera was not working properly and the pictures he thought he was taking, he wasn't.

Going forward, a monthly Time Line of Global Events will be included as it is important to understand that the 27ᵗʰ Infantry Division within which Martin served is just a snap-shot of the bigger picture of events happening around the world. And keep in mind, the war had been in process since September 1939!

WWII GLOBAL TIMELINE - JANUARY 1945

Day

1 The Germans begin a surprise offensive Operation Nordwind (North Wind) along the Saar and aimed at retaking Strasbourg.

2 The Japanese increasingly use kamikaze tactics against the US naval forces.

2 46 American B-29 bombers based near Calcutta, India attacked a railroad bridge near
Bangkok, Thailand and other targets in the area.

3 The Allies take the offensive east of the Bulge but they fail to close the pincers (which might have surrounded large numbers of Germans) with Patton's tanks.

4 US navy air attacks on Formosa (Taiwan)

5 The German offensive "North Wind" crosses the border into Alsace.

5 Japanese retreat across the Irrawaddy River in Burma with General Slim's troops in pursuit.

6 American B-29's bomb Tokyo again.

7 Germans, as part of the plan to retake Strasbourg, break out of the "Colmar Pocket," a bridgehead on the Rhine, and head east.

8 The battle of Strasbourg is underway, with Americans in defense of their recent acquisition.

9 Americans land on Luzon, the central island of the Philippines. There are more kamikaze attacks on the American navy.

12 The East Prussian Offensive, a major Red Army offensive in East Prussia, begins on January 13th.

13 1st Byelorussian Front launched its winter offensive towards Pillkallen, East Prussia, Germany, meeting heavy resistance from the German 3rd Panzer Army.

14 British forces clear the Roer Triangle during Operation Blackcock; it is an area noted for its industrial dams.

15 Hitler is now firmly ensconced in the bunker in Berlin with his companion Eva Braun.

15 The British commander in Athens, General Ronald Scobie, accepts a request for a ceasefire from the Greek People's Liberation Army. This marks the end of the Dekemvriana, resulting in clear defeat for the Greek Left.

16   United States First and Third Armies link up following Battle of the Bulge; Soviet troops meanwhile lay siege to Budapest.

17   Warsaw liberated by Red Army troops. A government favorable to the Communists is installed.

17   It is announced officially that the Battle of the Bulge is at an end.

18   Americans drive on Manila.

20   Franklin D. Roosevelt is sworn in as President (his fourth term); Harry Truman is sworn in as Vice President.

25   American navy bombards Iwo Jima in preparation for invasion.

25   The Allies officially win the Battle of the Bulge.

27   Auschwitz concentration camp is liberated by Soviet troops.

28   The Red Army completes the occupation of Lithuania.

31   Red Army crosses the Oder River into Germany and are now less than 50 miles from Berlin.

31   A second invasion on Luzon by Americans by inside to the Filipino soldiers and guerrilla fighters, this time on the west coast.

31   The whole Burma Road is now opened as the Ledo Road linkage with India is complete.

USS Columbia attacked by
a kamikaze *off Lingayen*
Gulf January 6, 1945.

LETTER 57

Pfc. Martin Paulson
Co D 105th APO 27
% PM San Francisco, Cal

Mr. A. Furford
Rt 1 Box 352
Kent, Wash

Postage: 6 cents airmail
US ARMY POSTAL SERVFICE APO
Feb 10, 1945

Dear Curly,   *February 7,*

Well Curly things are still just about as dead as ever around here. The only thing that changes is the weather and that sure changes and I mean fast. A hour ago there wasnt a cloud in the sky and it was hotter than the devil. A half a hour ago it was raining so hard that if you were out in it just a minuet or so you would be soaked. Now the sun is out and it is hot again. Some weather. Any rain we have at home is just a sprinkle along side of the way it comes down here.

To get a purple heart you dont have to be hurt very bad. Then again you have to be hurt really bad before they wont send you back to duty so it is hard to tell how bad Galdys husband was hit but it is most likely he wasnt hit very hard. He didnt stay in the hospital very long did he.

Well Curly I went in with another fellow the other night and bought a fifth of Shinleys Reserve. Its been so long since I had any whiskey that I didnt care much about it. You know it been almost a year since I had any.

You know there is one thing more on this island that I really hate and that is the flys. They are thicker than the devil and sticky as hell. You cant scare them and they are always landing on cuts and my mouth. One eaven landed on my mouth while I was taking a drink of water.

I suppose by this time you have seen the pictures I sent to Ruth. I sure hope they come out all right on the enlargements. I hope you can see the bones in the natives noses. They are a type of pigmy. Martin Johnson mentions them in one of his books. He visited them after the last war and then they were pretty wild. In fact he caught them roasting a human being.

I just heard Manila on the radio. I guess we just captured it. They are sure going to town arnt they. Well I guess I am just about run down. Take it easy Curly.

Martin

In this letter Martin further describes the island of Espiritu Santo as having rain and "flies!" Martin came from Seattle, Washington, where it rains abundantly, but the rains on this tropical island have made a greater impression on him. And unless one has lived in a place with high humidity, it is hard to explain how heat and humidity saps all energy from a person. Then to have to train in those conditions...with flies...can be very discouraging. The tone of his letter lets you know he is getting a little down with his comment, "*it is dead as ever around here.*" He must have just finished the morning runs, hikes, & training.

Glady is Curly's sister (Gladys 'Furford'). Her husband, Gene, had been wounded in battle while serving on the European Front, but went on to serve to war's end. As the 1953 picture shows, he returned from the war, married, and had children.

Glady & Gene Fluery and children 1953

Schenley was a liquor company based out of New York, NY with headquarters in the Empire State Building and a distillery in Lawrenceburg, Indiana. It owned several brands of Bourbon whiskey, including Schenley. They also owned a controlling interest in Blatzt beer, and made a Canadian whiskey called Black Velvet. Schenley's Black Velvet DeLuxe was the only liquor available to submarine officers at Midway in World War II where it was held in low regard and known as "Schenley's Black Death." [124]

1943 Schenley Royal Reserve Whiskey

Another "Gem" within Martin's letters is him mentioning the author Martin Johnson who wrote the book: Through the South Seas with Jack London in 1914. A great read! This led to another book by Martin Johnson's wife Osa Johnson: I Married Adventure: The Lives of Martin and Osa Johnson. The book includes their time on the New Hebrides Islands in 1919 when the natives were as Martin describes.

Another fascinating book to read is John G. Paton, Missionary to the New Hebrides – an autobiography. There are no pictures but his descriptions of events are very telling, like the chapter titled "*Cannibals at Work*" which makes the following picture come alive. At the beginning of the book John Paton describes an incident that took place when he and another missionary were building his dwelling shortly after arriving on the island.

---

[124] http://en.wikipedia.org/wiki/Schenley_Industries

Party after party of armed men going and coming in a state of great excitement (different village native groups who were curious)... We were informed that war was on foot, but our teachers were told to assure us that the Harbour people would act only on the defensive, and that no one would molest us at our work. One day two hostile tribes met near our station; high words arose, and old feuds were revived. The Inland people withdrew, but the Harbour people, false to their promises, flew to arms and rushed past us in pursuit of their enemies. ..... horrid yells of the savages soon informed us that they were engaged in deadly fights. Excitement and terror were on every countenance; armed men (natives) rushed about in every direction with feathers in their twisted hair – with painted red, black, and white, and some, one check black, the other red, others, the brow white, the chin blue – in fact, any color and on any part, the more grotesques and savage -looking, the higher the art! .... We were afterwards informed that five

Head Hunter of New Hebrides at Campfire 1919 (Used by permission of The Martin and Osa Johnson Safari Museum)

or six men had been killed; that their bodies had been carried by the conquerors from the field of battle, and cooked and eaten that very night at a boiling spring near the head of the bay, less than a mile from the spot where my house was being built. .... The next evening, as we sat talking about the people, and the dark scenes around us, the quiet of the night was broken by a wild wailing cry from the villages around, long-continued and unearthly. We were informed that one of the wounded men, carried home from the battle, had just died; and that they had strangled his widow to death, that her spirit might accompany him to the other world, and be his servant there, as she had been here. Now their dead bodies were laid side by side, ready, ready to be buried in the sea. Our hearts sank to think of all this happening within earshot, and that we knew it not!

John Paton arrived on one of the southern islands of the New Hebrides islands in 1859. In 1891 head hunters still existed on this island even though much work had been accomplished and many "heathens" as they were called had turned from their ways. However, it is mentioned in the last pages of the book that civil battles still arose occasionally and one of the *converted* headhunters mentioned that if it were not because of his conversion he would delight in eating the missionaries. It was a sobering thought to the missionaries!

Martin was on the largest of the New Hebrides islands and head hunters were still active inland ...some 50 years later! The picture of the head hunter Martin & Osa Johnson had in their book was taken in 1919...just 15 years before Martin was on the island. When John Paton arrived in 1859, the natives were naked (men, women, and children) except for the older women who wore grass skirts or leaves. When Martin was on the island of Espiritu Santo in 1944, the inland native men wore groan cloths and the women wore grass skirts. Martin said most of the native children were naked, but many native villages along the beaches wore "white people" cloths. There were missionaries and

New Hebrides women
1919 - Note bones in nose (Used by permission of The Martin and Osa Johnson Safari Museum)

some French people on the island in 1944. The French were clearing land and developing coconut groves. After the war, changes on the island occurred rapidly. Today, the New Hebrides islands are tropical tourist destinations![125]

Martin shakes his head saying he cannot believe the island is a tourist attraction today. He said, *"What I saw, you would never think it could ever be a tourist destination!"*

Part of the destruction of Manila

The *Battle of Manila*, also known as the *Liberation of Manila*, fought from February 3 to March 3, 1945 was part of the 1945 Philippine campaign. The one-month battle, which culminated in a terrible bloodbath and total devastation of the city ended almost three years of Japanese military occupation in the Philippines (1942–1945). The city's capture was marked as General Douglas MacArthur's key to victory in the campaign of reconquest.

Rear Admiral Iwabuchi Sanji was entrusted with the holding of the city Manila, and he was committed to defending it to the last man. He refused General Tomoyuki Yamashita's orders to evacuate Manila, and instead mounted the last stand of the Imperial Japanese troops. Prior to being promoted to admiral, Sanji had

---

[125]Book: John G. Paton – Missionary to the New Hebrides – An autobiography pgs 51-52

commanded the battleship *Kirishima* in 1942 when it was sunk by a US Navy task force off Guadalcanal. Feeling shamed at having lost a warship, he felt the need to redeem himself and so he ordered his Manila Naval Defense Forces, a motley assembly of sailors, marines and Army troops, into the city. They discovered several good defensive positions, including Intramuros [walled part of Manila; Latin for "*within the walls*"] and other nearby buildings. After blowing up every outlying facility of even marginal value, like bridges and footpaths, Iwabuchi had set up minefields, barbed wire,

Admiral Iwabuchi Sanji

interlocking trenches, and hulks of trucks and trolleys, to create bottlenecks and traps. He then ordered his ragtag troops into the defensive zone. Before the battle began, he issued an address to his men which went:

"We are very glad and grateful for the opportunity of being able to serve our country in this epic battle. Now, with what strength remains, we will daringly engage the enemy. Banzai to the Emperor! We are determined to fight to the last man.[126]

WW II GLOBAL TIMELINE - FEBRUARY 1945

Day

1   Ecuador declares war on Germany.

2   Naval docks at Singapore are destroyed by B-29 attacks.

3   U.S. forces enter Manila by helping with the Allied Philippine Commonwealth troops and recognized guerillas, Japanese forces in the city massacre 100,000 Filipinos civilians and devastates the city. A vicious urban battle ensues, to last for some weeks. Also known as Battle for Liberation of Manila

3   Heavy bombing of Berlin

4   Yalta Conference ("Argonaut" of Roosevelt, Churchill, and Stalin begins; the main subject of their discussions is postwar spheres of influence.

4   Belgium is now cleared of all German forces.

8   Paraguay declares war on Germany.

9   The "Colmar Pocket," the last German foothold west of the Rhine, is eliminated.

12   Peru declares war on Germany.

13   The Battle of Budapest ends with Soviet victory, after a long defense by the Germans.

---

[126]http://en.wikipedia.org/wiki/Battle_of_Manila_%281945%29

13/14   The controversial bombing of Dresden; it is firebombed by Allied air forces and large parts of the historic city are destroyed. Allies claim it is strategically important.

15   Venezuela declares war on Germany and Japan.

16   American naval vessels bombard Tokyo and Yokohama.

16   American paratroopers and the Philippine Commonwealth troops land on Corregidor Island, in Manila Bay. Once the scene of the last American resistance in early 1942, it is now the scene of Japanese resistance.

19   U.S. Marines invade Iwo Jima.

21   Vicious fighting in and around Manila was joint by Filipino and American troops.

23   U.S. Marines raise the American flag on Mt. Suribachi on Iwo Jima.

24   Egypt declares war on Axis.

24   Massive bombing of Germany by approximately 9,000 bombers.

25   US incendiary raids on Japan.

25   Turkey declares war on Germany.

25   After ten days of fighting, American and Filipino troops recapture Corregidor.

26   Syria declares war on Germany and Japan.

28   The Sixth United States Army captures Manila, capital of the Philippines by continued the Allied Philippine Commonwealth troops and recognized guerrilla fighters after an unyielding Japanese defense force. A Philippine government is established.

28   The combined Filipino and American military forces increase their presence in the Philippines by invading Palawan, a western island in the group.

February 16, 1945 indicates American naval vessels bombard Tokyo and Yokohama. Martin said in our interview that it was the Navy that made the winning of the war possible. He said land maneuvers would never have been possible if the Navy had not knocked out key Japanese ships, Japanese land holds, etc. with their destroyers and aircraft carriers.

USS Indiana *bombarding Kamaishi, Japan on 14 July 1945*

LETTER 58

Pfc. Martin Paulson
Co D 105th APO 27
% PM San Francisco, Cal

Mrs. A. Furford
Rt 1, Box 352
Kent, Wash.

Postage: 6 cents airmail
US ARMY POSTAL SERVICE APO
Feb 11, 1945

Dear Ruth,   *January 31*

We got the rest of the morning off I think so I will write this letter to you befor I go swimming. Just think it is only seven thirty now and I have been up two and a half hours already. It is also so hot already that I am sweating now. We moved out to an old Marine camp for a few days. This is sure a swell camp and I wish we could stay here all the time. We are real close to the ocean and can go swimming any time we are off. I havent been doing very much swimming because we have to go to far to get to a swimming place. You know the ocean is really to warm to swim in. I was swimming around last night and I noticed I was pretty warm so I went up on the beach and dried off my face and sure enough I was sweating. As cold as the ocean is back there it is hard to realize how warm it gets here.

Maybe I had better tell you a little bit about those pictures I sent to you. Those natives are some of the smaller ones they have around here. Some of them have loin cloths on and some have clothes they have gotten from Americans. Almost all of them have bones in their noses and some have them in their ears. Also notice if it shows the way one of them cut his stomache to get scars. The fellow standing with me with only our shorts on is one of my buddies. We were soken wet with sweat when the picture was taken. That big guy in a picture with four or five guys is another and that fellow standing in front of a sign with me is another. The last fellow is from Aberdeen, his name is Kirk and he used to know Sweede.

Well I guess I have run down again so I will have to sign off. Thanks a lot for sending me those clippings.   *Love   Martin*

PS By the way I dont think I ever told you I was a radio man now. I run one a little bigger than one of those Walki Talkies you probably have seen. The one I have now you put on your back like a pack.

Note the date on the letter, then the date on the envelope. The letter Martin wrote to Curly Feb 7, was received before this letter. Could it have been longer going through censorship? Unfortunately the pictures he mentions were not in his album. Martin said he later found the shutter on the camera did not work all the time due to the moisture in the air and a lot of the pictures he mentions in the letters were black on the roll of negative film when it got developed.

Espiritu Santo Lagoon

In our interview Martin said that swimming in the ocean was like having a vacation, most of the swimming was done in a lagoon in fresh water. It was still very warm, and clear enough to see to the bottom and see fish swim by and around you! He said he preferred swimming in the lagoons. The military personnel encouraged swimming as they wanted every soldier to know how to swim. Martin said he was surprised at the number of soldiers that did not know how to swim. The surface water temperatures near the Equator can be as high as 80° Fahrenheit.[127]

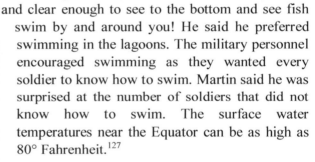

*Fish under water
at Espiritu Santo*

Avg. Seattle, Washington, ocean temperature
in Fahrenheit for each month

Jan	47	Jul	56
Feb	46	Aug	56
Mar	46	Sep	56
Apr	49	Oct	54
May	51	Nov	51
Jun	54	Dec	49

Ocean Shores, Washington

Ocean off Washington coast

---

[127]http://www.kidsgeo.com/geography-for-kids/0142-ocean-temperatures.php

Army B1000 Backpack Radio

Martin has officially become a Radio Man. There were two styles being used during WWII. The B1000 Backpack Radio and the EE-8 backpack phone. One disadvantage of the EE-8 phone was that it needed to be connected by wires to operate. Enemy soldiers could disrupt communications between commanders and the front simply by slicing the wires. The job of laying or repairing communication wire was very dangerous due to sniper fire. Martin was trained on the EE-8 on Espiritu Santo, laying wires and learning everything about the radio. However, he used the B1000 Backpack Radio on Okinawa.

The WWII US Army B1000 Backpack Radio was the first backpack style radio used by the different branches of the armed forces. The radio comes apart in two sections which are secured via the use of snaps. The lower portion of the radio was the receiver. The upper part is the transmitter. The radio has a built-in backpack with canvas straps. A pad is provided to help the bottom of the radio better rest in the lower back of the soldier. Wearing the radio was not a comfortable experience. It is heavy and restricts the movement of the soldier.

EE-8 Field Radio

Kirk (the person Martin mentions being in a picture) served in the same unit as Martin and was a good friend of his. He drove a jeep for one of the officers to drive reporters and other persons he was ordered to drive around. On his time off he was allowed to drive the jeep so took Martin and a few fellow soldiers on drives through the jungle. One day they went out farther than usual and came upon four native men. The natives started acting "mean" so they high tailed it out of there! He said they looked very frightening with their spears and weapons.

LETTER 59

Pfc. Martin Paulson
Co D 105th Inf Apo 27
% PM San Francisco, Cal

Mrs. A. Furford
Rt 1 Box 352
Kent, Wash.

Postage: 6 cents airmail
US ARMY POSTAL SERVICE APO
Feb 17, 1945

Dear Ruth,   February 14,

I am inclosing a form in this letter that you probably have started to wonder about already. All it is is a form to fill out if Dad moves and gets a different address. They have been having trouble back in Washington finding the relatives of some of the casualties so they gave these forms to us and are making us send them home. I would send it to Dad but you know how he would just worry about it when there isnt anything to worry about. The only thing we have to look out for is coconuts and they havent done any damage yet.

I would like to go to the show tonight because there is a good show on. From Bowery to Broadway. The trouble is it looks like it is going to rain. That is one thing you can allways depend on and Im not fooling. Its never safe to go to a show without a ran coat.

We sure had a good meal for supper tonight. In my opinion it is the best one we have had for quite awhile. We had meat loaf and it sure tasted good. All the beef we get comes from New Zealand and if that is the kind they have to eat down there I sure feel sorry for them. It never tastes right to me and is allways tougher than the devil.

Well that is about all I can think of now. I sure hope it clears up so I can go to the show. I hate to get soaked just to see a show.

Love   Martin

The military tried to make Espiritu Santo a place to raise moral as soldiers from previously fought battles needed a place to regroup. They would come to Espiritu Santo to recoup for possible future battles. As stated in earlier research the soldiers who arrived said Espiritu Santo was viewed *as a hell hole, ill-suited for rehabilitation and poorly chosen as a home for troops fresh out of a great battle.* As they arrived on the island, troops built their own camps in the great coconut plantations. There was no place to go even if the men got a pass. The original main base at Santo had a big Red Cross recreation center, an ice-cream parlor, and a beer garden, but it was inadequate for even the personnel on the island prior to the arrival of the 105th Division. Twelve open-air-theaters were constructed by the Division where second-rate movies were shown. No first-class theatrical troupes ever visited the area. A recreation hall was built, and this was served by two or three girls twice a week. On those occasions it served coffee and doughnuts.[128] Martin said he never saw any ice-cream parlor, beer garden or Red Cross recreation center. The military did send him and some other soldiers to a small island that had a building with entertainment and snacks, but no beer or ice-cream. He said the only beer they got was issued to them.

When Martin says he would need a raincoat to go to the movie, he didn't mean for just the walk to the theater. The theaters were literally "open air!" They would set up a screen under a tent for a projector, and the troops would sit on a bank of dirt/grass to view the movie.

You don't hear Martin mentioning going into town. It is said the town of Luganville on Espiritu Santo grew from the American military occupation of the island shortly after the bombing of Pearl Harbor (Ice-cream parlor, Red-cross recreation center, Beer Garden?). It was located on the Southeast side of the island, a long distance from where Martin's camp was located. During WWII about 40,000 United States military personnel were stationed in Luganville and it is estimated that 400,000 to 500,000 military personnel took R&R on the island, operating 3 bomber airfields, a huge wharf and a nearby dry dock.[129]

The movie Martin wanted to see: *"From The Bowery to Broadway"* – is a comedy. Bowery is a street/neighborhood in the southern portion of the New York City borough of Manhattan.

Movie description: 'Two Bowery vaudevillians find success in producing shows on Broadway, but when one of them suddenly departs to work for a beautiful woman, a feud erupts'.

Production comments: Before Ziegfeld launched his Follies, and before the Shubert brothers built their empire, Lew Fields' productions were the toast of Broadway. For the "smart set" in silk hats and evening gowns in the luxury box seats, and the shopkeepers and clerks in the gallery, an evening at the Weber & Fields Music Hall was the hottest ticket in town. The five year old named Moses Schoenfeld who crossed the Atlantic in steerage with his family in 1872 had grown up to become an innovative genius who helped raise the Broadway musical to the pinnacle of show business. Fields' influence was extraordinary: his raucous *"Mike and Meyer"*

---

[128]The 27th Infantry Division in World War II by Captain Edmund G. Love Pg. 521
[129]http://en.wikipedia.org/wiki/Luganville

knockabout comedy routines with his partner Joe Weber were the prototype for generations of acts to follow, from Abbott and Costello to Gleason and Carney, and the legacy of the dazzling satirical revues performed nightly at the Music Hall lives on in the irreverent topical humor of Saturday Night Live. "He was more than a gifted comedian," the late Helen Hayes wrote in the foreword to From the Bowery to Broadway. "For over a decade, he was Broadway's most inventive, extravagant, and prolific musical producer." Miss Hayes was but one of Fields' many stage "discoveries."

The form Martin mentions was still enclosed in this letter shows Martin's Dad, Adolf, did not move during Martin's military service as the form was never used. Martin knew he was being shipped to Okinawa when he was told to send out this form to his contact person. You can see it was a concern that his Dad not be the person to receive the form. The form follows:

Front of form....

HEADQUARTERS 105TH INFANTRY
A.P.O. 27 C/O POSTMASTER
SAN FRANCISCO, CALIFORNIA

NOTICE

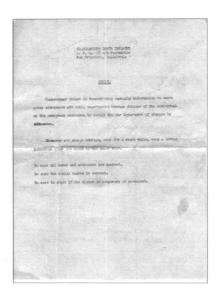

Unnecessary delays in transmitting casualty information to emergency addressees are being experienced through failure of the individual or the emergency addressee to notify the War Department of changes in Addresses.

Whenever you change address, even for a short while, send a letter patterned after the model on the other side.

Be sure all names and addresses are correct.
Be sure the serial number is correct.
Be sure to state if the change is temporary or permanent.

Back of form….

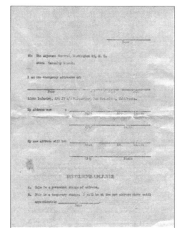

_____
Date

TO: The Adjutant General, Washington 25, D. C.
          Attn: Casualty Branch.

I am the emergency addressee of:

_____

Name   ASN   Bank   Unit

105th Infantry, APO 27 % Postmaster, San Francisco, California.

My Address was: _____

               Name   No,   Street

               City   State

My New Address will be: _____

               Name   No.   Street

               City   State

LINE-CUT EITHER A OR B BELOW

A.   This is a permanent change of address.

B.   This is a temporary change. I will be at the new address shown until approximately_____

Date

LETTER 60

Pfc. Martin Paulson
Co D 105th Inf APO 27
%PM San Francisco, Cal.

Mrs. A. Furford
Rt 1 Box 352
Kent, Washington

Postage: two 6 cent airmail
US ARMY POSTAL SERVICE APO
Feb 18, 1945

Dear Ruth,   *Tuesday*
*I havent much to write about but I thought I would drop you a short letter.
I suppose you are getting a lot rain now. I used to think it rained hard back there
in the Spring but that was before I came over here. It will just pour down for hours
and not let up for weeks. When I say pour down I mean all you have to do is step
out in the rain, turn around and come back in and you will be soaken wet.*
*I sure had a swell steak yesterday. You know all our beef comes up from
Australia and it is always tough and then it doesnt taste right. Well I had a T bone
steak off some meat that came from the States. Boy did it taste good. It is the first
piece of meat I have had like that for a year.*
*Im sure glad they put Curly in 4F. I thought maybe they would just overlook
his bad ear when he took his physical. Broken eardrums though are about the
easiest way to get out eaven over here. Is Sweede going to get a discharge. I know
there are lots of one eyed fellows in the Army so if the Navy gives him a discharge
the Army might grab him. That is if his other eye wasnt damaged to much.*
Well that is all I can think of to write now so I will have to close.
Love Martin
PS...

Note that the 'PS' section of the letter was torn off. The enlarged *censorship
stamp* above shows *"photo negatives"* written just above it. At the end of the
envelope the tape on the front side says "OPENED BY," and the back side of the
envelope says "U. S. ARMY EXAMINER."

The enclosed photo negatives and the *PS section with descriptions of the
negatives* must have made the examiner feel they were a threat to national security
(*or wanted them themselves*)! Martin does not remember what the negatives or the
descriptions were, but said (*with a smile on his face*) that maybe they were of a PT
boat moored close by (the Navy fellows who played basketball with the Army

fellows)..."*maybe it was the PT boat John Kennedy was on and the negatives showed him and I didn't know it. Or maybe they didn't want anyone to know the boat was there.*"

Martin may have Espiritu Santo and New Caledonia (where they played football with Navy) confused as PT boats moored at both locations. Kennedy's at New Caledonia in 1943. Kennedy's PT boat was hit and sunk in August of 1943. Never-the-less, censors may not have wanted anyone to know PT boats were at Espiritu Santo.

PT boats were a variety of torpedo-armed fast attack craft used by the United States navy in World War II to attack larger surface ships. "PT" is the US hull classification symbol for "*Patrol Torpedo*." The PT boat squadrons were nicknamed "*the mosquito fleet.*" The Japanese called them "*Devil Boats.*"

Model of PT-109

During World War II, American PT boats engaged enemy destroyers and numerous other surface craft ranging from small boats to large supply ships. PT boats also operated as gunboats against enemy small craft, such as armored barges used by the Japanese forces for inter-island transport. [130]

Lieutenant John F. Kennedy

The PT-109, commanded by future President John F. Kennedy, was made famous through the 1961 book PT 109: John F. Kennedy in World War II by Robert J. Donovan, and the 1963 film around sinking of the PT-109 and the survival of Lieutenant's men. Asked how he became a war hero, Kennedy once answered, "It was easy—they sank my boat."

In the *Blackett Strait* south of *Kolombangara* in the Solomon Islands on the starless, moonless night of August 1, 1943 (it was profoundly dark), Lieutenant Kennedy rendezvoused his boat with two others, PT-162 and PT-169. The three boats spread out to make a picket line across the strait. That night at about 2 a.m., the Japanese destroyer *Amagiri* [by accident or by design] bisected the much smaller PT-109 sending 26-year-old skipper, John F. Kennedy, into fiery waters killing two of his crew.

---

[130]http://en.wikipedia.org/wiki/PT_boat

Kennedy spent the rest of the night helping rescue injured and wave-tossed crew members. By dawn the survivors were all clinging to the still-floating bow. By afternoon they were making a several-hour swim—the strong towing the injured—to a deserted island. Despite a back injury, Kennedy himself pulled the worst case, tugging the sailor's life vest with his teeth. The following days

Japanese destroyer Amagiri - made famous for ramming the PT-109

saw several fearless attempts to be rescued. The men were weary with starvation and thirst when they were eventually rescued by Solomon Islanders loyal to the Allies. Two of them helped deliver to a coast watcher a coconut Kennedy famously carved with a rescue message. Six days after their stranding, Kennedy and crew were safe aboard a sister ship, PT-157.

Lieutenant John Kennedy (right) with his PT-109 crew.

The PT-109 survival story passed into popular culture and became perhaps Kennedy's greatest political asset. Kennedy the President had a PT-109 float in his inaugural parade, doled out 109 tiepins to visitors, and kept his medals on permanent display. And on his Oval Office desk sat, lacquered and almost illegible, the world's most important coconut. [131]

Curly was classified 4F in the Draft due to his broken eardrum. This meant he would not be drafted into service. His son, George, was always told his Dad was rejected due to Flat Feet. In World War II, the military rejected thousands of recruits because they had flat feet. However, Martin, clearly indicates that Curly was rejected due to a broken eardrum.

[131]http://news.nationalgeographic.com/news/2002/07/0709_020710_kennedyPT109_2.html

OKINAWA
Battle & Mopping Up

Beach landing on Okinawa

LETTER 61

Pfc. Martin Paulson
Co D 105th Inf APO 27
% PM San Francisco, Cal.

Mrs. A. Furford
Rt 1 Box 352
Kent, Wash

Postage: 6 cents airmail
US ARMY POSTAL SERVICE APO
Mar 22, 1945

Somewhere in the Pacific

Hello Ruth,   *March 11, 1945*

Well Ruth I dont get around to writing very often any more do I. There isnt a heck of a lot to say and I hate to just keep writing the same old thing. I wrote once and thanked you for the pictures but I was just looking at them a few minutes ago and I sure appreciate getting them. They are sure swell pictures and everyone looks so natural in them. Talking about pictures I have some more negatives to bother you with. Would you have one print made of them and keep it for me. Dont bother sending any to me. Also dont take them down right away because in a month or two you should get from the folks of one of my buddies. He had some film and we took a bunch of pictures. He sent the negatives to his folks and they will send them to you. I sure hate to put you to all this bother though. By the way be sure and take the money for these pictures out of my money. Talking about money I am sending you a money order with this letter and a piece of Jap money and a piece of New Caladonia money. Would you save them for me.

I also have a couple of pictures in this letter. One is of me hitch hiking. I didnt know the picture was being taken and I was looking at a Army Truck coming down the road. The other one you can get an idea what a jungle looks like. Just think how much rain it takes to keep it green in this hot weather and we sure get enough.

Well thats all I can think of now.

Love   Martin

First, note what is written above the date – *'Somewhere in the Pacific.'* Martin was on a transport heading around the island to Turtle Bay for beach landing training maneuvers. Until this research was complete, Martin did not realize Turtle Bay was on the same island (or that it was called Turtle Bay). All he knew was that they were on a ship and headed somewhere! When he had an opportunity to write, he says he appreciates getting the photos, he really meant it because though he did not know where he was headed, he did anticipate action.

Martin wishes he had all the pictures he mentions in the letters, but most of what he had in his album will be used within this book. One of the pictures mentioned in this letter was of his sister (Ruth), his nephew (George), and his Dad (Adolf). He lost his mother to cancer the year before he was drafted, so seeing a photo of his Dad was special.

Notice that Martin tells Ruth... *"Dont bother sending any to me. Also dont take them [negatives] down right away because in a month or two you should get negatives from the folks of one of my buddies."*

Martin knows where he is headed but cannot tell Ruth, nor does he want to worry her.

Ruth Furford, George Furford, & Adolf Paulson (Ruth's father & George's grandfather)

Also note that he is sending her his pay money via a money order, and some Jap and New Caledonia money (not in the letter).

At the writing of this letter, Martin was heading for beach landing training before landing on Okinawa. Turtle Bay was located on the east side of the Island. In the book: The 27th Infantry Division in World War II by Captain Edmund G. Love, and research from National Military Archives, College Park, Maryland.

Embarkation for Okinawa began during the first week in March. The nine infantry battalion landing teams held their dry runs at Turtle Bay during 15-22 March. The last elements of the Division boarded ship on 23 March in a driving rain that had continued for more than a week. The Division on that date was 1,793 men under strength, of whom 1,305 were shortages in the rifle companies. The average strength of line units within the Division was 152 mean as compared with an authorized strength of 193 men.

Throughout 24 March the transports remained anchored in the roadstead at Santo while the landing craft plied back and forth, finishing last-minute preparations for departure. Early on the morning of 25 March 1945, a sunny Sunday morning, the convoy filed out through the narrows and swung north. The stay at Santo was over.

Turtle Bay, Espiritu Santo

Martin said in our interview, *"We did not realize we were on the same island as we were never told where we were at or where we were going. We came upon hundreds of ships (looked like thousands) who were doing practice landings. It was an amazing sight. The ship they picked us up on was the one that came from Saipan. Some of the soldiers stayed on Espiritu Santo that would be shipped home. The practice landings were intense and an amazing sight to behold with all those ships. Once we left there, we were in the center of this humongous convoy on our way to Okinawa. Yes, we knew then where we were going."*

WWII GLOBAL TIMELINE - MARCH 1945[132]

Day

3:    The combined Filipino and American soldiers take Manila, the Philippines.

3:    Battle of Meiktila, Burma comes to an end with General Slim's troops overwhelming the Japanese; the road to Rangoon is now cleared.

3:    The allies attempted to destroy V-2s and launching equipment near The Hague by a large-scale bombardment, but due to navigational errors the Bezuidenhout quarter was destroyed, killing 511 Dutch civilians.

4:    Finland declares war on Germany, backdated to September 15, 1944.

6:    Germans launch an offensive against Soviet forces in Hungary.

7:    When German troops fail to dynamite the Remagen Bridge over the Rhine, Americans begin crossing the Rhine into Germany.

7:    Germans begin to evacuate Danzig.

9:    The US firebombs a number of cities in Japan, including Tokyo, with heavy civilian casualties.

10:   Japanese Fugo Attacks damage the Manhattan Project slightly but cause no lasting effects

11:   Nagoya, Japan is firebombed by hundreds of B-29's.

15:   V-2 rockets continue to hit England and Belgium.

16:   The German offensive in Hungary ends with another Soviet victory.

---

[132]http://en.wikipedia.org/wiki/Timeline_of_World_War_II_%281945%29#March_1945

16:     Iwo Jima is finally secured after a month's fighting; the battle is the only time that the number of American casualties is larger than the Japanese's. Sporadic fighting will continue as isolated Japanese fighters emerge from caves and tunnels.

18:     Red Army approaches Danzig (postwar Gdańsk).

19:     Heavy bombing of important naval bases in Japan, Kobe and Kure.

19:     Deutsch Schutzen massacre occurs, in which 60 Jews are killed

20:     German General Gotthard Heinrici replaces Heinrich Himmler as commander of Army Group, the army group directly opposing the Soviet advance towards Berlin.

20:     Mandalay liberated by Indian 19th Infantry Division.

20:     Tokyo is firebombed again.

20:     Patton's troops capture Mainz, Germany

20:     Mandalay, in central Burma, is now firmly under British and Indian control.

21:     British air raid on a Gestapo headquarters in Copenhagen, Denmark, in support of the Danish resistance movement takes place.

22-23: US and British forces cross the Rhine at Oppenheim.

23:     By this time it is clear that Germany is under attack from all sides.

24:     Montgomery's troops cross the Rhine at Wesel.

27:     The Western Allies slow their advance and allow the Red Army to take Berlin.

28:     Argentina declares war on Germany, the last Western hemisphere country to do so; its policies for sheltering escaping Nazis are also coming under scrutiny. Argentina had not declared war before due to British wishes that Argentine shipping be neutral (and therefore Argentine foodstuffs would reach Britain unharmed), this, however, went against the plan of the USA, who applied much political pressure on Argentina.

29:     The Red Army enters Austria. Other Allies take Frankfurt; the Germans are in a general retreat all over the center of the country.

30:     Red Army forces capture Danzig.

31:     General Eisenhower broadcasts a demand for the Germans to surrender.

LETTER 62

Pfc. Martin Paulson
Co D 105th Inf APO 27
% PM San Francisco, Cal.

Mrs. A. Furford
Rt 1 Box 342
Kent, Wash

Postage: 6 cents airmail
US ARMY POSTAL SERVICE APO

Note: Letter is Postage Dated April 17!

Dear Ruth,

There still isnt anything I can tell you. About the only thing I can say is I am still on a ship. Ive got a money order for fourty dollars that I have been carrying around in case I ever got a brake. I dont need it and it will run out in a few months so I am signing it and sending it to you.

It sure gets tiresome on a boat. You know they are always crowded and there isnt anything to do in my spare time except read or play cards and I have grown tired of both of them.

I would sure make a poor sailor. I have never been seasick yet but every time I get on a boat I dont feel good. This time I got disintary and couldnt eat for almost a week. I have started to feel pretty good now though. I think that is the first time I ever went a whole day without eating.

Well that is about all I can think of now. I will write more as soon as they let me.

Love   Martin

Important things to note:

1. There is no date on the letter, but the postage date stamp on the envelope is April 17. Martin's last letter was written on March 11.
2. Martin is feeling down (more from the dysentery than being on the boat) and he is giving a hint to Ruth by stating he would not need the money for a few months!
3. Between the time Martin wrote his last letter and when Ruth would have received this letter, many events will unfold of which (thankfully) declassified documentation help us understand all censored events going forward.

Dysentery (formerly known as flux or the bloody flux): is an inflammatory disorder of the intestine, especially of the colon, that results in severe diarrhea containing blood and mucus in the feces with fever, abdominal pain, and rectal tenesmus (a feeling of incomplete defecation), caused by any kind of infection. [133]

Poor Martin, he must have picked up a tropical infection during beach landing maneuvers at Turtle Bay. No wonder he didn't feel like playing cards or reading. He must have been very down especially knowing he was heading toward seeing action in Okinawa... and after being so sick!

SS Cecil (APA-96)

The transport ship Martin was on was the *USS Cecil* (APA-96) a Bayfield class attack transport. Launched as *Sea Angler* by Western Pipe & Steel, San Francisco, California, under a Maritime Commission contract, the vessel was acquired by the Navy on February 26, 1944 and renamed *Cecil* after a county in Maryland. She was placed in reduced commission February 27, converted at Commercial Iron Works, Portland, Oregon, and placed in full commission September 15, 1944, with Captain P. G. Hale in command. After her mission to Saipan, she headed to Espiritu Santo, where she loaded men and cargo of the 27th Infantry Division. [134]

The *Bayfield* class attack transport was a class of US Navy attack transports that were built during World War II. With the entry of the United States into the war, it was quickly realized that amphibious combat operations on hostile shores would be required, and that specialized ships would be needed for this purpose. The so-called "*attack transport*" ship type (hull classification symbol APA) was developed to meet this need. The early *Bayfield* class vessels were converted from existing cargo or transport ships. The first class of attack transports to be built in substantial numbers was the *Bayfield* class which began to enter service in 1943. The *USS Cecil* entered service in 1943. Martin said it was a beautiful ship!

---

[133] http://en.wikipedia.org/wiki/Dysentery
[134] http://en.wikipedia.org/wiki/USS_Cecil_%28APA-96%29

Beginning 15 March 1945 the Division combat-loaded at Espiritu Santo, still without any definite word other than that already received. The division departed from the New Hebrides on the morning of 25 March 1945.

While en route to Ulithi, the first port of call, the Division received a radiogram from Admiral Blandy that Captain Wright had not arrived aboard his ship in time to present the Division plans. ...No further word was heard from Captain Wright until the morning of 2 April 1945 when he radioed: "the Plan 3A will be used with modifications.

Meanwhile, the Division had been proceeding toward Ulithi where further instructions would be forthcoming. [135]

Ulithi Atoll

Ulithi is an atoll in the Caroline Islands of the western Pacific Ocean and was perfectly positioned to act as a staging area for the US Navy's western Pacific operations.

On September 23, 1944, an army regiment of the 81st Division landed unopposed, followed a few days later by a battalion of Seabees. The survey ship *USS Sumner* surveyed the lagoon and reported it capable of holding 700 vessels. It became the undisclosed Pacific base for the major operations late in the war, including Leyte Gulf and the Okinawa operation. The huge anchorage capacity was greater than either Majuro or Pearl Harbor, and over seven hundred ships anchored there at a time. Martin said he had never seen so many ships in one place and that it was actually a beautiful thing to see.

U.S. Naval forces including carriers in the distance at anchor in Ulithi, March 1945

The atoll is in the westernmost of the Caroline Islands, 360 miles southwest of Guam, 850 miles east of the Philippines and 1,300 miles south of Tokyo. It is a typical volcanic atoll, with a coral reef, white sand

[135]Book: The 27th Infantry Division In World War II by Captain Edmund G. Love pg. 525

beaches and palm trees. Ulithi's forty small islands barely rise above the sea, with the largest being only half a square mile in area. However the reef runs roughly twenty miles north and south by ten miles across, enclosing a vast anchorage with an average depth of 80 to 100 feet. The anchorage was well situated, but there were no port facilities to repair ships or re-supply the fleet.

Between 25 March and 3 April, when the convoy anchored in Ulithi Lagoon, the Division plan had been changed to some extent... Upon arrival, no communications could be established with Admiral Blandy. As a result, upon leaving Ulithi on 4 April 1945, the Division staff was still confused as to just what would finally develop.... Developments at Okinawa, however, were rapidly shaping the destiny of the Division. Information received regarding the Eastern Islands had convinced General Buckner that these areas were not heavily defended and might possible be taken with a much smaller force than the whole Division. Accordingly, during the early morning of 4 April 1945, he ordered the amphibious reconnaissance battalion attached to the Tenth Army to make a thorough reconnaissance in force no later than 6 April of all six of the Eastern Islands. This order was received aboard the USS Cecil at 1300 on 4 April, after leaving Ulithi....No further information regarding the mission of the 27th Infantry Division was received until 1900 on 8 April 1945. Developments at Okinawa had shaped final plans for the use of the troops en route. The result of the reconnaissance of the Eastern Islands had been to show that, with the exception of Tsugen Shima (Shima---Island), all other islands in the group were unoccupied by enemy garrisons.... at 1900, on 8 April, the 27th Infantry Division received orders to land on Okinawa the next morning.[136]

On April 9, 1945, USS Cecil landed the 27th reinforcements through high surf on Okinawa. She remained for a week continuing her unloading under enemy air attacks, aiding in fighting them off as she loaded and landed her boats.

It is at times such as this that talking with Martin was so very helpful. If just going by documentation, it would seem that Martin disembarked overnight April 8-9 and went into battle right away. As it was, only part of the 105th, 27th Infantry, left on transports the night of April 8-9 to Kerma Retto to "mop up" the fifth island from north to south of the Eastern Group lying off the coast of Okinawa, Tsugen Shima. Martin said he remained on the ship,

"And it was scary enough! The Japs were trying to Kamikaze the ships. The ships would send up smoke screens to try to camouflage and confuse the Jap pilots, but that would not stop them. Small boats would go out with smoke pots and circle the troop ships, but the masts would still stick up above the smoke. The convoy had

---

[136]Book: The 27th Infantry Division In World War II by Captain Edmund G. Love pg 525-526

Beach landing in Okinawa

destroyers surrounding the troop ships. When we heard the air-raid siren we were to head below deck. You would hear the sirens on other ships before you heard the siren on our ship... one siren would set off a chain reaction to other ships. I was always able to get below deck, but saw some of the carnage afterward. There was this Japanese plane in pieces in the water with a dead Jap floating close to the ship who had on a 'May West' life-jacket."

Kamikaze – were suicide attacks by military aviators from the Empire of Japan against Allied naval vessels in the closing stages of the Pacific Campaign of World War II, designed to destroy warships more effectively than was possible with conventional attacks. Numbers quoted vary, but at least 47 Allied vessels, from PT boats to escort carriers, were sunk by kamikaze attacks, and about 300 damaged. During World War II, nearly 4,000 kamikaze pilots were sacrificed. [137]

Supply ships were run in to the reef's edge, where they unloaded into trucks or amphibian vehicles.

---

[137]http://en.wikipedia.org/wiki/Kamikaze

The USS Cecil dropped anchor at 0900 ....preparations were begun at once to debark troops and supplies of the Division...at 1105 General Griner and his party returned to the Cecil with the information that the Division was assigned to XXIV Corps as of 1200, 9 April 1945, and would unload immediately over the Orange Beaches....the rest of the day the Division would be mainly concerned with establishing itself on Okinawa...By nightfall all troops, except ships' parties and rear detachments, were ashore on Okinawa and established for the night. For over three years the Division had lived in the tropics, and now the men found themselves, shortly after dark, in the midst of a cold, drizzling rain.

Because the Division had not begun unloading until almost noon 9 April, very little except the troops had come ashore that day...the Division's equipment did not begin to assemble until the morning of 10 April. Consequently there was little activity in the Division except for preparations for future movement, assembling of equipment, and organization of command. The two infantry regiments ashore were both in bivouac in the area directly east of Kadena Airfield. Since it had reached the eastern shore of Okinawa on the night of 2 April 1945, the 17th Infantry Regiment of the 7th Division had patrolled and protected this area.[138]

MAE WEST JACKETS: In 1942, midway through WWII, Hollywood actress Mae West discovered that RAF aircrew had taken to calling their life jackets "Mae Wests" — in part due to rhyming slang, and also as a result of their "bulging" shape when inflated. West, delighted to be playing even a minuscule part in proceedings, immediately wrote the following letter to the RAF. (Source: Air Force Association, 1943)

Dear Boys of the RAF

I have just seen that RAF flyers have a life-saving jacket they call a "Mae West" because it bulges in all the "right places." Well, I consider it a swell honor to have such great guys wrapped up in me, know what I mean?

Yes, it's kind of a nice thought to be flying all over with brave men, even if I'm only there by proxy in the form of a life-saving jacket, or a life-saving jacket in my form. I always thought that the best way to hold a man was in your arms — but I guess when you're in the air a plane is safer. You've got to keep everything under control.

Yeah, the jacket idea is all right and I can't imagine anything better than to bring you boys of the RAF soft and happy landings. But what I'd like to know about that life-saving jacket is — has it got shapely shoulders? If I do get into the dictionary — where they say you want to put me — how will they describe me? As

[138]Book: The 27th Infantry Division In World War II by Captain Edmund G. Love pg 525-526

a warm and clinging life-saving garment worn by aviators? Or an aviator's jacket that supplies the woman's touch while the boys are flying around nights? How would you describe me boys? I've been in Who's Who and I know what's what, but it'll be the first time I ever made the dictionary.

Thanks boys.

Sin-sationally,
Mae West

WWII GLOBAL TIMELINE - APRIL 1945

Day

1:   U.S. troops start Operation Iceberg, which is the Battle of Okinawa. It would have been a leaping off base for a mainland invasion.

1:   Americans retake Legaspi.

2:   Soviets launch Vienna Offensive against German forces in and around the Austrian capital city.

2:   German armies are surrounded in the Ruhr region.

4:   Ohrdruf death camp is liberated by the Allies.

5:   Po Valley Campaign begins in northern Italy.

7:   The Japanese battleship Yamato is sunk in the North of Okinawa as the Japanese make their last major naval operation.

9:   Battle of Koingsberg ends in Soviet victory.

9:   A heavy bombing at Kiel by the RAF destroys the last two major German warships.

9:   Pastor Dietrich Bonhoeffer is executed at Flossenburg prison.

10:   Buchenwald concentration camp liberated by American forces.

11:   Spain breaks diplomatic relations with Japan.

11:   Japanese kamikaze attacks on American naval ships continue at Okinawa; the carrier Enterprise and the battleship Missouri are hit heavily.

12:   U.S. President Franklin D. Roosevelt dies suddenly. Harry S. Truman becomes president of the United States.

13:   Vienna Offensive ends with Soviet victory.

14:   Large-scale firebombing of Tokyo.

15:   Bergen-Belsen concentration camp is liberated by the British Army.

16:   The Battle of the Seelow Heights and the Battle of the Oder-Neisse begin as the Soviets continue to advance towards the city of Berlin.

18:   Ernie Pyle, famed war correspondent for the GI's, is killed by a sniper on Ie Shima, a small island near Okinawa.

19:   Switzerland closes its borders with Germany (and former Austria).

19:    Allies continue their sweep toward the Po Valley.

19:    The Soviet advance towards the city of Berlin continues and soon reach the suburbs.

20:    Hitler celebrates his 56th birthday in the bunker in Berlin; reports are that he is in an unhealthy state, nervous, and depressed.

21:    Soviet forces under Georgiy Zhukov (1st Belorussian Front), Konstantin Rokossoviskiy (2nd Belroussian Front), and Ivan Konev (1st Ukrainian Front) launch assaults on the German forces in and around the city of Berlin as the opening stages of the Battle of Berlin.

21:    Hitler ordered SS-General Felix Steiner to attack the 1st Belorussian Front and destroy it. The ragtag units of "Army Detachment Steiner" are not fully manned.

22:    Hitler is informed late in the day that, with the approval of Gotthard Heinrici, Steiner's attack was never launched. Instead, Steiner's forces were authorized to retreat.

22:    In response to the news concerning Steiner, Hitler launches a furious tirade against the perceived treachery and incompetence of his military commanders in front of Wilhelm Keitel, Hans Krebs, Alfred Jodl, Wilhelm Burgdorf, and Martin Bormann. Hitler's tirade culminates in an oath to stay in Berlin to head up the defense of the city.

22:    Hitler ordered German General Walther Wenck to attack towards Berlin with his Twelfth Army, link up with the Ninth Army of General Theodor Busse, and relieve the city. Wenck launched an attack, but it came to nothing.

23:    Hermann Goring sends a radiogram to Hitler's bunker, asking to be declared Hitler's successor. He proclaims that if he gets no response by 10 PM, he will assume Hitler is incapacitated and assume leadership of the Reich. Furious, Hitler strips him of all his offices and expels him from the Nazi Party.

23:    Albert Speer makes one last visit to Hitler, informing him that he ignored the Nero Decree for scorched earth.

24:    Meanwhile, Himmler, ignoring the orders of Hitler, makes a secret surrender offer to the Allies, (led by Count Folke Bernadotte, head of the Red Cross) provided that the Red Army is not involved. The offer is rejected; when Hitler hears of Himmler's betrayal, he orders him shot.

24:    Forces of the 1st Belorussian Front and the 1st Ukrainian Front link up in the initial encirclement of Berlin.

24:    Allies encircle last German armies near Bologna, and the Italian war in effect comes to an end.

25:    Elbe Day: First contact between Soviet and American troops at the river Elbe, near Torgau in Germany.

26: Hitler summons Field Marshal Robert Ritter von Gerim from Munich to Berlin to take over command of the Luftwaffe from Göring. While flying into Berlin, von Gerim is seriously wounded by Soviet anti-aircraft fire.

27: The encirclement of German forces in Berlin is completed by the 1st Belorussian Front and the 1st Ukrainian Front.

28: Head of State for the Italian Social Republic, Benito Mussolini, heavily disguised, is captured in northern Italy while trying to escape. Mussolini and his mistress Clara Petacci, are shot and hanged in Milan the next day. Other members of his puppet government are also executed by Italian partisans and their bodies put on display in Milan.

29: Dachau concentration camp is liberated by the U.S. 7th Army. All forces in Italy officially surrender and a ceasefire is declared.

29: Allied air forces commence Operations Manna and Chowhound, providing food aid to the Netherlands under a truce made with occupying German forces.

29: Hitler marries his companion Eva Braun.

30: Adolf Hitler dictates his last will and testament. In it Joseph Geobbels is appointed Reich Chancellor and Grand Admiral Karl Donitz is appointed Reich President.

Pfc Martin Paulson in Jungle
of Espiritu Santo

LETTER 63

Pfc. Martin Paulson
Co. D 105th Inf APO 27
% PM San Francisco, Cal.

Postage: Free
US POSTAL SERVICE NO 2
Apr 29, 1945 2 PM

Mrs. Ruth A. Furford
Rt 1 Box 352
Kent, Wash.

Dear Ruth   *April 16, 1945*

I havent been able to write for quite awhile and I still cant say very much. I suppose you read the paper so you will know that I am in Okinawa. If you dont hear from me too often you will know that is probably because I cant get any paper or they cant take mail. Up until now I havent been able to get any paper. Then before that I was on the boat and they wouldnt take any mail. Just remember that if you dont hear anything dont worry. There isnt any too much danger and you know me. I wont be sticking my nose into any trouble.

Well that is all for now. I will write as often as I can.

Love   Martin

Note the postage date, it is 13 days later than the date on Martin's letter. Ruth would be reading the news in the paper before getting this letter...and yes, she would worry as she would not have heard from Martin. In the previous letter which she would have received in the latter part of April, Martin was still on the ship.

About 350 miles from the Japanese mainland, U.S. invasion forces establish a beachhead on Okinawa Island. Pouring out war supplies and military equipment, the landing crafts fill the sea to the horizon, where stand the battleships of the U.S. fleet. (AP Photo)

There are books, films, and plenty of information surrounding the Battle of Okinawa. What follows will be specific to what Martin experienced as well as facts surrounding the battle itself. Declassified Top Secret documents refer to the Battle of Okinawa as *"Operation Iceberg."* The 105th (Martin's Infantry Division) was part of the Tenth Army.

Landings were taking place along the full stretch of beach front. Martin said, *"It is not a sight you forget."*

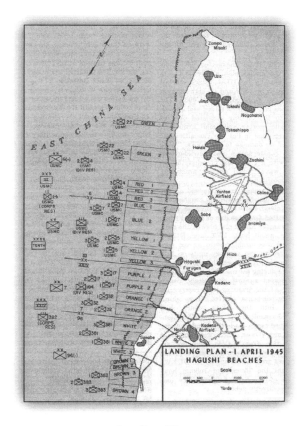

Landing Plan

Control of operations on the beaches, initially in the battalion landing teams, passed step by step through the echelons of command until Tenth Army, acting through the Island Command and the 1st Engineer Special Brigade, assumed responsibility on 9 April. The difficulties in initiating so intricate an undertaking near the enemy's homeland were prodigious, and it required time and the process of trial and error to overcome them. Suicide planes and suicide boats were a constant menace. On 10 April surf backed by a high wind brought work to a standstill, and on 11 April conditions were but slightly improved. Rain accompanying these storms made quagmires of the roads and further complicated the supply problems. Despite these handicaps, the assault shipping was 80 percent unloaded by 16 April, and 577,000 measurement tons had crossed the Hagushi beaches, a larger amount than had been anticipated in the plans. [139]

On the following page is the "declassified" Operation Report cover of the 105th Infantry on the battle of Okinawa, and a portion of the first page with first paragraph.

---

[139]http://www.ibiblio.org/hyperwar/USA/USA-P-Okinawa/USA-P-Okinawa-3.html

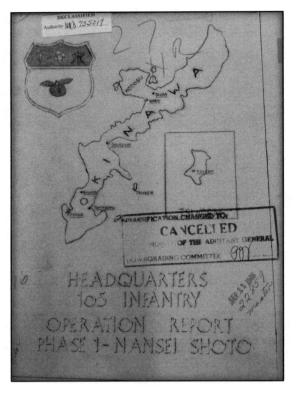

CONFIDENTIAL
HEADQUARTERS 105TH INFANTRY
APO 27th
1 July 1945
ACTION REPORT
NANSEI SHOTO – PHASE I
I
GENERAL

The purpose of this report is to NANSEI SHOTO operation (ICEBERG) as it concerned the 105th Infantry. This will include the training phase January 1 to March 15, preliminary planning by all sections, rehearsals, loading, embarkation, debarkation, unloading phase, **and most important of all, the combat period.**

The above mentioned report as well as the declassified OPERATION ICEBERG manual will be the basis of the facts of the battle as presented in these writings. As mentioned earlier, what is documented below only pertains to the positions, actions, etc., of the 27th Infantry of the 105th. Martin was with the 1st Battalion, Company D. What follows is directly from declassified documents.

OVERVIEW

The mission of RCT (*Regimental Combat Team*) 105 and the 27th Infantry Division was that of the Tenth Army Reserve.

On 14 April 45 90% of RCT 105th troops were ashore on OKINAWA in staging area near CHATAN (*Chatan Beach was the site of the U.S. forces' first landing*). 105th Infantry moved South into assembly areas on 15 April and on 16 April relieved elements of 381st Infantry on the line and occupied the left flank of the 27th Division sector. 105th Infantry attacked with rest of 27th Division on 19 April and engaged in fierce and bloody combat with the enemy until 1 May 45. Until arrival of about 600 replacements on 27 April, many rifle companies were greatly reduced in strength. 105th Infantry was relieved by the 5th Marine Regiment of 1st Marine Division at 1700, 1 May 45 and moved into assembly area near

GINOWAN-EURA (was city of approx. 12,000 citizens at time of invasion). The regiment was assigned the task of mopping up the area around MOTOBU Peninsula and on 2 May 45 moved to positions in the above area. Mopping up was still in progress on Northern OKINAWA at the date of termination of this report, 30 June 45.

DAY TO DAY BATTLE

Japanese cave positions near Ginowan

16 April: Relief of units of 381st was completed by 1st battalion (Martin was part of the 1st Battalion) at 0900 (9am). 1st Battalion strengthened defensive positions and registered artillery and mortars. Enemy mortar fire was received sporadically by 1st Battalion and enemy artillery fell in both forward and rear area as Heavy Blue artillery barrage was laid down in front of 1st Battalion lines at 1900 (7pm).

17 April: Front lines remained the same throughout the day. Continuing softening up of enemy positions on KAKAZU Ridge and KAKAZU Village was carried on using artillery, naval gunfire support, air support and mortars. Division Artillery fired missions throughout the day with large concentrations on KAKAZU Village. Two hundred fifty (250) civilians interned from forward areas, one POW captured.

GI checks surrendering Japanese soldier on Okinawa (US Army Photo)

18April: Orders issued for attack at 0730 on 19 April 45. General plan called for attack by 1st Battalion at 0730 with 2nd Battalion to follow... Attack is to be preceded by heavy artillery concentration and have tank support.....In preparation for the attack, front lines of 1st Battalion moved forward to position. Four POWs were captured by 1st Battalion. Artillery and Naval Gunfire fired missions in sector all day. Enemy artillery was heavy during the evening hours.

19 April: Artillery preparations for attack were fired from 0645 to 0730 and at 0730 the 1st Battalion jumped off in the attack. 1st Battalion advanced steadily against heavy enemy machine gun, rifle, mortar and artillery fire, and by 0940 had advanced to north and east edge of KAKZAU Village. Tanks aided greatly in this advance. Our troops were then held up at this point. 1st Battalion became pinned down...105th ordered the 3rd Battalion to move into line on right of 1st Battalion....advance of 3rd Battalion was very rapid and by 1430 (2:30pm)

had advanced beyond the stalled 1st Battalion and held position. At 1225 2nd Battalion order to bypass KAKAZU Village to east...1st Battalion, still held back by continuous enemy fire of all types, was ordered as regimental reserve with mopping up KAKAZU Village...2nd Battalion in attempting to bypass KAKAZU Village was halted by enemy fire and took route around west. At 1530 2nd Battalion attempted to swing to left of 3rd Battalion when they were held up for the day. Our right was in position but the left was bent back considerably. 1st Battalion requested permission to move to a more favorable location

The last picture of General Simon Bolivar Buckner, Jr., right, the day before he was killed by Japanese artillery on 19 June 1945

for the night defense and it was granted. Co. B 165th Infantry was attached to 105th Infantry for night defense and went into position at 2100. Fighting for the day was fierce and our loses heavy. Our lines advanced 1500 yards in the days fighting. Orders issued at 1700 called for continuance of attack by 2nd and 3rd Battalions with 1st Battalion to mop up KAKAZU Village and Ridge.

20 April: 0730 strong enemy small arms. 1G and Mortar slowed up the attack. 2nd and 3rd Battalion moved forward making slow progress. At 1500 an enemy counterattack and drove

Japanese gun emplacement and concrete pillbox - type of enemy fire power used

2nd Battalion back leaving 2nd Battalion in same position as when they started the day's fighting. Almost all line company officers of 2nd Battalion were wounded or killed in this action and troops were temporarily disorganized. Our right advanced about 400 yards but the left was bent back to form a U-shaped line. 1st Battalion assisted by 27th Cav Rcn Trp (*Calvary Reconnaissance Troop*) from 1200 mopped up positions on KAKAZU Ridge, but in attempting to enter KAKAZU Village ran into concentrated machine gun and mortar fire, and by dark had not taken the village over. At 1700, 1st Battalion was ordered to bypass KAKAZU and form line left of 2nd Battalion to strengthen front lines. Battalion was in position and dug in by 2200. Fighting again was heavy for the day and our losses were high. Tanks could not be employed because of mined roads.

21 April: 105th Infantry resumed attack at 0630 [only the 1st Battalion is covered in these writings, but you can see it takes the "whole" to do the job]. 1st Battalion moved forward against machine gun and mortar fire from ESCARPMENT RIDGE... 1st Battalion advanced to the top of the ridge at 1530. 1st Battalion at close of day's fighting was forced to withdraw down the ridge. 1st Battalion sent patrols to its rear near KAKAZU Village and patrols encountered heavy machine gun fire. Air strike employing 118 rockets and 110 one-hundred

pound bombs was run on AMACHA Village and in vicinity of village. Naval Gunfire and artillery concentrations were heavy throughout the day. All rifle companies of all battalions are deployed on the line with Antitank Company as regimental reserve.

21-22 April: an infiltration attempt on our left flank was stopped by friendly artillery and mortar fire, 68 dead Japs were counted in the morning. 105th Infantry lines remained the same during the day except that our right flank was withdrawn slightly …. Three air strikes were run and one strike started fires and caused a large

TWO DIVISIONS OF VMTB-231 fly over the scarred terrain of southern Okinawa while returning from a strike

explosion. 500 rounds of naval shells were fired in support of 105th with air support, good results were obtained. Effective strength of riflemen in rifle companies has been reduced to about 35%. Enemy artillery and mortar fire was heavy during the period.

23 April: 105th Infantry lines remained the same during the period. Enemy pocket located on pinnicle of ridge...25 Jap dead in area...plans made for clean-up of KAKAZU Ridge and KAKAZU Village by a special task force...

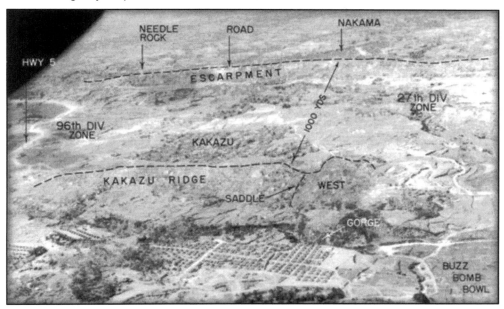

Note 27th Div. Zone at right, Kakazu Ridge, Escarpment Ridge, and Kakazu Village between.

The battle wages on. The next entry is important in that it concerns Martin's line of work. Martin's job was to radio position locations of the enemy to the Mortar men. Enemy snipers were always searching for and trying to take out radio men as they were key to killing large groups of their men. Martin said he would hear the bullets only if they ricocheted off the trees. When asked how often he heard the ricocheted bullets, he hesitantly said, *"quite often, but you didn't think about that...you just did your job."*

25 April: By 0600, Antitank Company relieved 2nd Battalion....2nd Battalion relieved 165-2. 1st and 3rd Battalions moved front lines forward 100-200 yards to more favorable positions. Patrols were sent out by all units...Enemy snipers harassed our troops all day and enemy mortar concentrations were heavy *(Martin said fighting was very heavy, very gruesome!)*

26 April: Enemy artillery fire was heavy throughout the night...all three Battalions jumped off in the attack. Advance was steady... 1st Battalion on the right moved forward about 600 yard and 3rd Battalion moved into the village of AWACHA assisted by tanks and flame-thrower tanks. 2nd Battalion was employed in cleaning up pockets of resistance on ESCARPMENT RIDGE and by 1230 had knocked out four machine guns and two mortar positions. 3rd Battalion reached south

US flamethrowers used to dislodge the Japanese from their bunkers

edge of village at 1400, an advance of 800 yards from original position...2nd Battalion was ordered at 1530 to establish contact between left of 3rd Battalion...our lines at this time were spread very thin due to heavy losses since April 19th...106th Infantry was to attach to 1st Battalion to strengthen the lines...At 1730, Cannon company was ordered into position in secondary defensive positions.

27 April: (there was battle through the night and all morning)...starting at 1630 (4:30pm), replacements began to arrive and were pushed right into the front lines to strengthen our over-extended positions. 629 were received, 35% of which went to rifle companies, the balance to Heavy Weapons companies and Medical Detachment....

28 April: During the night, forty Japs attempted to break through 3rd Battalion's lines and 30 Japs were killed by machine gun and mortar fire...elements of 1st Battalion moved with left

of 106th Infantry in attack. Attack went well for 300 yards when enemy machine gun and mortar fire pinned our troops down. 381st Infantry and 381st Cannon company went as scheduled and they passed through our 2nd Battalion lines about 0900. 2nd Battalion mortars assisted in attack on objective which was village south of Hill 196. Opposition was severe and unit withdrew through our lines at 1800. Net results of day's operation was a gain of 300 yards on our right flank. Air strike in town of DAWSHI with 50 five hundred pound bombs and 180 rockets was successful and many explosions resulted. Cannon company was again placed in secondary position for night....

29 April: No change in our front lines for the day. Stubborn enemy pocket in gulch studded with machine guns and prevents further advance by right or left. Gulch was worked over all morning by artillery, mortars, SPMs, 57MM guns, and flame throwing tanks. An attempt to close gap between 1st and 3rd Battalions was unsuccessful due to heavy enemy machine gun and mortar fire. Company "A" was sent into gulch at 1400 but made little progress due to intense enemy machine gun fire.

Satchel Charges, such as this one being flung into an enemy dugout were often the only means of silencing Japanese opposition

30 April: During the night, two infiltration attempts in 3rd Battalion sector were repulsed, 60 dead Japs were counted in the morning. Movement of 105th Infantry today will be governed by advance of 307th Infantry on our left.... There was no change in our front lines. Definite plans were made for relief of 105th Infantry...

1 May: Twenty Japs were killed during the night when they attempted to penetrate our 2nd and 3rd Battalion lines. Battalion of 307th Infantry passed through our 2nd Battalion at 0900 to attach Hill 196 from flank. 2nd and 3rd Battalions of 105th Infantry supported the attack with mortar fire. Relief of front line units of 105th Infantry began at 1000 and was completed at 1700....

2 May: Enemy activity during the night was negative. Organic vehicles of the regiment began movement northward at 0600 (Regiments that replaced the 105th Infantry). Foot troops were loaded on trucks as follows: 2nd Battalion at 1125, 1st Battalion at 1330 and 3rd Battalion at 1440. 105th Infantry established CP near MEJIYA at 1500. Other units were located as follows: 1st Battalion near village of UNTEN, 2nd Battalion near HAMASAKI, 3rd Battalion near MEJIYA, Antitank and Cannon Companies near NAKAO. Rain and poor road conditions made travel difficult. All units closed in new areas by 2400.

MARTIN IS OFF THE FRONT LINE!

Readers must keep in mind that the battle you just read about was just a tiny fraction of all the battles that were taking place all over the island ...at the same time, not to mention around the world! The invasion of Okinawa began April 1 and lasted until June 21, with "mopping up" during and following. Not all aspects of each days battle is presented in this writing. At the NATIONAL MILITARY ARCHIVES in College Park, MD, one can research and read World War II documents which are now declassified. Each person there was wonderful in helping to locate information specific to the Division of which Martin served.

AIRDROP was often the only means by which front line troops could be supplied.

Martin's comments from interview:

"Kakazu Ridge was a horrible battle. When we tried to get over the top, it was very tough as they had caves dug in that ran through the ridge so they could escape on-coming fire and could get reinforcements if needed through the tunnels from the other side of the ridge. There was LOTS of mortar fire. Just lots of fire period! If you had a radio (like me), you were shot at all the time and you would hear the bullets ricocheting all around you. It was times like this that you were thankful for the repetitive training (even if it was BORING doing the same thing over and over again!) so that you were able to do what you needed to do without thinking. During battle, flame throwers were used. I looked in a few caves afterward (we had to, to make sure there were no Japs inside), but sometimes it was a horrible site seeing burned bodies. There was once I saw an explosion and guessed they had

hit an ammo storage. Shortly after that a hand full of Japs jumped out of a line of trees and charged us while the others escaped (they didn't have any more ammo). Japs would charge and shoot until their fingers could no longer pull the trigger. They did not surrender and didn't have respect for those who did surrender so no US soldier wanted to be captured by the Japanese as they were terrible to POW's. We had orders not to take prisoners. We did at first, but it took manpower to watch over them and move them to POW locations. Once the battle started in earnest is when we were given the orders. My battalion moved to the right and went up the ridge and was on the ridge for some time and took Shuri Castle. There was another time that 15-20 Japs jumped out of a line of trees, rolled on the ground, zig-zaged back and forth, then ran back into the trees. We got off a few rounds at them, but our commander knew what they were doing and we did not go after them. They wanted us too! It was a trap! We needed to get by them as we needed to get to the ridge top. We set up mortar fire to take them out." When asked how that worked, as we knew he was a radio man and was with front man observer, he said, *"the observer would give me the coordinates and I would give the orders. We had 6 tubes in each group. I would radio the orders to the #1 Tube, and the other five would see where he shot and they would shoot in the same spot. Once we took out the Japs we then made it to Shuri Castle and took it. We spent a long time on the ridge.*

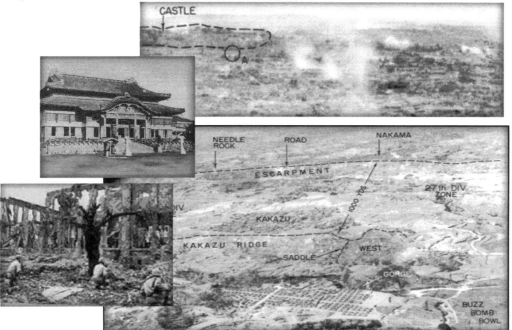

Note 27th to right. The 27th, 1st Battalion moved to right and up and along the escarpment ridge to take Shuri Castle. Shuri Castle (upper left). Shuri Castle during battle in WWII (lower left).

263

Once Martin finished talking about the ordering of mortar fire, he didn't want to talk about the battle anymore. He once said that you could always tell another man who had been in a terrible battle by the "zombie" look in their eyes when talking about it. The author saw this look many times when he would stop a moment in thought... then would quickly change the subject or say he no longer wanted to talk about it (the battle, other instances of killings, or reminders of fallen comrades).

Shuri Castle is believed to have been built by King Satto at the end of the 14th century and stood on a hill (130 meters above sea level). The castle was the headquarters of the Sho dynasty for 450 years -- from 1492 (when three kingdoms were unified on Okinawa) through 1879. During WWII, the Japanese military set up its headquarters in the castle underground. Martin was part of the first military group to take the castle. However, due to the underground tunnels and operation, on May 25, 1945, the American battleship *USS Mississippi* (BB-41) shelled it for three days. On May 27, the castle burned. Shuri Castle was designated a national treasure of Japan in 1928. The castle was restored and reopened to the public in November of 1992.

This photo of Shuri Castle was taken in 1937 after the era of the Okinawan kings, but it still gives you an idea of what it might have been like training in unarmed combat to protect the king. This was just 8 years prior to the Battle of Okinawa.

LETTER 64

There is no date on the letter. The date on the envelope: May 10, 1945

This letter was written sometime during the battle. Martin said they tried to write a couple of times, but they didn't know if the mail got out!

Dear Ruth,

I got some V-mail today so I am dropping you a short letter to let know that I am still allright. We have been having some hard fighting but it looks like things are going our way now. I guess by the time you get this things will be pretty well along. One thing I found out that you can eaven get a good nights sleep in a fox hole. I lost my pack about five days ago. That night I picked up a Jap shelter half and then the next night I picked up a Jap rain coat. I still slept pretty cold with these but then last night I found a blanket and I sure slept warm. As soon as I get another chance I will write again. Love Martin

Ruth received the last three letters about the same time … after Martin was off the Front! If received before, she would have been very worried about her brother.

Two Japanese soldiers with a Shelter Half WWII

SHELTER HALF: Although small by American or British standards, the shelter half is very serviceable. As a rain cape it provides excellent protection against wetness and is preferred by many Japanese soldiers to the issue raincoat. A cord is attached to the middle of one end so that the shelter half can be suspended from the shoulders and tied under the chin. Loops through the eyelets on one of the sides then may be slipped through the eyelets on the opposite side to close it securely in front. Two of the corners rest approximately elbow high, allowing the arms freedom of movement. The shelter half also is used as a ground sheet, or to roll up in for protection in a foxhole. It can

Japanese Rain Cape 1944

be pitched as a tent, either alone or in combination with varying numbers of others. A standard method of pitching requires 28 shelter halves.

JAPANESE RAIN CAPE: Cotton raincoats with hoods are issued to Japanese soldiers, but in most theaters they prefer to use the shelter half as rain protection. JAPANESE BLANKET: Wool blankets were issued to Japanese soldiers. [140]

Martin spoke of carrying a shelter-half in his pack (he called it a half-rack). Each soldier was issued a shelter-half (half a pup tent). Martin indicated that it was standard issue and kept in your pack at all times. It was used in the South Pacific as a half shelter between men so that the soldier beside you could not cough on you (to discourage the spread of malaria). In battle it kept the rain off of you, or from under you!

16. TENT, SHELTER. (FM 20–15.) a. General. The old-type shelter tent and the new-type shelter tent differ in one respect. The old has a single closure provided by a triangular piece of canvas sewed to one end of the shelter half, and the new has a double closure provided by triangular pieces of canvas sewed to both ends. When authorized for a unit, the shelter half is issued on the basis of 1 per enlisted man, with 1 tent pole, 5 tent pins, and 1 guy line; and 2 per officer, with 2 tent poles, 10 tent pins, and 2 guy lines. The tent, shelter half, is also used as a fly.

b. Tent, shelter (old-type). (1) *General.* The tent is made of light, water-repellent cotton canvas and is constructed in two sections, which are buttoned together to accommodate two men. It has a ridge height of 43 inches. The tent may be ventilated by opening the closed end.

12

Half this pup-tent is a "Shelter Half"- note how it snaps together at top

Inspection time - note two soldiers per tent and inspection of issued items at front of tent

[140]http://ftp. ibiblio.org/ hyperwar/Japan/IJA/HB/HB-11.html

LETTER 65, 66, and 67

Letter: April 30
Letter: May 5
Envelope: May 10

Envelope: May 9

NOTE DATE ON LETTERS & ENVELOPES

Letter: May 10
Envelope: June 4

Dear Ruth,   *April 30, 1945*

I still cant say very much but that I am still in one piece and almost as good as new. I am kind of tired but I guess I should expect that. I cant say very much about the circumstances but I think I have done all the fighting I am going to do in this place. The last time I mentioned how well the weather was it started to rain. I hope it doesnt do it again when I say we are having swell weather the days are nice and warm and then it cools off at night so I can sleep good.

I havent picked up any souvenirs at all. I think most of it is just junk and not worth monking with. Most of them would just collect in the attic anyway. Well so long for now.

Love   Martin

Hello Ruth,   *May 5, 1945*

Well Ruth everything is pretty quiet now, I am off the front and back in a rest camp. It sure seems nice and quiet here. There are lots of civilians around but they act at least like they are glad to see us. The kids are always hanging around our camp. We got a book that gives drill orders in Jap and some of the guys got some of the Jap kids out doing close order drill. These kids were smaller than George so you can see how they train the kids. The grown ups seem real friendly in fact too friendly and are always looking for something to eat.

I sure like the climate over here but every time I mention it it rains. I guess though we have to expect rain this time of year.

Im glad you found out what was keeping Georges weight down. He has always looked good and healthy but he always seemed a little underweight. I can imagine he has changed a lot since I seen him last. How is Curly feeling now days. By the way how much weight did Curly loose while he was sick. [family members do not remember any illnesses, & George does not remember any medical issues]

267

I sent another money order to you just before I landed on this place because I didnt want to carry it into combat with me. I signed it but I dont know if I signed it correct or not. Try to cash it if you can. If you cant I dont know what to do with it.

After I came off the front I went over to some engineer outfit that had fixed up a shower and took a hot shower. After sixteen days laying in dust and mud I am telling you it sure made me feel good. Well that is all I can think of now.

Love   Martin

The April 30 Report indicated definite plans were made for relief of the 105th. Martin's position of radio man was passed to another on the front lines in preparation for this relief and he pulled back. You can almost see the commanding officers handing their men paper and pen and saying write home! The only problem is that the V-Mail process was so slow Ruth received them much later! And it must have been wonderful for Martin to get letters from home after being in battle.

After reading the first letter, you would not realize all that he had gone through in battle except for this statement, *"I am still in one piece and almost as good as new."* How can anyone who has not gone through battle know the depth of that statement? And you can't help but chuckle at his, *"I am kind of tired but I guess I should expect that."*

In the second letter, he gives a hint to what the state of his mind was like before heading into combat, *"I sent another money order to you just before I landed on this place because I didnt want to carry it into combat with me. I signed it but I dont know if I signed it correct or not."*

Martin also mentions the things that give him delight after his battle experience... quietness... kids.... climate... family.... and a long HOT SHOWER!

Dear Ruth,   *May 10, 1945*

There is a stamp shortage around here so I will have to use V-Mail again. I guess we are supposed to be in a rest camp or something but there is sure a lot of work connected with it. At least I have had to work every day.

The people around here sure seem strange to me. They always stop and bow raising their hands above their heads and taking off their hats when they meet you. They are also always so polite and smile and will do anything for you. It gets kind of tiresome their being so polite.

Did you notice anything in the papers about the 27th while we were fighting. I hear we got some pretty good write ups back there and I think we really deserve them. I guess I cant say very much about that though.

Did you ever send those pictures out of my money. Would you try to get some film at Eastman Kodak in Seattle. One fellow got some from his wife and she got them there when she told them they were for someone over seas. Dont make a special trip though.

Love   Martin

One of Martin's camps - from his photo album

CONTINUATION OF ACTION REPORT....
3 May – 18 May, 1945

3-5 May   The period of 3-5 May was used by units to set up base camps. [Martin's complaint of being kept busy!] Five separate camps were established on MOTOBU Peninsula at the following places:

Rgtl Hq plus Hq Co, Sv Co, and AT Co	– TAIRA
Cannon Company	– IZANCHA
1st Battalion	– near COECHI
2nd Battalion	– HAMASAKI
3rd Battalion	– near MEJIYA

The 105th Infantry was assigned an area to patrol and search out scattered groups of enemy army and navy personnel that remained. This area was then divided into battalion areas of responsibility. Cannon and Antitank Companies were held responsible for patrols in all directions.... 50% of all personnel, less overhead, were sent on patrol each day. On Sundays, 10% of personnel patrolled assigned areas... At night, ambush patrols were sent out by all units.

1st Bn

2nd Bn

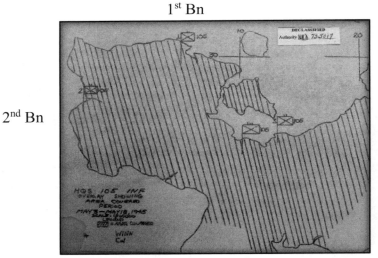

3rd Bn (at right of 105 HQ - at entrance to bay - above 105)

105 Headquarters (at entrance to Peninsula)

MOTOBU Peninsula - overlay showing area covered by
1-5 Inf 3-18 May 1945

On 17 May orders were received by 27th Inf Division. The order provided for a mop-up of Northern OKINAWA by the 27th Inf Div starting at ISHIKAWA Isthmus... On 18 May troops were moved into assembly areas in the vicinity of NAKADONARI in preparation for H-Hour at 0730 on 19 May 45 (ISHIKAWA Isthmus is the narrow waist of the island leading off to the north).

Okinawa is barley the size of Rhodes Island. Sixty miles long and 18 miles wide where the MOTOBU Peninsula extends into the China Sea. Just below is the ISHIKAWA Isthmus, only two miles across, the narrowest part of the island. The Isthmus divided OKINAWA into two very different regions for military planners to deal with in preparing operations. To the North lay 2/3 of the islands land mass, mountainous and heavily wooded with sheer coastal cliffs, all sparsely populated. In sharp contrast the southern part of the island, except for a narrow rugged section just below the isthmus that was rolling and lightly wooded. The southern part of the island was home to 2/3 the islands population.

Northern Okinawa - Ishikawa Isthmus is at narrowest point of island below Motobu Peninsula

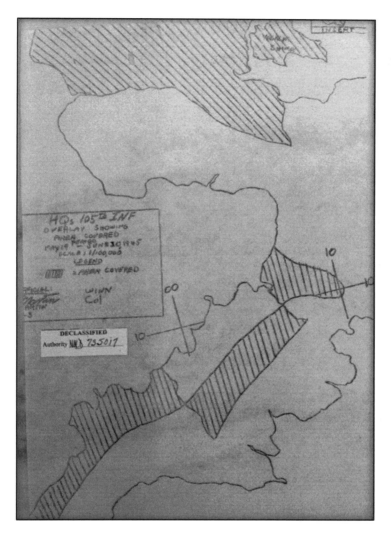

Overlay showing area (shaded) covered 19 May -
30 June 1945

LETTER 68

Letter: May 16, 1945
Envelope: May 17, 1945
Postage: 6 cents airmail

Dear Ruth,   *May 16, 1945*

I'm still not doing very much except going out on patrols and staying on outpost over night. I cant kick as long as that is all I have to do. Our kitchen also got a bunch of canned stuff that isnt the regular field rations so I guess we are supposed to have a regular meal tonight. This will be my first one since I left the boat. The field rations they give us now are darn good but then the same thing always gets tiresome and you cant replace a regular meal.

I guess I might as well tell you about the close call I had. The Japs started dropping some of their biggest artillery around me one night and I didnt have a chance to get back to my hole or eaven find a hole so I had to hit the ground right where I was. Two of their shells landed about five feet from me. That is the craters edge was five feet from me. I thought that I was pretty lucky then not to be hurt. About that time I heard another whistling in towards me and it really came close. It made a crater about six feet in diameter and I was covered up with almost a foot of dirt right on the edge of the crater. It shook the devil out of me, nocked the wind out of me, gave me a bloody nose and lots of skined places all over my legs and back and one on my face but that is all. No one can understand how I came out of it alive. I guess God was just on my side. It was also hard on my ears but I guess they arnt broken allthough they, or one anyway still bothers me.

The people around here sure have a funny custom of taking care of people after they die. They put them in a coffin for, I have heard a year and also three, I dont know which is correct. Then they take them out and take all the meat off the bones and wash them in salt water or alchohal. They then put the bones in big jars and set them in big vaults or tombs. I guess they believe in their ancestors living after death and they seem to put more work in their family tombs then they do in their homes. You see these tombs scattered out all over this place.

I was just reading an article in the Readers Digest about all the Red Cross is doing over here. If they are doing so much I would sure like to see some of it. The only good I have seen is they give us cigaretts and toilet articles once in awhile. For my part they could cut the Red Cross out and it wouldnt hurt my feelings.

That is about all I can think of now so I will have to close.

Love Martin

This was one letter that was so hard not to mention earlier. The letter doesn't tell all, but Martin never wanted to "*worry*" his sister. The areas of "skinned" arms, legs, etc. were burned off areas from the heat of the explosion. Today he still has problems with one ear....and he spent 3 months at the end of the war in a hospital before they released him to go home! When asked if they sent him to the back of the lines, he had a surprised look on his face and said,

This picture gives you an idea to the type of explosion that landed next to him!

"No, it happened in the middle of the night. I was in my fox hole and had to go to the bathroom so got out and was walking away when a barrage of artillery (mortars) came in. I hit the ground. One mortar landed right next to me but did not go off so I thought it was a dud and about that time it blew. I awoke to the men removing the 1-2 feet of dirt from on top of me. They couldn't believe I was still alive. There was a 6' wide crater next to me. My right ear was bleeding and my eye was sore… I was pretty sore all over with the burns on my face, arms, and legs from the explosion. I went to the Aid station. It was a 'family tomb' in the side of the hill. That is where you want to be as the mortars seem to bounce off them. The only lights were inside that tomb, no lights outside. There was a guard outside and after looking me over with his pen light, said I wasn't critical and would be attended to in the morning and told me to lie down just outside. They had canvas strips on the ground. I laid there awhile but didn't have my gun with me and didn't feel secure so went back to my foxhole. In the morning I went and got my helmet which was twisted up so bad they had to give me a new helmet. I talked with my commander and he told me to rest a couple of days. We were given orders to pull back about that time as our company was VERY TIRED and battle worn. There wasn't time to rest, though. I had a job to do. When we arrived at our location for rest, we had to work hard in building our tent camp!"

This triggered a memory by Martin...
"The Japs had what they called 'Flying Boxcar Mortars.' They were mortars shot from a 12" pipe and you had to really look out for them as they were not accurate and you could hear them coming but not know where they would land. They made big holes and lots of noise."

Research referred to this same item as a "Knee Mortar." The artillery fire Martin was under was very heavy. You could see him mentally go to another place when talking about it. He had a neighbor who served in the South Pacific and actually shipped overseas on the same ship, and they would share stories of their experiences... except when it came to the battle. Martin's son, Marty, said that when it came to the talk of the battle and killings his Dad would

The 12 mortar Japanese used to fire mortar rounds. Note the mortar rounds in the hands of the Japanese soldier at left.

stop the talk and change the subject. Martin had once said he saw hundreds of men killed.

Martin had said in one of our phone conversations that the memories were to gruesome to remember and he didn't want to talk about them. In that statement, he said all that needed to be said and his wish was respected. He was never asked how he felt about the fighting. During research when studying the day to day battle, one officer radioed in and said one of his soldiers saw a Jap behead his friend and wanted to know if he could send this soldier to the back lines. He was told to send him to the Medical unit at the rear.

Once Martin was off the Front Line did not mean he saw no further action. He said there was a lot of "*mopping up*" to do. It is important to mention at this time what Martin himself has stated....

> *"It was a different time. Japanese at that time were coming out of a Samurai culture and they fought to the death and were very vicious in the way they dealt with the enemy. Some of the Japanese officers and soldiers wore their ancestral samurai swords into battle. They hated us, we hated them knowing what they did. That was then, this is now. Times have changed."*

As stated before, the radio man was a major target of the enemy (on both sides). Martin's job was to radio the position of the enemy to the Mortar Teams and where to "lob" their shots. Therefore, he was always a major target, especially of the snipers. The following excerpt from the book: CROSS IN THE BACKGROUND by Randy D. Horsak illustrates this danger.

Mortars lob small "bombs" to distances ranging from a few hundred yards to a few miles. Mortar fire was extremely effective in breaking up infantry attacks, since a three-mortar team could launch a hundred rounds or more in a five-minute period of intense fire. At first, it would appear that this is a fairly safe job in combat since you are not eyeball-to-eyeball with the enemy. This attitude, however, callously ignores a key principle in warfare – first kill the enemy that is doing the most damage to your troops. In many cases, it was the mortar squad, and specifically the radio man directing the Mortar Team. The Japanese military records indicate that they hated the American mortar squad.

In Okinawa, almost one million mortar rounds were fired by the US Military. If Japanese could locate US mortars they would attempt to neutralize them with artillery fire.

Turtle Back Tomb – These tombs were found all over Okinawa

Martin standing beside a family tomb

Notice how the memory of his close call made Martin think of death, then gave an interesting description of the Okinawan death ritual. The tombs are still seen across their landscape today.

Due to fears concerning their fate during and after the invasion, the Okinawan people hid in caves and in family tombs. Below is an interesting story around the use of caves which also helps to understand the mentality of *suicide over capture.*

After the beginning of World War II, the Japanese military conscripted school girls (15 to 16 years old) to join a group known as the *Princess Lilies (Hime-yuri)* and to go to the battle front as nurses. There were seven girls' high schools in

Okinawa at the time of World War II. The Princess Lilies were organized at two of them, and a total of 297 students and teachers eventually joined the group; 211 died. Most of the girls were put into temporary clinics in caves and tombs to take care of injured soldiers. With a severe shortage of food, water and medicine, many of the girls died while trying to care for the wounded soldiers.

The Japanese military had told these girls that if they were taken as prisoners, the enemy would rape and kill them; the military gave hand grenades to the girls to allow them to commit suicide rather than be taken as prisoners. One of the Princess Lilies explained: "We had a strict imperial education, so being taken prisoner was the same as being a traitor. We were taught to prefer suicide to becoming a captive." Many students died saying "*Tenno Heika Banzai,*" which means "*Long live the Emperor.*"[141]

Ariel view of a WWII village in Okinawa

---

[141]http://en.wikipedia.org/wiki/History_of_the_Ryukyu_Islands

LETTER 69, 70, & 71

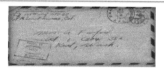

Letter Date: May 24
Envelope Date: none

Letter Date: none
Envelope Date: Jun 22

Letter Date: June 1
Envelope Date: June 12

Dear Ruth,   *May 24, 1945*

I wont have many chances to write to you for awhile so if you dont hear from me regular you will know why. I'm not up on the front now or anything like that. I dont know how much I can say about what we are doing but is sure a lot of work. If I had Bert following me over these hills he wouldnt have to worry about a diet. I guarantee that. In that news you saw about Okinawa did you remember seeing a picture of the 27th marching up to the front. I was in that picture. Im sure getting a beard now. I havent shaved for a week now and If I dont get a chance to shave until I think I will I will really have one. Well that is about all I can think of now. I will write again as soon as I can.   *Love   Martin*

Dear Ruth,   *June 1, 1945*

I havent much time to write but I will write a short note to you and send some Jap money to you. There are fourteen fifty yen notes and then one war bond. I have some change but I can't put that in a letter. I want to get rid of it before I ruin it in the rain. It has been raining almost steady for a couple of weeks now and I have been out in all of it day and night. I can sleep now wet or dry hot or cold. By the way any time you find anyones address that you think is near me let me know what his address or at least outfit is and I can look him up. If you just say engineers there are always all kinds of them around. That's all I have time for now.   *Love   Martin*

No Letter Date
Envelope Date: June 22

Dear Ruth,

Everything has been going pretty smooth today. We have been just sitting around taking it easy. I expect an order any time to get ready to move out though. This mopping upstarted out pretty tough but lately it hasnt been too bad. The rain seems to have let up and that alone is a great help. Do you know one night I was soaken wet and laid down and the water made a stream under me and I still slept good. I got more sleep than usual because the two fellow that were with me couldn't sleep and so they pulled all the guard.

By the way I had better let you know that I have started putting my money in the Soldiers deposite. We dont need any money here yet so I signed over a couple of hundred of my back pay into it. This will save you a lot of trouble and I can always get it if I need it very bad. I am glad you came through your check up OK.

Love   Martin

CONTINUATION OF ACTION REPORT....

19 May – 30 June 1945: The sweep of Northern OKINAWA started on schedule at 0730 on 19 May. In the zone of action of the 105th Infantry, only small groups of enemy personnel were encountered. All civilians were interned and transported to Military Government Camp in Eastern OKINAWA. ...

The nature of the terrain, steep razor-back ridges with numerous valleys

The torturous terrain that had to be taken by the Americans

- Complications arose from heavy rainfall

and heavy vegetation, made progress slow and contact very difficult. The problems of supply and evacuation were many. In addition, during the period of 20 May to 2 June, heavy rains made quagmires out of the roads and trails.

By 24 May the line of the regiment had advanced to the vicinity of ONNA, a gain of five miles. At this point, the advance was held up because the 106th Infantry encounters organized resistance on ONNA TAKE... during the period of 24 May to 2 June, our score in enemy killed was high because the enemy flushed from ONNA TAKE were on the move and wandered into our lines at night or were surprised in the daytime by our patrols. The lines were stable again on 4 June.

On 9 June, the general advance was resumed....our objective was KUSHI TAKE, a

ONNA TAKE (shaded area), KUSHI TAKE is to the right of ONNA TAKE

hill mass that was reported to have organized enemy positions. The enemy must have flown as no contacts were made and our advance continued to a line from YOFULE east. This line was absorbed by the 106th Infantry while the balance of the division prepared for the mop-up of the MOTOBU Peninsula. This was begun on 19 June 45, included in our zone of action were two islands off East coast of the Peninsula – YAGACHI SHILA and KOURI SHIDA.

WWII military camp with mountains in background

ONNA TAKE coast line

On 30 June, plans were in the making for the continuing sweep of Northern OKINAWA SHIMA (Okinawa Mainland). This mission was scheduled to start on July 2, 1945.

SHIMA: means island

Yagachi Island is in the bay between Motobu Peninsula and the mainland.

Kouri Island is north of Yagachi.

279

Many of the caves had rear entrances which went right through the ridge. Besides offering protection from bombardment, the caves allowed the Japanese to move back and forth between the front and rear slopes of Okinawa's many hills undetected. If Americans made it over a ridge, they could be attacked from the rear.

Caves Japanese soldiers hid out in and fought from

27th DIVISION PATROL scouts a stream bed during the three-month mop-up drive in northern Okinawa (Army Photograph)

Soldier washing up in rain-filled foxhole! (Looks like Martin)

Photo re at right: *In process of Mopping Up. Note the terrain*

Martin spoke of the many pillbox caves the Japanese used. He said they were too small for an American to get in and the Japanese, if spotted, could go back through the mountain through all their tunnels.

They did not use Flame Throwers during mop up, but did use containers of fluid that they lit and threw into the caves which sent flames through cave. He said the mopping up was exhausting, dangerous, and the mountain terrain was horrible! [The picture at left of a pillbox cave is from Martin's photo album]

WW II GLOBAL TIMELINE - MAY 1945[142]

Day

1: As one of his last acts Reich Chancellor Joseph Goebbels has sent German General Hans Krebs to negotiate the surrender of the city of Berlin with Soviet General Vasily Chuikov. Krebs is not authorized by Goebbels to agree to an unconditional surrender, so his negotiations with Chuikov end with no agreement.

1: Partisan leader Tito and his troops capture Trieste in northwest Italy. New Zealand troops play a supporting role. Goebbels and his wife kill their children and then commit suicide.

1: The war in Italy is over but some German troops are still not accounted for.

1: Australian troops land on Tarakan Island off the coast of Borneo

2: The Battle of Berlin ends when German General Helmuth Weidling, commander of the Berlin Defence Area, (and no longer bound by Goebbels commands), unconditionally surrenders the city of Berlin to Soviet General Vasily Chuikov.

3: Eamon de Valera, Taoiseach (prime minister) of Ireland, offers regrets for Hitler's death to German officialdom.

3: Rangoon is liberated.

4: Neuengamme concentration camp is liberated.

4: German troops are surrendering throughout Europe. Troops in Denmark, Northern Germany and The Netherlands surrender to Montgomery.

5: Czech resistance fighters started Prague uprising.

5: Soviets started Prague Offensive.

5: Mauthausen concentration camp is liberated.

5: German troops in the Netherlands officially surrender; Prince Bernhard of the Netherlands accepts the surrender.

5: Formal negotiations for Germany's surrender begin at Reims, France.

5: Kamikazes have major successes off Okinawa.

5: Japanese Fire balloons claim their first and only lives

---

[142]http://en.wikipedia.org/wiki/Timeline_of_World_War_II_%281945%29#May_1945

6:      This date marks the last fighting for American troops in Europe.

6:      German soldiers open fire on a crowd celebrating the liberation in Amsterdam.

7:      Germany surrenders unconditionally to the Allies at the Western Allied Headquarters in Rheims, France at 2:41 a.m. In accordance with orders from Reich President Kaarl Donitz, General Alfred Jodl signs for Germany.

7:      Hermann Göring, for a while in the hands of the SS, surrenders to the Americans.

8:      Ceasefire takes effect at one minute past midnight; V-E Day in Britain

8:      The remaining members of the Prime Minister Jozef Tiso's pro-German Slovak Republic capitulates to the American General Walton Walker's XX Corps in Kremsumster, Austria.

8:      Germany surrendered again unconditionally to the Soviet Union army but this time in a ceremony hosted by the Soviet Union. In accordance with orders from Reich President Karl Donitz, General Wilhelm Keitel signs for Germany.

8:      In accordance with orders from Reich President Karl Donitz, Colonel-General Carl Hilpert unconditionally surrenders his troops in the Courland Pocket.

8:      Prague uprising ends with negotiated surrender with Czech resistance which allowed the Germans in Prague to leave the city.

8:      Soviet forces capture the Reichstag during which the soviets install the famous flag of Soviet Union over Reichstag.

8:      Vietnam is considered a minor item on the agenda; in order to disarm the Japanese in Viet Nam, the Allies divide the country in half at the 16th parallel. Chinese Nationalists will move in and disarm the Japanese north of the parallel while the British will move in and do the same in the south. During the conference, representatives from France request the return of all French pre-war colonies in Indochina. Their request is granted. Viet Nam will once again become French colony following the removal of the Japanese.

9:      Red Army entered Prague as part of the Prague Offensive.

9:      Soviet Union officially pronounces May 9 as the Victory Day.

9:      German garrison in Channel Islands agreed to unconditional surrender.

9:      German troops on Bornholm surrender to Soviet troops.

11:     Prague Offensive ends with Soviet capture of the capital city, the last major city to be liberated, though the war is over. Eisenhower stops Patton from participating in the liberation.

11:     German Army Group Centre in Czechoslovakia surrenders.

11:     War in New Guinea continues, with Australians attacking Wewak.

14:     Nagoya, Japan is heavily bombed.

14:      Fighting in the southern Philippines continues.

14–15: The Battle of Poljana, the last major battle of World War II in Europe, is fought.

18:      Continued fierce fighting on Okinawa.

20:      Georgian Uprising of Texel ends, concluding hostilities in Europe.

23:      British forces capture and arrest the members of what was left of the Flensburg government. This was the German government formed by Reich President Karl Donitz after the suicides of both Adolf Hitler and Joseph Goebbels.

23:      Heavy bombing of Yokohama, an important port and naval base.

23:      Heinrich Himmler, head of the notorious SS, dies of suicide by cyanide pill.

29:      Fighting breaks out in Syria and Lebanon, as nationalists demand freedom from French control.

NOTE: May 18th states there is '*continued fierce fighting on Okinawa*'

Below are the operation notes for Martin's division for May 18th and the following days:

On 17 May orders were received by 27th Inf Division. The order provided for a mop-up of Northern OKINAWA by the 27th Inf Div starting at ISHIKAWA Isthmus… On 18 May troops were moved into assembly areas in the vicinity of NAKADONARI in preparation for H-Hour at 0730 on 19 May 45 (ISHIKAWA Isthmus is the narrow waist of the island leading off to the north).

19 May – 30 June 1945: The sweep of Northern OKINAWA started on schedule at 0730 on 19 May. In the zone of action of the 105th Infantry, only small groups of enemy personnel were encountered. All civilians were interned and transported to Military Government Camp in Eastern OKINAWA. …

    The nature of the terrain, steep razor-back ridges with numerous valleys and heavy vegetation, made progress slow and contact very difficult. The problems of supply and evacuation were many. In addition, during the period of 20 May to 2 June, heavy rains made quagmires out of the roads and trails.

What this report does not tell you is what the soldiers witnessed or encountered. It states that "only small groups" of enemy personnel were encountered. However, it does not tell of what happened in those encounters, or what our soldiers saw within caves. Martin spoke of seeing "gruesome sights," but would not describe them. He also said it was horrible trying to move through the terrain with the mud and rain.

LETTER 72, 73, & 74

Letter Date: June 29   Envelope Date: Jul 6

Envelope Date: Jul 5

Letter Date: July 4

Letter Date: Jul 12
Envelope Date: Jul 21

Dear Ruth,   *Okinawa, June 29, 1945*

I havent very much to write about. I havent been doing much lately except stand out on an outpost. I am through with that now though for awhile and I guess we are going to move to another part of the island. I will sure be glad when we get this place in shape and settle down in a base camp. I suppose we will go back into training then but at least we will get something to eat besides rations and have a tent and cot to sleep on. By the way I finally got a Jap flag. It isnt a good one but its a flag any way. I also got a navy or marine Japs medal.

I was sure surprised the other day. I got a letter from Mickey [a hometown friend]. It sure surprised me. I guess he is in Aberdeen now and is working in a Radio repair shop.

The women over here sure have a tough life. They are always working and carrying big loads. You never see a man carry anything unless his wife has such a big load she cant carry any more and that has to be a lot.

Myrtle told me you bought a place out at the lake. Are you going to move out there or keep the place you are living in. I suppose you will just stay out there this summer.

Well I am about run down so I will close now.

Love Martin

PS. Would you save this Jap money for me. [no money was in envelope]

Hello Ruth,   *Okinawa, July 4, 1945*

Today is the fourth but it doesnt mean much over here. Its just another day. A couple of guys took a machine gun out and shot it awhile to celebrate and that is about all. I went swimming in the China sea but the water is too warm and so it isnt much fun. Its pretty warm over here now. We sure have it easy in one way over here though. When we stay in one place like this we can get the Gooks (natives,

284

Okinawans, Japs or whatever you want to call them) to do all the work for you. Women and kids are always hanging around just hoping you will let them do something for you so you will give them some cigarettes. I guess they get tired of sweet spuds and rice. One fellow eaven had a kid holding his mirror while he shaved.

I have some Jap money and I am going to start putting some in each letter I send to you. Will you save it for me? If you want any take it (Ruth must have taken some as there is Jap money in this letter). I have a couple of flags and a few other souvenirs I will send as soon as I can. They arnt very good flags but I guess everyone cant find good ones.

Well I cant think of anything more now so I will have to close. The sun is setting now and one thing they have here is beautiful sunsets. I can look out across the ocean and the sun is setting behind a group of small islands.

Love   Martin

Hello Ruth   *July 12, 1945*

Well Im back in the hills again so I have to use V-Mail again. When we first got on the island it was pretty cold especially at night. Its gotten so its seems just as hot here now as it was in the tropics. What I hate worse than the heat though is the flies and mosquitoes. There is always a swarm of flies around in the day time and then when it starts to get dark the mosquitoes take over. We have to have misquote leans to sleep because they can bite right through our clothes.

Im not in the mortar platoon now. I am in Company headquarters. The job I am doing now is in charge of communications and so I should make sergeant. They are pretty slow at giving ratings out around here so I might not get it for quite awhile. I have to wait until a fellow with a lot of points gets his discharge.

Love   Martin

Islands off coast of Okinawa

Martin got relief from the 'mopping-up.' Then got to swim in the China Sea, which means he was on the west side of Okinawa. He said he could see islands off in the distance.

The 4th of July celebration may have been small then, but the 4th of July celebrations after the war were celebrations to remember. The author was born just after the war and can remember being told many times she was a "new generation" baby. Fourth of July celebrations were community celebrations and lasted all day culminating in a big fireworks display after dark.

Okinawa Island

There will be some who will think it is terrible that the soldiers were collecting souvenirs. The policy at that time was to report all items found. Martin was frustrated as he had found some very nice swords and the officers would take them for themselves and not return them. The items found were pretty much a reward for what the men had been through. At the end of the war, he had a few 'souvenirs'...a couple Jap rifles, money, and some swords. He gave one of the swords to his nephew, George, who has it to this day. Below are the front and back of the money Ruth had in this letter.

front & back   *front & back*

front & back

Martin said the "mopping up" was in some ways worse than Front Line battle as it was more hand-to-hand/fact-to-face battle. Again, he would go to another place then say, "They would not surrender." Research revealed that Okinawan civilians had been told such horrible tales of what would happen to them if captured so they would commit suicide rather than be captured. Sometimes whole families who hid in caves would commit suicide, and those were not easy scenes for the soldiers. Civilians, and the Japanese soldiers who were captured and became prisoners of war, were surprised at how well they were treated. At the beginning of the military operations the inhabitants took refuge in caves and in the mountains;

as soon as possible they were concentrated in AMG camps (American Military Government).

During the battle, U.S. soldiers found it difficult to distinguish civilians from

Japanese Flag

soldiers. It became routine for U.S. soldiers to shoot at Okinawan houses, as one infantryman wrote, "*There was some return fire from a few of the houses, but the others were probably occupied by civilians – and we didn't care. It was a terrible thing not to distinguish between the enemy and women and children. Americans always had great compassion, especially for children. Now we fired indiscriminately.*" When the American forces occupied the island, many Japanese soldiers put on Okinawan clothing to avoid capture. Many of the Okinawans came to the Americans' aid by offering simple ways to detect Japanese in hiding. [143]

The standard of living of the Okinawan people was low. The Japanese made no attempt to raise it as they regarded the Okinawan people as inferior rustics. Martin said the Japanese considered them inferior because they were of Korean decent. Most of the inhabitants subsisted on small-scale agriculture. Every foot of usable land was planted, even extending far up the narrow valleys dissecting the northern peninsula, and terracing was extensive. Crops were sugarcane, sweet potatoes, rice, and soybeans. Livestock (cattle, horses, goats) were apparently abundant before military occupation. In 1940, the human population of the island was 435,000. Since many Okinawan residents fled to caves where they subsequently were entombed, the precise number of civilian casualties will probably never be known. At the conclusion of hostilities around 196,000 civilians remained.[144]

Okinawan girls with bundles on head

Martin often mentioned the fly and mosquito problem when talking about Okinawa during battle. Excerpts from the following report has historical information on how the Army dealt with the mosquito problem in Okinawa. However, most was accomplished "after" the initial invasion and, therefore, did not relieve Martin's misery in battle or mopping up.

---

[143]http://en.wikipedia.org/wiki/Battle_of_Okinawa
[144]http://en.wikipedia.org/wiki/Battle_of_Okinawa

U.S. Army Medical Department
Office of Medical History

    This report is concerned with the history of malaria and other insect-borne diseases on Okinawa and adjacent islands in the Ryukyu Islands Command from the initial landings on 1 April 1945 until late in the fall of that year, after the end of the war. ...

    The military invasion and the occupation of the Ryukyus (Okinawan Islands) was the first step in the plan of the United States to penetrate the inner ring of Japanese defense. In addition to cutting the enemy's air communications through the Ryukyus and flanking his sea communications to the south, Okinawa furnished airbases within medium bomber range of Japan and an advanced naval base. The plan was to use it as a supporting position for the invasion of Kyûshû and Honshu. The calendar of operations was as follows:

> Assault landing, Kerama Islands, 26 March, secured 29 March 1945.
> Assault landing, Okinawa Island, 1 April, secured 30 June 1945.
> Assault landing, Ii-shima Island, 16 April, secured 21 April 1945.

    This campaign, as is well known, was marked by some of the bitterest fighting and by the heaviest Allied casualties of the war in the Pacific. Severe combat on Okinawa was concentrated in the southern half and especially in the southern one-third of the island. Before the military occupation of Okinawa, it was known, through Japanese reports, that malaria was endemic in the Ryukyu Islands. ...By 18 April, the entire northern peninsula of Okinawa had been captured.... The entire central part of the island and the north, freed of all except occasional guerrilla actions, was available for rear-area installations. Military government installations and native camps were located in the north of the island, and airfields, dumps, hospitals, and camps were set up in the flatter central region...

    The mean annual moisture content of the air around the Ryukyu Islands is excessive, averaging 76 percent or more. Humidity is highest during the April-September period, when it averages about 80 percent. ...Mosquitoes became very active at dusk. If one stood outdoors, or in the doorway of a house, dozens of mosquitoes would land and attempt to bite within a short period of time. Even indoors, mosquitoes would be found to have entered freely and to be attempting to feed.

    ...Because of the ever-present danger of sniper action, long after the island was declared secure, airplane spraying was largely limited to the areas of troop concentration in the southern half of the island during May and June [*note. After the first major battles*] and was infrequent over the northern half. Moreover, the mountainous terrain in the north forced the planes to fly high and so decreased efficiency. Consequently, in many regions of northern Okinawa, mosquito populations had the opportunity to and did maintain themselves in considerable numbers. [145]

---

[145]http://history.amedd.army.mil/booksdocs/wwii/Malaria/chapterVIII-2.htm

Memories Martin had of how they protected themselves from mosquitos...

"Each soldier was issued a half-rack (half a pup tent) which we used to wrap ourselves up in, and we had Mosquito nets that we kept inside our helmets which we put on over the helmets when mosquitos were really bad. At night we wore gloves to protect our hands. When new fellows came onto the field and asked where we got them, they were told if they weren't issued one they would have to pick up helmets on the ground and see if there was a net inside as that was where we kept them. The half-racks were lost quickly during battle."

Then Martin became quiet. You could tell he was back seeing the scenes. There were so many times you could tell he was '*back there*' and he didn't really want to be '*back there*.' In June of 2013, WWII Veterans from across the nation gathered in Atlanta, Georgia. One Vet was asked what this meant to him and he replied, *"It is great as you can talk about things you can't talk about to your family. We don't want to talk about them and usually don't, but you know they (fellow soldiers) understand what you went through and it is a good feeling to know that someone knows what you are feeling."*

WWII GLOBAL TIMELINE - JUNE 1945

Day

2:     Air Group 87 aircraft from USS Ticonderoga struck airfields on Kyushu, Japan in an attempt to stop special attack aircraft from taking off.

5:     A huge Pacific typhoon hits the American navy under Admiral Halsey; the fleet suffers widespread damage.

5:     Allies agree to divide Germany into four areas of control.

10:     Australian troops land at Brunei, Borneo.

13:     The Australians capture Brunei.

15:     Osaka, Japan is bombed heavily.

16:     The Japanese are in a general retreat in central China.

17:     Japanese Admiral Ota Minoru committed ritual suicide for failing to defend Okinawa, Japan.

19:     The United Kingdom begins demobilization.

20:     Schieromonikoog, a Dutch island, is the last part of Europe freed by Allied troops.

21:     The defeat of the Japanese on Okinawa is now complete.

26:     The United Nations Charter is signed in San Francisco.

27:     The first oil pump is restored at Tarakan Island.

LETTER 75 & 76

Letter Date: July 20, 1945
Envelope Date: July 21,

Letter Date: July 28, 1945
1945 Envelope Date: July 29, 1945

Somewhere in West Pacific
July 20, 1945

Hello Ruth,

Well Ruth I guess in about three weeks we will be through with these darned hills. I sure hope so because this is really tough work. I thought basic was hard but that was just a picnick. When you climb around these hills for about ten or more hours you know you have put in a hard day.

Did I tell you I got a letter from Mickey [a neighborhood friend]. He is working down in Aberdeen now but doesnt intend to stay long. He said Len [another neighborhood friend] was up in Everett [Washington] now.

On those negatives that were supposed to be sent to you. The people lost your address and I had to give it to them again. I thought it would be easier now if I sent them to Myrtle. At least it would be less confusing.

I bet George does get a big kick out of staying out at the lake. He should be learning how to swim pretty soon shouldnt he. That isnt a very good place for him to learn how though. By the way I have swam in the Coral sea and the East China sea and the Pacific of course.

Well there isnt much to write about so I will have to close.

Love Martin

Hello Ruth,   *July 28, 1945*

Ive a lot of spare time right now but nothing much to write about. We have been resting a few days getting ready to finish up the mop up. I guess we have only about a week more of actual working. I will sure be glad when we finish and set up some sort of a camp. Some of the fellows have been working making the camp so it should be pretty well along when we get there. They have a kitchen set up and a shower. They are setting up the tents now and I hear all of them leak. That will sure make it nice [Martin is being sarcastic] because it really likes to rain.

Would you tell Myrtle to get some of the D72 or D76 instead if she can. Any one of the three will work but I would rather have any kind of fine gran developer because the pictures will come out better.

I suppose you keep Curly pretty busy now fixing up the cabin. Doesnt it need a new float under it. It seems to me the float used to be pretty low. I bet George really does have a good time out there but doesnt he miss Donnie. It seems like it would be lonesome for him.

Well Ive finally got fifteen months over seas now. By the time the war ends I should have enough points for a discharge. If they are as slow then as they are now though it will sure take a long time. We have lots of fellows with way over a hundred points and no one has left for home yet. A couple are supposed to leave soon but they havent yet.

I cant think of anything more now so I will have to close for now.

Love   Martin

Mountain area in Northern Okinawa

Note that Martin is using "Red Cross" stationary and envelopes. Martin has spoken of the mopping-up and said it was very hard and not nice. He said the Japs were very fierce and did not want to give up. Martin often used the word *"gruesome"* in describing war and the sights he wishes he could forget, *"but you cannot forget."*

Mountain ranges in Northern Okinawa were not only steep and jungle in nature, but also very hot and humid with insects (including the pesky misquotes and flies), snakes, etc. Although deserts and savanna (grassland) climates are common in this latitude, Okinawa is Subtropical in climate. A warm ocean current effects Okinawa's climate. These subtropical forests are not found anywhere else in Japan. [146]

Once south Okinawa was taken, America considered the battle over. What you do not read about is the continued 'mopping-up' phase. Below is the account of the *'mopping-up'* of the Southern part of Okinawa. Martin also participated in the mopping-up of Northern Okinawa which took longer.

On 23 June 1945 Tenth Army began a thorough and coordinated mop-up campaign to eliminate the disorganized remnants of the 32d Army in southern Okinawa at the southern end of the island, then turn and advance northward through two successive phase lines. A blocking line was established along the Naha-Yonabaru cross-island road to prevent any Japanese soldiers from infiltrating to the northern part of the island.

*Raising the American Flag - Jun 22
denoted the end of organized
resistance*

The troops first cleaned out some strong pockets of unorganized resistance in the sweep to the first phase line in the south. Cave positions were systematically sealed up by flame throwers and demolitions, with hundreds of Japanese entombed within. Several bloody skirmishes ensued when well-armed groups of the enemy attempted to infiltrate the American lines and make their way to the north. Extensive patrolling ferreted out individual Japanese soldiers hiding in cane fields and rice paddies. Once the American troops turned northward, fewer and fewer of the enemy were found, and the third and final phase line was reached with comparative ease [according to declassified reports stated earlier, 'mopping up' in the North had been on-going]. [147]

Evan as late as July 28, 1945 they were still mopping-up! And Martin indicates they have maybe a week remaining which would put them into August. The battle of Okinawa ended June 21! It must have been nasty business. No wonder he is looking forward to getting into a camp. Imagine having to fight the enemy, build your own living quarters... and eat rations day after day!

---

[146] http://www.history.army.mil/books/wwii/okinawa/chapter18.htm#b3
[147] http://www.history.army.mil/books/wwii/okinawa/chapter18.htm#b3

Ruth and Arvid (Curly) Furford had purchased a house on Lake Tapps in Sumner, Washington where Martin and Ruth's sister, Myrtle, already lived. The houses were literally built on large floating logs over the water. George remembers living there that summer. He was 8 yrs. old, and no, he did not know how to swim. He doesn't remember why

Ruth & Curly's lake house on Lake Tapps - Sumner, WA

WWII Army rubber flotation life belt

they did not teach him to swim, but he loved it at the lake. He said he had to wear this big ugly brown rubber tube around his body when he went into the water or got in a boat. The rubber tube he is referring to is a WWII Army rubber flotation belt that was wrapped around his chest under his arms.

Martin asked his sister, Myrtle, to get D72 or D76 which is film developer. There were some men in a company that set up a developing station and the soldiers helped to get supplies so they could get their film developed. When writing his letter, Martin knew he would soon be at camp and his unit would be guarding an airport. The group that developed film established themselves in a building near this airport.

In this letter and in letters to come, Martin talks about points associated to discharge. He wants so badly to get home.

POINT SYSTEM

Initially proposed by General George C. Marshall, and amended by Secretary of War Henry L. Stimson on May 10, 1945, the *Adjusted Service Rating Score (ASRS)*, was based on the "Point System." A soldier was awarded a number of *Points* for his months of service, for the medals he received, for the combat stars earned by his unit, and for the number of children he had ... the higher the score, the higher the probability to be sent home for demobilization and discharge! The "Credit" or "Points" were indicated and totaled on the *Adjusted Service Rating Card (ASRC)*, W.D., A.G.O., Form N°.163 – these cards were filled by Army Personnel Offices and checked by the individual serviceman before being signed and sent in. At the end of WWII, servicemen were constantly harassing Company Clerks to get their *Adjusted Service Rating Cards* corrected and updated (subject Cards listed Service Credit + Overseas Credit + Combat Credit + Parenthood Credit).

"**Points**" for discharge from the Army were to be totaled as follows:
1. Each Month in Service.. 1 Point
2. Each Month in Service Oversea....................................... 1 Point
3. Each Combat Award (including each Medal and each Bronze Service
4. Star, or battle participation star) .... 5 Points
5. Each dependent Child under 18 (maximum 3 Children)....... 12 Points

The above 4 items are the *only criteria* for which "Points" were awarded (for total time of service performed since 16 September 1940). No "Points" will be awarded for age, marriage, or dependents other than children under 18. The magic number of "Points" to be obtained was <u>85</u>. With fewer "Points," further service would be required! [148]

WWII GLOBAL Timeline - JULY 1945

Day

1: Australian troops land at Balikpapan, Borneo in the Western Allies last major land operation of the war
4: General MacArthur announces that the Philippines have been liberated.
6: Norway declares war on Japan.
10: US Navy aircraft participate in attacks on Tokyo for the first time.
14: Italy declares war on Japan.
16: U.S. conducts the Trinity test at Alamogordo, New Mexico, the first test of a nuclear weapon.
17: The Potsdam Conference begins. The Allied leaders agree to insist upon the unconditional surrender of Japan.
24: Truman hints at the Potsdam Conference that the United States has nuclear weapons.
24: British and Americans commence the Bombing of Kure.
26: The Labour Party win the United Kingdom general election by a landslide. The new United Kingdom Prime Minister Clement Attlee replaces Churchill at the negotiating table at Potsdam. Potsdam Declaration is issued.
28: The Japanese battleship Haruna is sunk by aircraft from US Task Force 38.
30: The USS Indianapolis is sunk shortly after midnight by a Japanese submarine after having delivered atomic bomb material to Tainan; because of poor communications, the ship's whereabouts are unknown for some time and many of its men drown or are attacked by sharks in the next four days.
31: US air attacks on the cities of Kobe and Nagoya in Japan.

---

[148]http://users.skynet.be/jeeper/point.html

JAPAN

Photo from Martin's Album

LETTER 77, 78, & 79

Letter Date: Aug 11, 194   Letter Date: Aug 12, 1945   Letter Date: Aug 24, 1945
Envelope Date: Aug 10, 1945   Envelope Date: Aug 13, 1945   Envelope Date: Aug 25, 1945

(Did Martin or Postal Service make mistake on the date of letter #77?)

Hello Ruth,   *August 11, 1945*

Well I guess the war is just about wound up. You should have been here last night when the news came in. You might think you have seen some fourth of July fireworks, well you should have seen the one we had. All the anti aircraft opened up, the searchlights were turned on and then they shot up a bunch of flares. I was at a show when they started and we knew what it must mean when they started it without the air raid signal. Everyone was sure happy. Maybe I will get home in six months or so now. I would sure like to know how they are going to work it. I am so close to Japan maybe they will send us up there.

I found a place to develop film and sent my two rolls in. I should get them today and I am sure anxious to see them. There should be some good ones.

I spend most of my spare time playing contract bridge now. There is sure a lot to the game isnt it. They are waiting for me to play right now and I cant think of much more now. We finally finished the mop up the other day and at the present we are guarding an airport. The way it looks there isnt much we will have to do around here and that is the way it should be. If anyone needs a rest we sure do. With the war almost over it may not last long now though. Will that is all I can think of now. I got two rolls of film from Karen.

Love   Martin

Hello Ruth,   *August 12, 1945*

Thanks a lot for the box of candy and the film. I got it yesterday and it was all in good shape. It sure tasted good because it has been hard to get any candy lately. By the way keep your eyes on the papers and you might see our division mentioned in them.

The Japs giving up sure came as a pleasant surprise. I thought they might but something like that is something that was to big to hope for. You would agree on that if you saw how they never give up. They havent signed anything yet maybe Im getting to fast.

I sent some film in the other day to get developed and now the outfit broke down that does them and maybe I wont be able to get them now. We were on a airport guarding it but now we are back in another area. I sure hope I get a chance to go back to the airport and get them. We sure move around a lot dont we.

By the way we are back in Okinawa again. First they let us say we are here then they say no, then they say yes, then no again, and now they say yes again. Some deal or what.

I am writing this by candle light and it sure makes it hard to write. I sure hope you can read this. By the way I sent the last letter I wrote to you to your winter address. I hope you get it. Well that is all I can think of now.

Love,   Martin,

Okinawa

August 24,

Hello Ruth,

I suppose by the time you get this letter you will be back to Kent again. I imagine it would be kind of hard to send George to school from the lake.

Thanks for the pictures. You sure look natural in them. Has George got a BB gun now. Bet George would sure get a big kick out of one now. By the way I have some pictures printed that I took on this island. I will send some of them to you. Some of the fellows want prints of them so I wont send the negatives to you until I get some more printed.

By the way I am a sergeant now. They sure arnt particular who they make sergeant anymore are they.

It looks to me like I will have to stay over here for awhile yet. I dont imagine I will make it until after the first of the year. They will either have to lower the points or make them easier to get or I will be over here a year more at least.

Well I cant think of anything else now so I will have to close.

Love,   Martin

The above three letters go together in that they all have one message. Martin says they told him one time it was okay to say he was on Okinawa and another time he couldn't, then he could, and then he couldn't! Martin was *always* on Okinawa. He mentions in one letter that he finished mopping-up and then they were guarding at an airport, and he made it sound so routine. There was nothing routine about it. He wasn't just guarding an airport, he was guarding the airport that planes were flying from that were continuously fire-bombing Japan. The information below is one area that the United States is not proud of, but was very necessary in that the Japanese would not stop their vicious fighting. When you finish reading it, the comment at the end of the following statement Martin makes in his letter (and so many times to the author) has so much more depth of meaning:

"The Japs giving up sure came as a pleasant surprise. I thought they might but something like that is something that was to big to hope for. You would agree on that if you saw how they never give up."

Martin said he was depressed the last 2-3 months in Okinawa as he knew they were to invade Japan and he did not want to go there knowing how the Japanese fought. He saw some very gruesome things during the fighting and mopping-up process on Okinawa and knew they would fight harder on their homeland...and not just Japanese men. He said they were informed the women and children would be fighting them too, and that was not something he wanted to do. His concerns were justifiable. He also said, *"I was fearful*

Super fortress is a four-engine propeller-driven heavy bomber

in that I had been 'lucky' so far and afraid if I went into battle in Japan my time might be up." What an awful thing to have to carry with you. Remember he was very battle worn and had seen many fellow soldiers (friends) killed.

Firebombing of Japanese cities during WWII

Planes flew from the airport Martin was guarding to firebomb Japanese cities. B-29 raids from the islands began on 17 November 1944 and lasted until 15 August 1945, the day Japan surrendered. Fire-bombing of Japanese cities wrecked more death and destruction than the atomic bombs. Anyone who has seen the Miyazaki film GRAVE OF THE FIREFLIES (*A tragic film covering a young boy and his little sister's struggle to survive in Japan during World War II.[149]*), already have an idea just how horrible this process was.

---

[149] Grave of the Fireflies 1988, "Hotaru no haka" *(original title)* Writers: Akiyuki Nosaka (novel), Isao Takahata

The dissatisfaction with damage results of high-altitude bombing with conventional explosives renewed interest in incendiary bombing, a tactic adopted by Army Air Forces personnel as early as the 1920's. For those not familiar with history, the Air Force was not always a separate branch of the military, but fell under the *guidance and control of the Army*.

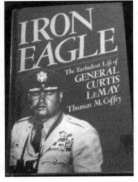

Shortly after Gen. Curtis LeMay assumed control of the bomber groups based in the Marianas (*arc-shaped summits of fifteen volcanic mountain islands in the north-western Pacific Ocean*) in January 1945, he prepared for night-time firebombing of Japanese cities. Things did not immediately improve. The damage the bombers did was too little, and the losses to high. In February of 1945 he changed tactics. Instead of the planes simply carrying bombs, they started to carry a mix of incendiaries and fragmentation bombs.

Iron Eagle - The turbulent life of General Curtis LeMay by Thomas M. Coffey

Incendiary Device: *Bombs designed to start fires or destroy sensitive equipment using materials such as napalm.*

Fragmentation Bomb: *The process by which the casing of an artillery shell, bomb, grenade, etc. is shattered by the detonating high explosive. The resulting high velocity fragments produced are the main lethal mechanisms of these weapons.*

Napalm bombing

The first test of this was Kobe, a major shipyard city, and 159 tons of firebombs and 13 tons of high explosives were dropped resulting in the destruction of 1,000 buildings and severely damaging two of the shipyards. The next attack was a complete failure as 47 of the 97 bombs dropped on the Nakajima plant in Ota were duds. So it was time to change tactics again. This time they decided to give the bomber crews intensive training and napalm (*a thickening/gelling agent generally mixed with petroleum or a similar fuel for use in an incendiary device*) was picked as a substance to be used during the bombings. A test of this was an early bombing of Tokyo, and the results were about a square mile of the city being destroyed. LeMay decided to have the planes carry heavier bombs and fly at a lower altitude.

Bombing of Tokyo

The testing of the new tactics began with the bombing of Tokyo on March 9 in which 334 B-29s bombers took part flying far lower than ever before on a bomb run. Planes dropped napalm bombs every 100 feet to make an "X" on the ground, a target for the rest of the planes to attack. The attack itself took over three hours. The Japanese later listed over 83,000 dead in the attack; over 40,000 wounded and a total of 15.8 square miles of the city were burned to ashes with the destruction of 265,171 buildings. The intensity of the fire was so much that the water in the rivers reached the boiling point.

The bombing was continued and within ten days 32 square miles of Japanese cities basically ceased to exist. Bomber losses decreased during the process. By the end of April, eleven more square miles of cities had been destroyed. Smaller targets were also hit. Toyama, a small urban area of 128,000, was 100% destroyed. From May to August, 1945, U.S. planes firebombed fifty-eight Japanese cities. Four cities were kept off the firebombing list; those included Hiroshima, Nagasaki, Niigata and Kokura.

Reports seldom mentioned civilian casualties, even when describing a Japanese city as '*a flaming cauldron.*' Most people accepted the bombing of urban areas, especially Japanese cities. The lack of reference to civilian losses also reflected the pervasive notion that incinerating civilians, however regrettable, was justifiable if it ultimately saved American lives. The firebombing

Tokyo after Allied firebombing

went so well that the military was actually running out of reasonable targets to firebomb and an estimate by General LeMay said they would run out of targets by Christmas of 1945.

In July of 1945 the U.S. dropped leaflets on some Japanese cities, warning them that they could end up being firebombed. The general effect was to try and

299

demoralize the enemy population by showing the Japanese just how totally helpless they were, and that their own military could not prevent Japanese cities from being attacked directly and bombed.... something that had not happened on any scale ever in the entire history of Japan.

What is astonishing is that despite the incredible losses, and the fact that there was virtually nothing Japan could do to stop the bombing, the country kept fighting. No matter how many square miles were destroyed, *no matter how many civilians died, the Japanese military wanted to keep fighting.* The Japanese beach hold would eventually have to be extended further and further for allied landings. Perhaps intense firebombing of adjacent areas and all crops could possibly have allowed the U.S. military to eventually conquer Japan, but the loss in civilian lives would have been almost unimaginable. Landing troops might have prevented the need for using the atomic bomb, but at what cost (to both Japanese and American troops)? It's one of those historical questions that can never really be answered.[150]

Now one can understand why Martin was depressed and not wanting to invade Japan. Per declassified documents, plans to invade had been in place prior to landing on Okinawa, and the Army troops would be the first to land.

Letter dated August 11: *"Well I guess the war is just about wound up. You should have been here last night when the news came in. You might think you have seen some Fourth of July fireworks, well you should have seen the one we had. All the anti aircraft opened up, the searchlights were turned on and then they shot up a*

bunch of flares. I was at a show when they started and we knew what it must mean when they started it without the air raid signal."

Letter dated August 12: *The Japs giving up sure came as a pleasant surprise. I thought they might but something like that is something that was to big to hope for. You would agree on that if you saw how they never give up. They havent signed anything yet maybe Im getting to fast [ahead of myself].*

Martin said he was watching a movie when everything erupted and he was really excited in one way, but had a hard time getting a handle on the fact that the Japanese would surrender. He said even after the second bomb and they said they were surrendering, he doubted it.

The mushroom cloud over Hiroshima after the dropping of Little Boy

---

[150]http://www.bookmice.net/darkchilde/japan/fire.html

He had seen some horrific things and was very doubtful they would "*really*" surrender.

On August 6, 1945, during World War II (1939-45), an American B-29 bomber dropped the world's first deployed atomic bomb over the Japanese city of Hiroshima. The explosion wiped out 90 percent of the city and immediately killed 80,000 people; tens of thousands more would later die of radiation exposure. Three days later on August 9, a second B-29 dropped another A-bomb on Nagasaki, killing an estimated 40,000 people. Japan's Emperor Hirohito announced his country's unconditional surrender in World War II in a radio address on August 15, citing the devastating power of "a new and most cruel bomb." [151]

The 'Fat Man' mushroom cloud resulting from the nuclear explosion over Nagasaki rises 60,000 ft. into the air from the hypocenter.

Martin had received film for his camera from two of his sisters which lifted his spirits. He had been getting the film developed by a group that opened a film developing business in one of the buildings at the airfield. However, after the bombing of Hiroshima the outfit they belonged too, were being shipped home. Once an outfit was ordered to move, things happened quickly. Martin's outfit were preparing to move again also...to land in Japan. Martin said he never did get the pictures he had last dropped off, but he was happy to get film and especially the candy!

Through troop movements a position opened and Martin was made Sergeant over communications. That meant he was responsible for all radios his outfit used. He did not personally maintain the radios, but was responsible to see that they were repaired and fit for duty. His disappointment is that making Sergeant did not bring his points up enough... to go home!

WWII GLOBAL TIME-LINE - AUGUST 1945

Day

1: Ukrainian insurgents attack the police station in Baligrond, Poland. Polish soldiers defend the station, driving off the attackers, who torch several houses as they retreat.

6: Enola Gay drops the first atomic bomb "Little Boy" on Hiroshima.

8: Soviet Union declares war on Japan; the Manchurian Strategic Offensive Operation begins about an hour later which includes landings on the Kurile Islands. The Japanese have been evacuating in anticipation of this.

---

[151] http://www.history.com/topics/bombing-of-hiroshima-and-nagasaki

9: Soviet troops enter China and Korea.

9: Bockscar drops the second atomic bomb "Fat Man" on Nagasaki.

14: An attempted coup by Japanese military and right-wingers to overthrow the government and prevent the inevitable surrender.

14: Last day of United States Force combat actions. All units frozen in place.

15: Emperor Hirohito issues a radio broadcast announcing Japan's surrender; though the surrender seems to be "unconditional," the Emperor's status is still open for discussion.

15: World-wide celebration of VJ Day.

16: Emperor Hirohito issues an Imperial Rescript ordering Japanese forces to cease fire.

17: Indonesia declares independence from Japan. General Order No.1 is approved by the President of the United States.

19: At a spontaneous non-communist meeting in Hanoi, Ho Chi Minh and the Viet Minh assume a leading role in the movement to wrest power from the French. With the Japanese still in control of Indochina in the interim, Bao Dai goes along because he thought that the Viet Minh were still working with the American OSS and could guarantee independence for Vietnam. Later, Ho Chi Minh's guerrillas occupy Hanoi and proclaim a provisional government.

19: Hostilities between Chinese Nationalists and Chinese Communists break into the open.

22: Japanese armies surrender to the Red Army in Manchuria.

27: Japanese armies in Burma surrender at Rangoon ceremonies.

30: Royal Navy force under Rear-Admiral Cecil Harcout liberates Hong Kong.

31: General MacArthur takes over command of the Japanese government in Tokyo.

Pictures Martin sent home from Japan

302

LETTER 80 & 81

Letter Date: Sept. 6, 1945
Envelope Date: Sept. 7, 1945

Sgt Martin Paulson

Letter Date: Sept. 10, 1945
Envelope Date: Sept. 11, 1945

*Sgt. Martin Paulson's
arrival in Japan*

Okinawa
Hello Ruth,   *September 6, 1945*
They finally lifted our censorship so now I can write anything I want to. It looks like I am going to have to go to japan. We have been alerted for a month waiting to be sent up by airoplane. Right now we are just sitting around waiting and it looks like we may leave today or tonight. We have had our bags packed for a month though now and all we have been told is we will leave Monday then Wednesday and that has been going on for a month. Last night they said we would leave at two in the morning and we are still here. When the war ended we were down at the airport that those atomic bombs were sent from.
We are sure getting lousy chow. You would think with the war being over that now we would get something decent to eat but it is the same old spam, stew, and dehidrated junk. We havent had any fresh meat at all for three weeks now. You would also think we would be able to get some beer once in awhile too. They have only given us fifteen bottles since the first of March. You would think combat outfits would get a break when they possibly could when it comes to food but instead we get the worst.
When is Curly leaving to go fishing and who is he going in on a boat or what. What is Dad doing now. I havent heard from him for quite awhile and no one ever mentions anything about him.
Well there isnt much more I can think of now to write about. I had my picture taken by a reporter from the Star a few days ago.   *Love Martin*

Japan
Hello Ruth,   *September 10,*
Well here I am finally in Japan. We flew in from Okinawa on a C54. They are large transports that look like passenger airliners back in the states. We eaven took some of our jeeps right with us. We are stationed in a small town a little ways

303

from Tokyo. It looks to me like the people here must be pretty tired of war and they try to be good to us eaven if you know they dont like us. It was kind of hard to see all these dammed soldiers walking around without being able to do anything about it. They havent given us any trouble though so far. Some of our own soldiers raised a little trouble though. You know most of our soldiers that raise cane are the ones we got as replacements and just came over from the states.

We are stationed in some buildings that used to be living quarters for workers in the mint that makes the Jap money. The mint is just a few yards from us. Maybe we out to crack the joint. Getting back to the quarters they are the best we have ever had allthough they arnt to hot. The rooms have mats for floors and are pretty dirty and full of fleas. We have cleaned it up pretty well and are supposed to get it sprayed tomorrow. After that it should be pretty good. There arnt any toilets or showers either but we will be able to fix that up. We do have electric lights and are inside a building and thats a break anyway.

I have still got some Jap money that I got in Okinawa and we can use it here. I sure wish I had picked up all I could have now. I sure didnt ever expect to spend it.

By the way we were getting our outfit ready to start training for a beach head operation when the war ended and it would probably have been here we would have made it. Hardly anyone in our outfit said much or did any cellebrating when we heard they (the Japs) wanted to call it quits. It sounded to good to be true.

That is all I have time to write so I will close.   *Love Martin*

Graves of fallen American soldiers on Okinawa

You can hear the depression in Martin's letters. With all that the soldiers experienced to this date, you can understand what a simple meal and a bottle of beer would mean to them. Yet, even with all they have been through they continued to remain professional [well, most of them]. Amazing!

The picture above and below helps us to understand the high and low emotions of the soldiers.

Newspaper clipping: WHERE'S MY BUDDY? Doughboys of the 27th Division, back from the front lines on Okinawa face the grim task of searching of buddies slain fighting the Japs in earlier stages of the island invasion.

Pictures of Martin at different times on Okinawa in 1945. He looks too young to have participated in such a horrendous battle. One can understand how he would struggle emotionally when learning the Japanese had surrendered…. *doubting it was true.* Even after landing in Japan and while the nation celebrated, you can hear it in the letter... the mistrust and insincerity he feels about Japanese motives.

The headline below is from the *Seattle Post Intelligencer* newspaper dated September 15, 1945 that Martin's sister had with the box of letters.

Troops awaiting transport

While the world was celebrating, Martin was on his way to Japan. It should be noted that in Martin's letter he said he was at the airport the atomic bomb planes flew from. Many *fire-bombing missions* to Japan flew from the airport in Okinawa. The two planes carrying the atomic bombs flew from Tinian, one of the three principal islands of the Northern Mariana Islands. Martin would not have known that until later. In our interview, Martin said they picked up a fighter escort from their airport. One of his neighbors, Ralph Williams, was stationed on Tinian.

The devastation Martin observed upon arrival in Japan

One of the moral boosters for the soldiers on Okinawa was a little Orphan. It is at this juncture that the story should be told.

There have been many times if *just going by documented facts*, accurate as they may be, what the author would have written "as fact", would not have been accurate. One example: Martin was assigned to the 27th Division in Espiritu Santo and on the way to Okinawa his ship stopped at a small island so that the 27th could be part of *"mopping up"* the remaining part of that Island. The 'facts' stated the 27th mopped up the island. Though Martin was part of the 27th, he was not part of that mission. He, along with others of the 27th, stayed on board ship. Another is the newspaper article on the Okinawan orphan, Junior.

If taken strictly from the newspaper account on the story of "Junior," Martin and another soldier from Seattle were his primary care givers. However, Martin said a reporter from the Seattle Star wanted men from Seattle to pose with Junior for the newspaper. Martin said we all loved this kid and were all his care givers, but there were a couple of the guys who hoped they could adopt the little fellow and take him home with them when the time came. Martin did say aside from the fact they were not the primary caregivers, the rest of the article was correct.

Newspaper article:

GI'S SEEK WAY TO BRING NATIVE BOY PAL TO CITY
by Stuart Whitehouse

Seattle very possibly may have as an honored guest – even a resident – a grinning, cheerful six-year-old Okinawan native boy.

That was the word today from William Holloman, editor of the Aero Mechanic,

THE OKINAWA KID, 6 year old war orphan, is shown between two of his pals on the war-torn island: S/Sgt. Berton J. Williams, (left) of 616 E. Thomas Street, and Sgt. Martin Paulson, of Auburn. The men of Co. D of the 105th infantry hope to bring the lad back to America with them.

newspaper of the Boeing workers. Holloman is just back from Tokyo and other U.S. Far Eastern bases, which he visited as guest of the government with a group of American labor editors.

His story of the Okinawan youngster, now under guardianship of two G.I.'s from Seattle, is one of the most typically American to come out of the war, and one which exemplifies the great American love for Children.

"I suspect when Co. D of the 105th infantry, in the 27th division, comes back home, Junior will be with them," Hollomon said today.

The Lad's special guardians in Co. D are S/Sgt. Berton J. Williams, of 616 E. Thomas Street, a former Seattle service station operator and Sgt. Martin Paulson, of Rt 2, Box 574B, in Auburn.

The boy is a waif of war. He was found by a machine gun company during the final mopping up of Okinawa. His father, mother, and several sisters and brothers had been killed during the initial onslaught on the island.

"He could not speak a word of English," Holloman relates. "Co. D adopted him, and made him a lieutenant's uniform, borrowing a sewing machine from a nearby Sea-Bea outfit. It has gold bars on the shoulders."

The boy whose real name is Sachi, Quickly started picking up English – but the wrong kind. The company passed a rule of speaking only "good" English in his presence, but that didn't stop the bad words, so they threatened using soap in washing out his mouth at each innocently-spoken swear word. When Holloman saw him, only the purest words passed his lips.

Toys were sent to him from America – but Junior will have no part of them. He prefers to play real-life soldier by riding around with his G.I. Pals in jeeps.

"His favorite is his mess kit. Holloman tells. "He keeps it shining like silver, and washes it after every meal. At first, he would be a "chow hound" and try to muscle into the chow lines, but now he takes his place at the end of the line."

Both Williams and Paulson told Hollomon the company intends to bring Junior to America – so they, as his special pals, probably will bring the lad to Seattle. If army and immigration rules allow, Holloman believes.

"And when a bunch of G.I.'s put their mind to something, they usually succeed," Holloman points out.

Martin said "Junior" was with them for several months and rode on the C54 plane with them to Japan. What an experience for this young 6 year old!

United States Douglas C-54 Skymaster transport - WWII

"He was a very sweet kid, a quick learner, and picked up 'all the wrong words' from us to where we had to really buckle down on our language around him. He mimicked everyone and drilled and trained right along with us. He was an amazing kid."

When asked why Junior was not mentioned in his letters, Martin said it is because Junior was Japanese and most people back home would not have been happy knowing the soldiers were caring for a Japanese child. Also, letters were censored on what we could write about. Washington State was interning Japanese citizens in holding camps for fear some may be spies or saboteurs. This is a period of history the USA is not proud of and

Lieutenant Junior"

apologized for in 1988, and gave a cash settlement to each person who had been interned in one of the camps.[152]

It is wonderful to know our soldiers knew the difference between Japanese men trained to kill and innocent children who looked up to and learned from the adults around them. It was gut wrenching for our soldiers to see children who had committed suicide with their families, or seeing Okinawan's who were slaughtered by the Japanese soldiers. Keep in mind, *that was then... it is not today.*

SURRENDER OF JAPAN, TOKYO BAY, 2 SEPTEMBER 1945[153]

Wallet card souvenir of the occasion, issued to Lieutenant Robert L. Balfour, USNR, a member of Admiral Halsey's staff. These cards were designed by Chief Shipfitter Donald G. Droddy and produced by USS Missouri's print shop. One was issued to each man who was on board the ship on 2 September 1945, when the surrender of Japan was formalized on her decks. The cards contain the facsimile signatures of Captain Stuart S. Murray, ship's Commanding Officer, General of the Army Douglas MacArthur, Fleet Admiral Chester W. Nimitz and Admiral William F. Halsey.

Navy carrier planes fly in formation over USS Missouri (BB-63) during the surrender ceremonies, 2 September 1945. Photographed by Lieutenant Barrett Gallagher, USNR, from atop Missouri's forward 16-inch gun turret.

[152]http://www.archives.gov/education/lessons/japanese-relocation/
[153]http://www.history.navy.mil/photos/events/wwii-pac/japansur/js-8.htm

LETTER 82 & 83

Letter Date: Sept. 18, 1945
Envelope Date: Sept. 19, 1945

Letter Date: Oct. 8, 1945
Envelope Date: Oct. 9, 1945

Adarawa [Koriyama], Japan
Sept. 18, 1945

Hello Ruth,

Im on guard today and havent much to do so I thought I would drop you a line. It sure has been windy here last night and today. These Jap buildings are made out of cheap, light material and I have been expecting them to blow apart any time. It has been blowing windows out and doors off. In weather like this I am sure glad Im not a private and have to stand a post.

There are a lot of rumors going around that men who have been in combat will be sent back pretty soon. It is hard to imagine them doing a thing like that though. I still think im stuck in here until at least the first of next year.

The Japs dont seem to have much left now. All their stores are closed except a very few and then they dont have anything worth while. The only thing we can get to drink is a little of their beer. That is pretty hard to get. I have only had two bottles. Their beer is a lot like ours only it tastes a little flat.

Japan is sure a stinking hole. A few places are nice an clean and all the Japs keep their floor real clean but otherwise their places stink. The buildings we moved into I could hardly stand it until we got it aired out. And then their floors are covered with mats and they are all full of fleas. By the way what is Curly doing now. Is he still welding at the yards or has he gone fishing all ready. It seems pretty late in the season to start fishing now. Who does he intend going fishing with.

We aren't working very hard now. We march around the streets every day to impress the Japs and then we have a little practice with the weapons and have a little exercise. We usually get a half a day off but then we are usually busy cleaning up the buildings and around them.

I dont think you know much about the size of a division or anything so I will try to tell you. I am in the 27th Division which has three regiments with quarter master, ordinance, artillery, tanks and medics attached. The regiments are broke down into three battalions each. I am in the 105th regiment and the first battalion. The battalion is broke down into three rifle companies of about 180 men each, one heavy weapons company of about 160 men and the Battalion headquarters which has about 100 men. Each regiment besides the 3 battalions have a anti tank company, service company and a headquarters company. Maybe that will mix you up more than ever.

I can't think of anything more now so I will have to close. Let me know how Dad is getting along will you? I havent heard anything from him for a long time.

Love Martin

Koriama [Koriyama], Japan

Hello Ruth, *October 8,*

Well Ruth I came pretty close to getting a furlough home today. All us fellows that have been over here longest drew for a forty five day furlough at home. There was only one fellow going for sure and a chance that another would out of our company. Well my name was drawn in case they gave us two furloughs in our company but I guess they arnt. If I would have gotten it I would have had to come back over seas again but I didnt have to sign up to stay in so when my points came up I would still get discharged. They are still up pretty high on them though. Everyone that has eighty points or more has gone home and that is all. I only have forty six. The way they set up those points they sure didnt give me a break. I could have had a purple heart which would give me five more points but I didnt want one at the time because I didnt think I earned one. Since though I have seen lots of guys get them with a lot less.

We are sure picking up lots of Jap equipment and getting lots of nice souvenirs. You can guess though who is getting to keep them. The dammed officers are getting everything. Eaven the ones that just came over and didnt see any combat. Of course they were generous enough to offer me a old bayonet. When there was any fighting to be done they werent too bad, but now there isnt a one that wouldn't take every advantage they can of you. Some of the fellows that just came over dont eavn rate the bayonet.

What is Curly doing? Is he using Ralph's boat now or what. There isnt much to go fishing for this time of year is there. I always thought the best fishing was in the summer. I been thinking maybe I will try fishing when I get out. I imagine by that time I wont be able to find any kind of job. The only trouble is I wont know anything about fishing. I imagine though I can always learn. George sure did get a good tan didnt he. Tell him thanks for the picture will you. What surprised me most was the way he has grown. Gosh, he looks lots older than I pictured him. Well I cant think of anything more now to write about. I told you I had fifty yards of silk for you, Karen and Myrtle didnt I. I got it just in time because it is hard to get now. We cant buy over two and one half yards at a time now. I will send it as soon as I can.

Love Martin

311

Martin did not know how to spell the name of the town and wrote it the way it sounded. Koriyama is located north of Tokyo as shown on the map.

What Martin did not know at the time was that a typhoon was the reason for the high winds. The following article tells how damaging it was.

THE MAKURAZAKI TYPHOON
(*TYPHOON IDA*)

Beginning late at night on September 17, 1945 and continuing through the next day [*note the date of Martin's letter*], the huge Makurazaki Typhoon raged over the scorched plain. On a par with the Muroto (1934) and Ise-wan (1959) typhoons, the Makurazaki was one of the three most devastating typhoons of the Showa era (1926-1989). Assaulting Japan with a low barometric pressure of 963.93hp and heavy rain, it left some 3,746 dead. Some were killed by landslides, many simply disappeared. Water flooded central Nobori-cho to a depth of over 20 inch, and the entire city suffered water damage. Bridges that had remained standing after the atomic bombing were washed away. Railroad tracks and roads under construction,

Path of the Makurazaki Typhoon. Koriyama is at top right just below the path line of the Typhoon, just under where the land dips inward

surviving company buildings whose employees had only recently come back to work, all were drenched – efforts to rebuild lives were washed away. Water drove people out of the tiny air-raid shelters and barracks where they were sleeping and carried off the few possessions they had left. Some residents who had come back from their places of evacuation and refuge finally gave up on the burnt plain and returned to the countryside. It was a year before people returned in significant numbers to the A-bomb desert [Nagasaki].[154]

The typhoon moved north across Japan with Koriyama receiving the same damaging winds. It will not be until years later that the American people understood the depth of devastation the bombs had on the Japanese people. Then to be hit by a Typhoon!

The following pictures were taken by Martin. They are not in the best of

---

[154]http://www.pcf.city.hiroshima.jp/Peace/E/pHiroshima1_4.html

condition, but help us to understand what Martin saw in Japan. As you can see, this town was not one that was hit by fire-bombs.

STARTING FROM BURNT RUINS
The Recovery and People's Lives
[From: Hiroshima Peace Memorial Museum Website]

At 8:15 on August 6, 1945, the atomic bomb "Little Boy" was dropped over the center of Hiroshima City. With energy reportedly equivalent to 16 kilotons of TNT, its heat rays and blast burned and completely or partially destroyed 90% of the roughly 76,000 houses in the city.

From burnt bodies, homes, and places of work, the people of Hiroshima made a new start in an utterly burnt-out plain of rubble. Lacking materials or assistance, that new beginning was filled with suffering.

After the fierce fires subsided, the people looked out over a burnt plain extending in every direction. The surviving articles of daily life lay burned and smashed where they had fallen. Unrecognizable bodies lay everywhere. The survivors' hauled away debris, mourned over the bodies, and began eking out a life in the rubble. They hid from the elements in damaged air-raid shelters, huts of burnt tin sheeting, or emergency barracks built by soldier rescue teams.

Mother and child in burnt ruins after bombings

For ten days starting immediately after the bombing, area towns and villages sent food to the city. Then, the food rationing system floundered. To prevent starvation, people

313

supplemented rations with food from kitchen gardens dug near their makeshift dwellings. They went to the countryside to get food from farmers, typically by barter. Many survivors had nothing to barter. The food for sale was nicknamed "Eba dango" (rice balls from Eba). These "substitute" rice balls were mixed with grass or gulfweed growing along the railroad

Burnt Ruins of Hiroshima

track in Eba and other suburbs. Such food staved off hunger, and nothing more.

     Martin so wants to go home. Can you blame him? The long training months, the Battle at Okinawa, his close call with death, mopping up, the constant reminder of war, and missing family.... then to have to wait! He is beginning to think ahead to what he may do when he gets out. Curly worked on fishing boats that went to Alaska for King Crabs, and he is considering working with Curly.

Fishing Boat - The Deutz 1946

Fishing boat - Wilma S" on way to Alaska

Martin gave a good description to Ruth of the Regiment structure. Below is a graph with descriptions as given in www.UnitHistories.com.

The structure of a typical WWII U.S. Army Infantry Division

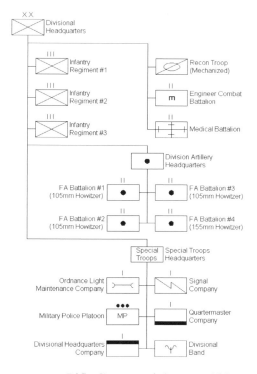

Each Infantry Regiment (approx. 3250 men, commanded by a Colonel) consist of the following units:
- 1st Battalion (approx. 870 men, commanded by a Lieutenant-Colonel)
- 2nd Battalion (approx. 870 men, commanded by a Lieutenant-Colonel)
- 3rd Battalion (approx. 870 men, commanded by a Lieutenant-Colonel)
- HQ Company (approx. 110 men, commanded by a Captain)
- AT Company (approx. 165 men, commanded by a Captain)
- Cannon Company (approx. 120 men, commanded by a Captain)
- Service Company (approx. 115 men, commanded by a Captain)
- Medical Detachment (approx. 135 men, commanded by a Major)

Each Battalion consist of the following units:
- Rifle Company * (approx. 190 men, commanded by a Captain)
- Rifle Company * (approx. 190 men, commanded by a Captain)
- Rifle Company * (approx. 190 men, commanded by a Captain)
- HQ Company (approx. 125 men, commanded by a Captain)
- Heavy Weapon Company * (approx. 165 men, commanded by a Captain)

The Companies where:
o   A, B, C and D (Heavy Weapons) for the 1st Battalion of a Regiment
o   E, F, G and H (Heavy Weapons) for the 2nd Battalion of a Regiment
o   I, K, L and M (Heavy Weapon) for the 3rd Battalion of a Regiment

Each Rifle Company consist of three Rifle Platoons, a Weapons Platoon and a HQ Section.
Each Heavy Weapon Company consist of two Heavy Machine Gun Platoons, a Heavy Mortar Platoon and a HQ Section.
Each of these Platoons was commanded by a Second Lieutenant or a First Lieutenant.

"George sure did get a good tan didnt he. Tell him thanks for the picture will you. What surprised me most was the way he has grown. Gosh, he looks lots older than I pictured him."

This picture has been one of the favorite of the Furford family over the years. Everyone smiles when they see the picture and the stories told of how they had to really bribe him to pose for the picture. Martin said it was pictures like this that brightened his days overseas!   *(Yes, the picture is used by permission of George)*

8 yr. old George after a summer at the lake!

WWII GLOBAL TIMELINE[155] - SEPTEMBER 1945

Day

2: The commander of the Imperial Japanese Army General Tomoyuki Yamashita surrenders to Filipino and American troops at Kiangan, Ifugao in Northern Philippines.

2: The Japanese Instrument of Surrender is signed on the deck of the UUSS Missouri in Tokyo Bay.

2: Ho Chi Minh issues his Proclamation of Independence, drawing heavily upon the American Declaration of Independence from a copy provided by the OSS. Ho declares himself president of the Democratic Republic of Vietnam and pursues American recognition but is repeatedly ignored by President Harry S. Truman.

5: Singapore is officially liberated by British and Indian troops.

13: British forces under Major-General Douglas Gracey's 20th Indian Division, some 26,000 men in all, arrive in Saigon which is in turmoil, South Vietnam to disarm and accept surrender of Japanese Occupation Forces in South Vietnam south of the 16th parallel. 180,000 Chinese Nationalist soldiers, mainly poor peasants, arrive in Hanoi, North Vietnam to disarm and accept surrender north of the line. After looting Vietnamese villages during their entire march down from China, they then proceed to loot Hanoi.

16: Japanese garrison in Hong Kong officially signs the instrument of surrender.

22: The British release 1,400 French Paratroopers from Japanese internment camps around Saigon. Those French soldiers enter Saigon and go on a deadly rampage, attacking Viet Minh and killing innocent civilians including children, aided by French civilians who joined the rampage. An estimated 20,000 French civilians live in Saigon.

---

[155]http://en.wikipedia.org/wiki/Timeline_of_World_War_II

WWII GLOBAL TIMELINE - OCTOBER 1945
DAY

1: In southern Vietnam, a purely bilateral British/French agreement recognizes French administration of the southern zone. In northern Vietnam, Chinese troops go on a "rampage." Ho's Việt Minh are hopelessly ill-equipped to deal with it.

The non-fraternization directive for U.S. troops against German civilians was rescinded. Previously even speaking to a German could lead to court martial, except for "small children", these had been exempt in June 1945.

25: General Rikchi Ando, governor-general of Taiwan and commander-in-chief of all Japanese forces on the island, turns over Taiwan to General Chen Yi of the Kuomintang (KMT) military. Chen Yi proclaims that day to be "Retrocession Day of Taiwan" and organizes the island into the Taiwan Province. Taiwan has since been governed by the Republic of China.

Retrocession Day is an annual observance in the Republic of China to commemorate the end 50 years of Japanese colonial rule of Taiwan on October 25, 1945. Taiwan, then more commonly known to the Western world as Formosa, became a colony of the Empire of Japan when Qing China lost the first Sino-Japanese War in 1894.

Celebrating Taiwan's retrocession at Taipei City Hall following Japan's defeat in WWII.

LETTER 84 & 85

Letter Date: Nov. 20, 1945
Envelope Date: Nov. 21, 1945

Postage: 12 cents
Postage: 6 cents

Letter Date: Dec. 2, 1945
Envelope Date: Dec. 3, 1945

Sgt. Martin A. Paulson
(He did not like this picture as it
made him look like a "child")

Koriyama, Japan
November 20, 1945

Hello Ruth,

I suppose you are beginning to wonder when I would write. The trouble is I hurt my right hand playing basketball and as you can see it is still bothering me by my writing.

I have just about given up being sent home. I should make it after the first of the year but I am not too sure of that. They got us over here and intend to keep us. Our division is leaving pretty soon but I think they will kick most of us into another outfit. The way it looks only eight fellows from my company will get to go.

Its sure getting cold over here. We are expecting snow any time now. I am freezing with all the clothes I have and these people go around with hardly any clothes and only wooden sandles on their feet. I sure cant see how they do it. Over here about the only ones that have shoes are the guys that have been demobilized [discharged from military service or use]. They have their regular Army shoes. When it comes to having anything these people are sure out of luck. They dont have anything at all including food. They are sure afraid we are going to move out and let the Chinese or Russians take our place here. We tell them they are coming and you ought to see them blow up. They say "You Stay Americans Okay, Chinese, Russians no good." They dont like us but they would rather have us then anyone else. They sure try to cooperate in every way but I still just dont trust them.

I got a Jap flag with Georges name on it, written in both Jap and English. I will put it in this letter. I cant think of much more now so I better close.

Love, Martin

318

If you can get any films now would you send them to me airmail. If you cant get them right away dont bother though.

Koriyama, Japan
Hello Ruth,   *Dec 2, 1945*
           I had some pictures taken at a Jap Studio and I am sending one to you. I think they make me look a little younger than I really look. I got a couple more if you think Jennie [friend of family] would want one send me her address and I will send her one or I can send it to you and you can give it to her.
           Well they are sending my division home but are taking most of us out and keeping us here. In fact they are taking about 90% of us out. I dont know for sure where I will go but I imagine it will be the 81ˢᵗ Division. Im not sure about that though they could send me most any place. I sure wish they would send me down around Tokyo so I could get a few breaks. They have PX's, ice cream and everything down there and we haven't anything up here but the <u>cold</u>. And after the tropics this place is cold.
                                                                                    Martin

Not only is Martin sounding very *down* about not going home... he is getting COLD! He looks very thin in the picture at right which was taken after he got to Japan. His comment says it all...

"I sure wish they would send me down around Tokyo so I could get a few breaks. They have PX's, ice cream and everything down there and we haven't anything up here but the <u>cold</u>. And after the tropics this place is cold."

Martin with a Japanese Flag

           The postage on the first letter was an additional 6 cents because Martin had included the small Japanese flag for George. George does not remember the flag, but said he would have really enjoyed getting it!

           As mentioned previously, the author was born November of 1945 and though her family struggled following the Great Depression and WWII, she and her siblings talk about growing up in the best generation ever. It was a time of peace and slow prosperity, and the nation as a whole would celebrate their freedom in large scale every 4ᵗʰ of July.

           Martin talks about not trusting the Japanese. An interesting fact arose during research ... the youth of Japan during WWII grew up not trusting the military as

319

they suffered greatly from pressure under their own military during that time. Research unveiled a trove of information on the atrocities of the Japanese military toward allied soldiers, POW's and civilians in the countries in which they fought. But it also is important to understand the role of the Japanese philosophy of honor for their emperor which extended to all Japanese, not just the military.

It is not clear whether the Japanese believed that soldiers of lesser ranks were mentally inferior, and therefore incapable of making complex moral and ethical decisions in a wartime situation, but they were very superior to those below them. Subordinate ranks were not treated with the same reverence and respect that their superiors demanded. Nor were they taught the same ethical considerations with which officers were instructed. Within such an authority-based system of morality, the worth of individuals was conceived of in terms of their proximity to the emperor. Despite the fact that the Constitution ostensibly guaranteed equality to citizens beneath the emperor, the everyday reality was that those who carried out his wishes represented the most worthy and valuable citizens.

During WWII the Japanese command structure was lacking in that individual officers and company commanders were allowed to carry out their own will, without the oversight of a greater authority. Even though the instructions may have been passed down through rank-and-file, the individual Japanese appeared to have an insatiable barbaric appetite that bordered on inhumanity and sadism.

The Japanese have denied such action in World War II because **World War II is the first war that the Japanese had lost in two thousand years** and thus, their actions and behaviors in those two thousand years were only judged from the perspective of *what was effective*. Because they have established a premise of *just war,* their honor, valor, and virtue have been maintained. Yet for them, *their action was just because it was effective, not because it was moral*. The loss of World War II was the first time that *their actions and decisions had been called into question as being dishonorable and immoral by a superior foe.* [156]

Yutaka Mio, 84, the first Japanese to officially testify on the Japanese imperial army's biological warfare program in the 1930s recalls how he was tutored to become an unquestioning subject of the emperor (who was considered a god in Japan until the end of the war), and how he had believed he was doing his duty. He said that Japanese unwilling to comply with the daily rituals of bowing so low that their noses touched the ground before photographs of the Emperor, and of singing Japan's national anthem many times a day, were whipped or tortured by superiors.

"I am fighting for the truth to be told in Japan. No Japanese must go through again the unbearable pain I have endured," Mio said softly.

---

[156]   http://www.militaryhistoryonline.com/wwii/articles/bushido.aspx

Japanese students are not taught about Japan's role in WWII. They are only taught about the fire-bombings, the A-Bomb, and the Big Boy bombings the Allies inflicted upon Japan.

Japan surrendered to the Allies on August 14, 1945. On the following day, Emperor Hirohito announced Japan's unconditional surrender on the radio. The announcement was the emperor's *first ever radio broadcast and the first time most citizens of Japan ever heard their sovereign's voice.* This date is known as *Victory over Japan*, or V-J Day, and marked the end of WWII and the beginning of a long road to recovery for a shattered Japan. On V-J Day, United States President Harry Truman appointed General Douglas MacArthur as Supreme Commander for the Allied Powers (SCAP), to supervise the occupation of Japan.

The Allies knew of this unquestionable loyalty to the emperor. Even in Okinawa they strove to get the Japanese soldiers to surrender by implementing the following plan.

OWI Leaflet 1050

The Tenth Army Combat Propaganda Team put together a very detailed campaign to motivate the Japanese defenders of Okinawa to surrender. On 10 June 1945, Canisters were dropped with a letter from U.S. Army Lieutenant General Simon B. Buckner to Lieutenant General Ushijimi Mitsuru. The letter was a personal request to surrender. The Japanese commander ignored the request as might be expected, so on 12 June 1945, 30,000 leaflets reproducing the letter with an appeal to Japanese officers were dropped. This letter explained that their commander had no regard for their safety, so as educated officers they should take responsibility for the care and welfare of their own men. On 14 June, 25,000 leaflets entitled "Think this over carefully" were addressed to Japanese soldiers and dropped on Okinawa. The leaflet pointed out that although the Americans were trying to save their lives, their own officers were willing to see them all killed. Before the island was declared "secure" on 21 June, hundreds of thousands of surrender leaflets were dropped, enough for one leaflet for every square yard of enemy territory.

Leaflet 1050 is an appeal to Japanese enlisted soldier and depicts Japanese POWs on the front and the title:

WE ARE GOING TO LIVE!

Morning roll call at the Japanese prisoner of war camp on Okinawa

生きぬくぞ

沖縄の日本停虜収容所——朝の点呼

THE BACK IS ALL TEXT AND SAYS IN PART:

The commander of the American forces is well aware of the relationship which exists between you and your commanding officer. Therefore, he first made his intentions known to your commanding officer. You know what effect that had.

Now the only choice is to deal with you directly. ...We would like you to consider carefully whether there is any point in dying...If you think there is no sense in dying, please persuade your esteemed commanding officer to cooperate with you.

If he is a commanding officer who lacks any sense of right and wrong and any trace of magnanimity and affection, and who is interested only in flaunting his rank, part from him without hesitation...Let those who would live be cautious and calm, and, at the first opportunity, let them be resolute and let nothing hinder them from taking the decisive step! One last word – you can be sure that the Americans will not kill you.

There have been many testimonies from Japanese POW's as to how surprised they were with the treatment they received at the hands of Americans. They had been expected to be tortured and killed, but found they were treated kindly.

AMERICAN OCCUPATION OF JAPAN AFTER WORLD WAR II[157]

The American occupation of Japan began immediately after the war was over and lasted for six years and eight months. The primary goals were demilitarization, democracy and decentralization. The terms of surrender included the occupation of Japan by Allied military forces, assurances that Japan would never again go to war, restriction of Japanese sovereignty to the four main islands *and such minor islands as may be determined,* and surrender of Japan's colonial holdings.

[157]http://factsanddetails.com/japan.php?itemid=526&subcatid=110

☐ After the surrender treaty was signed MacArthur immediately established a military occupation. American troops went ashore to liberate war prisoners and make sure the terms of the surrender were complied with. All Japanese military forces were disarmed and sent home. It was the first time ever that Japan was occupied by foreigners. Japan did not become a sovereign nation again until 1952.

☐ Under the direction of General Douglas MacArthur, the Supreme Commander for the Allied Powers (SCAP), Japan's army and navy ministries were abolished, munitions and military equipment were destroyed, and war industries were converted to civilian uses. War crimes trials found 4,200 Japanese officials guilty; 700 were executed, and 186,000 other public figures were purged. State Shinto was disestablished, and on January 1, 1946, Emperor Hirohito repudiated his divinity. MacArthur pushed the government to amend the 1889 Meiji Constitution. Constitutional reforms were accompanied by economic reforms, including agricultural land redistribution, reestablishment of trade unions, and severe proscriptions on zaibatsu. The relatively rapid stabilization of Japan led to a relaxation of SCAP purges and press censorship. Quick economic recovery was encouraged, restrictions on former zaibatsu members eventually were lifted, and foreign trade was allowed.

☐ After the war American soldiers were told to be respectful to ordinary Japanese, and do things like remove their shoes when entering homes, direct traffic in front of train stations and help malnourished children. Many Japanese were shocked by the courtesy. To this day some elderly Japanese bow to American-looking foreigners to say thank you for all that American did for Japanese after the war.

☐ One of the first thing that Japanese officials did in preparation for the American occupation was to set up hundreds of brothels and comfort stations to prevent them making unwanted advances on Japanese women. Some Japanese women were so worried about attacks they cut their hair short and tried to pass themselves off as men. There were reports of some Japanese women carrying cyanide tablets, ready to commit suicide before being raped.

For their part American soldiers arrived in full-combat gear and were ready for attacks from the general public. *No-fraternization orders* were given and *no contact with the "indigenous population"* was allowed. But in the end, the Japanese population turned out to be so complaint and cooperative the non-fraternization order was rescinded after six months and many American soldiers felt safe enough to walk around without their weapons.

MACARTHUR AND JAPAN AFTER WORLD WAR II
Gen Douglas MacArthur, acting as Supreme Allied Commander for the Allied Powers, established his office in downtown Tokyo on September 7, 1945. Known as the "American Shogun," he ruled Japan like a godlike dictator for six years. Even so he was widely respected by Japanese. Some of his most fervent supporters in his 1948 bid for the U.S. presidency were Japanese.

- A conservative Republican, MacArthur arrived with a staff of New Dealers who were intent on setting up an American-style democracy and doing to Japan what Franklin Roosevelt did to the United States. At MacArthur's request, immediately after the war was over, an infusion of U.S. aid was brought into Japan to stave off famine and political unrest. Among the reforms introduced with help of MacArthur were school lunch programs.

- MacArthur guided Japan's transition to a democratic form of government. In a testimony before Congress MacArthur called Japan a "boy of 12" in need of instructions on the basics of Western democracy and capitalism. Among his first actions was confiscating 5 million swords.

Many historians, believe that the role MacArthur played "in starting Japan on the path from feudal militarism toward modern democracy represented a greater triumph than any the old warrior had won on the battlefield."

FOR MORE INFORMATION ON JAPAN AFTER WWII, go to…

http://factsanddetails.com/japan

for the complete article on:

JAPAN AFTER WORLD WAR II: HARDSHIPS, MACARTHUR, THE AMERICAN
OCCUPATION AND REFORMS.

THE PRICE OF WAR AROUND THE GLOBE
IN PICTURES …

WWII GLOBAL TIMELINE[158] - NOVEMBER 1945

Day

29: The prohibition against marriage between GIs and Austrian women was rescinded on November 29. Later it would be rescinded for German women too. Black soldiers serving in the army were not allowed to marry white women, (in the case that they remained in the army) so they were restricted until 1948 when the prohibition against interracial marriages was removed. (Yes, only one item was listed)

---

[158]http://en.wikipedia.org/wiki/Timeline_of_World_War_II

LETTER 86

Letter Date: Dec 12, 1945
Envelope Date: Dec 15, 1945

Sapporo, Japan
Hello Ruth,   *Dec 12, 1945*

Well they kicked me out of the 27th and they are going home. You should see some of the guys because they will most likely go through Seattle. I will send you one of my old patches so you will know one when you see one. Most of them are probably be from different outfits because only a very few old fellows got to go along. I am now in the 77th. I haven't been assigned to any company yet. They sent us way up North and it is colder than the devil up here. We eaven have snow here. This is the first snow I have ran into for a long time.

From what I have seen around here I dont think I am going to like it at all, so if you hear I am a Pvt. again dont be surprised. From everything I have seen and heard a Sgt. has to be one of those rough tough guys you always hear a Sgt. is supposed to be and I dont intend to go around hollering at guys. In a combat outfit it doesnt pay to do it but that is what they seem to want here. I guess I can stand it for two or three months and that is the longest they can keep me here. I hope. If it is too bad I can allways enlist in the regular army for a year and get a three month furlough. By the way how does it look back there about getting jobs. I imagine they are pretty scarce. I sure dont know why I sent that picture to you I had taken. It sure doesnt look like me and it looks like I am about fifteen years old or so.

Well I cant think of much more to kick about now so I will close. I got your Christmas box just before I left. Thanks a lot. You sure picked good things. I guess you have noticed I am using the paper and that shaving soap is just what I have been hoping to get. All we get is brushless stuff over here and its no good. Well so long for now and Merry Christmas to you and Curly and George.

Love   Martin

MARTIN IS NOW IN SAPPORO, JAPAN!

Sapporo is located on the West Coast of the northern island of Hokkaido. No information could be found on the role Sapporo played militarily during WWII.

The only accounts listed are through current tourist information and they only tell of the fire-bombings by allied forces.

Sapporo is the capital of Hokkaido Prefecture located in upper left on the Japanese island of Hokkaido

The early years of the 20th century Sapporo grew in size both in development and commercially as well as in industry and transportation. Sapporo was scheduled to hold the Winter Olympics in 1940, but with the onset of war it was canceled. The Okadama Airport was constructed in 1942 [note that it was built well after WWII began and indicates strong war involvement]. Sapporo was then the fifth largest city of Japan, and the largest city of Hokkaido Island in Northern Japan.

Towards the very end of WWII (July 1945) Sapporo was attacked by approximately 30 bomber planes, dropping

Ice Sculpture at Sapporo Snow Festival

almost 900 tons of incendiary and fragmentation cluster bombs. The resulting firestorm led to the death of some 168 civilians, just under 7,000 injuries, and almost 80,000 people were left homeless. Many buildings were obliterated and roughly 20 percent of the city was left destroyed. It was the most tragic event in the history of Sapporo, but over the next few years, the destroyed areas of the city were steadily reconstructed and redesigned, where necessary. [159]

Sapporo has a humid continental climate with a wide range of temperature between summer and winter. Summers are generally warm with July and August the warmest months with temperatures up to 79° F but not humid, and winters quite cold and snowy with an average snowfall of 248". The city's annual average precipitation is around 43", and the mean annual temperature is 47 °F.

_____

[159] http://www.sapporo.world-guides.com/sapporo_history.html

Today Sapporo is known outside Japan for having hosted the 1972 Winter Olympics, the first ever held in Asia, and for the city's annual *Yuki Matsuri*, internationally referred to as the Sapporo Snow Festival which draws more than 2 million tourists from around the world. [160]

In this letter you get a good idea of Martin's character. All who know him cannot see him "yelling" at another person, and his having to maybe be that person does not sit well with him. His character again shows through in the pride he has in his fellow soldiers who are going home by providing Ruth with one of his patches so that she can identify them upon their arrival in Seattle. Soldiers were greeted home with great pride and celebration after the war.

In 1943 Martin said he was one of the "old" ones as he did not get drafted until he was 25 yrs. of age. Now he is saying only the "old" ones are getting to go home, but unfortunately, he is not one of them.

At left is the 27th Infantry Division shoulder sleeve insignia that was in this letter. The red circle and stars depict Orion, a *pun* on "O'Ryan," the name of the division's World War I commander John F. O'Ryan.

The younger generations may be asking, "What is *brushless soap*?" When Martin was referring to 'brushless soap', he was

talking about the Army issue bar soap (picture below). Aerosol cans of shaving cream, and the ever popular electric razors were not available back then, and most men had a brush and a soap cup with a special shaving soap inside. This soap foamed

US Army WWII soap bar shaving- laundry - cleaning   *Old Spice soap mug with brush and razor*

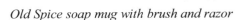

when the men would wet the brush and swivel it around in the soap cup. They would then apply the foamed soap to the face and shave.

As time gets closer to going home, soldiers begin to wonder if there will be jobs for them. All they have seen is the devastation of war...no food, no houses, no businesses... just people struggling to meek out a living with what is left. Even villages that were not fire-bombed were struggling.

Many Americans feared that the end of World War II and the subsequent

---

[160]http://en.wikipedia.org/wiki/Sapporo#History

drop in military spending might bring back the hard times of the Great Depression. But instead, pent-up consumer demand fueled exceptionally strong economic growth in the post war period. The automobile industry successfully converted back to producing cars, and new industries such as aviation and electronics grew by leaps and bounds. A housing boom, stimulated in part by easily affordable mortgages for returning members of the military, added to the expansion. The nation's gross national product rose from about $200,000 million in 1940 to $300,000 million in 1950, and to more than $500,000 million in 1960 [the amount seems very low compared to the trillions of today, but was considerable back then]. At the same time, the jump in postwar births, known as the "baby boom," increased the number of consumers. More and more Americans joined the middle class. [161]

WWII GLOBAL TIMELINE - DECEMBER, 1945

Day
28: The US Coast Guard was transferred under the US Treasury Department.
31: The British Home Guard is disbanded.
     The US prohibition against food shipments to Germany is rescinded. "CARE Package" shipments to individuals remained prohibited until June 5, 1946.

---

[161] http://economics.about.com/od/useconomichistory/a/post_war.htm

LETTER 87 & 88

Letter Date: December 30, 1945   Letter Date: January 22, 1946
Envelope Date: January 2, 1946   Envelope Date: January 22, 1946

Asahigawa [Asahikawa], Japan
Dec 30, 1945

Hello Ruth,

I havent much to write about but I thought I would drop you a line. Im kind of getting used to the cold now so it isnt quite as bad now as it was. The temperature is below freezing all the time and it goes below zero quite a bit. Just think last year it was the other extreme. Then the temperature was always above 100 and I was sweating all the time.

Well tomorrow night is new years eve and I guess I will celebrate it by pulling guard. I sure hope their arnt too many guys from the 27th getting tight and start raising hell, because then I will probably have to stay up and try to keep them quiet. I wont have to worry about these other guys they havent enough pep to do anything. You know last New Year we celebrated with almost every weapon we had. There were eaven mortars firing. You would think there was a full scale war going on. These rear achilon [a level of command, authority, or rank] commanders around here wouldnt do anything like that.

Do you know I have more time over seas than anyone else in this battalion. One fellow that came up here with me is tied with me, we both came over on the same ship.

Well thats all I can think of now so I will have to stop.

Love, Martin

PS I have a couple of money orders Ill stick in here too.

Asahikawa, Japan
January 22, 1946

Hi Ruth,

Well Ruth I can finally write to you and tell you something I have been waiting a long time to write. I will be on the long trip home. Dont expect me for at least a couple of months or more though because I will have to go through several replacement depos. In fact it will take me a couple of weeks to just get to Yokohama from here. That is if a snow storm doesnt come up and slow us down eaven more. It seems kind of foolish to me the way the Army sent me way up here to just stay one month. Its quite a ways up here. We are the fatherest North of any American troop in Japan. I found out one thing though and that is I am never going to go any place where it gets cold if I can help it. I have had all I want of the cold here.

Well I cant think of much more now so I will have to close.

Love, Martin

Martin on left - Asahikawa, Japan
Dec 1945

Martin is getting used to the cold. The picture at left tells it all! As we learn below, Asahikawa was a military city prior to WWII and therefore reason the American forces sent soldiers to Northern Japan to let their presence be known. Again, military information on Asahikawa as with Sapporo was not to be found.

Asahibashi Bridge

Asahikawa thrived as a military city before World War II when the IJA 7th Division was posted there. Today, the second division of the northern army of the Japan Ground Self-Defense Force is headquartered in Asahikawa.

Asahikawa is the second largest city in Hokkaido, Japan after Sapporo. On August 1, 1922, Asahikawa was founded as Asahikawa *City*. As the central city in northern Hokkaido, Asahikawa has been influential in industry and commerce. There are about 130 rivers and streams including the Ishikari River and Chūbetsu River, and over 740 bridges in the city. Asahibashi, a bridge over Ishikari River, has been one of the

Zoo Photo: A polar bear attacks the seal which comes out from under the drift ice. There is a capsule to experience a seal's viewpoint.

symbols of Asahikawa since its completion in 1932, and it was also registered as one of the Hokkaido Heritage sites on October 22, 2001

The city is currently well known for the Asahiyama Zoo and Asahikawa ramen.

AVERAGE TEMPERATURES BY MONTH

	Jan	Feb	Mar	Apr	May	Jun	Jul	Aug	Sep	Oct	Nov	Dec	Annual
Min	7.9	8.2	17.2	30.7	41.0	51.3	60.1	61.7	51.6	39.2	29.3	17.1	34.7
Avg.	15.3	17.1	26.1	40.3	52.2	61.2	68.4	69.4	59.7	47.3	34.7	22.8	42.8
Max	23.2	26.1	34.7	50.0	63.3	72.0	78.3	79.3	70.2	57.7	41.7	29.1	52.2

Ramen: A Japanese noodle dish which consists of Chinese-type wheat noodles served in a meat- or (occasionally) fish-based broth, often flavored with soy sauce or miso [*also called bean paste, is fermented soybean paste with a salty earthy flavor*], and uses toppings such as sliced pork, dried seaweed, kamaboko [*a cured, processed seafood product of Japan*], green onions, and occasionally corn.

Shōyu (soy-based broth) ramen

Weary worn Martin on way home! 1946

When Martin was sent north, he was no longer a part of the 27th Infantry Division and was assigned to the Headquarter Battery of 305th Field Artillery, 77th Infantry Division. To him, he was still a 27th Infantry Division soldier. Although he was with them just a few months, he trained and fought with them in battle and became one with them. The army apparently agreed with him as his discharge papers show him as being with…

Company D
105th Regiment Infantry
27th Division

Martin thought it would take a couple of months or more to get back to the states. His discharge papers show he left from overseas on January 28, 1946 arriving in the US on February 8, 1946 – 11 days. These same documents show he left the US for overseas duty on May 8, 1944 arriving May 29, 1944 – <u>21 days</u>! Martin said he was very happy to arrive in the US, but that he probably didn't show it as he was "very tired," which is reflected in the picture of him on the ship.

Golden Gate Bridge - from Martin's Album

Martin said the first thing he saw upon entering the US was the Golden Gate Bridge in San Francisco, CA … *"A beautiful site!"* They were not a part of the original troops who arrived right after the war so did not expect to be greeted upon arrival and were really surprised when a boat pulled up alongside with a large "Welcome Home" banner on its side. He said there were not a lot of people outside as it was very windy and cold that day, but they made a lot of noise. He was surprised how it lifted his spirits.

Martin in hospital

"Remember the song, 'Sentimental Journey' where it said 'get on the train at Seven'...I got on the train at Seven! We went by way of Alaska. They were first going to have us get off in Seattle, but it was full of guys so they took us on down to San Francisco to Camp Stoneman for 2 days then again by train to West Oregon to Fort Lewis. I could have gotten out right away but I got banged up pretty good and I knew I was supposed to report it so they put me in hospital for over two month! Had trouble with my ear and my eye. They found scar tissue in my ear and scar tissue on my eye which I still have today. My eye was still sore and my ear had drainage for a long time. Ear still gives me problems today."

Martin

Boat with a 'Welcome Home' banner!

Martin was discharged
April 10, 1946

*WELCOME HOME
SERGEANT MARTIN A.
PAULSON!!
&
TO ALL WHO SERVED TO
GIVE US A FREE
COUNTRY!!*

The photos on the last two pages are from Martins photo album of the 105th Regiment Infantry, 27th Division, and Company D. It is an honor to print the faces and names of these men with whom Martin served (apologies for names that are not complete). Martin wrote the names himself as he tried to remember all the names when he first got the photo 68 years ago. We thank each one for their sacrifice and love of their country.

1st Row	2nd Row	3rd Row
Dennis Bellas	Nicky Montesano	John Majocha
Cecil H. Covington	Joseph Asien	Jerry Ciullo
Charles H. Collins	Vernal P Goody	O.B. Self
Paul E Coffman	William Jackson Jr.	Mickey Grovine
Wilmon A. Coco	Nathan Abbos	Robert L Anderson Andrews
Morris Lookout	George Walker	Sam Agote
John M. Christian Jr.	Wilson E Champagne	Dick Duley
	George S. Amaral	Frank Capote Slapky
	Earnest C. Chastain	Ray Hill
	Walter Amell	Crouch
	Joseph E Hoffman	J Pearson
	Hernandez	Cecil C. Jones
Harry E Chambers	Joseph A Angelesta	Howard Clement
Ernest Chapman	Alferd Wagoner	Robert C Anderson
Anthony	Nelvin K Helms	Stanley C. Ainsworth
Migul Alira	William Hooker	Richard C. Hill
John B Elmer	Delmar Aders	Peter C. Collins
Francis Harrmann	Burton Williams	A. M. Welch
	Alfred Hanson	Jack Harp
		John M. Lopez

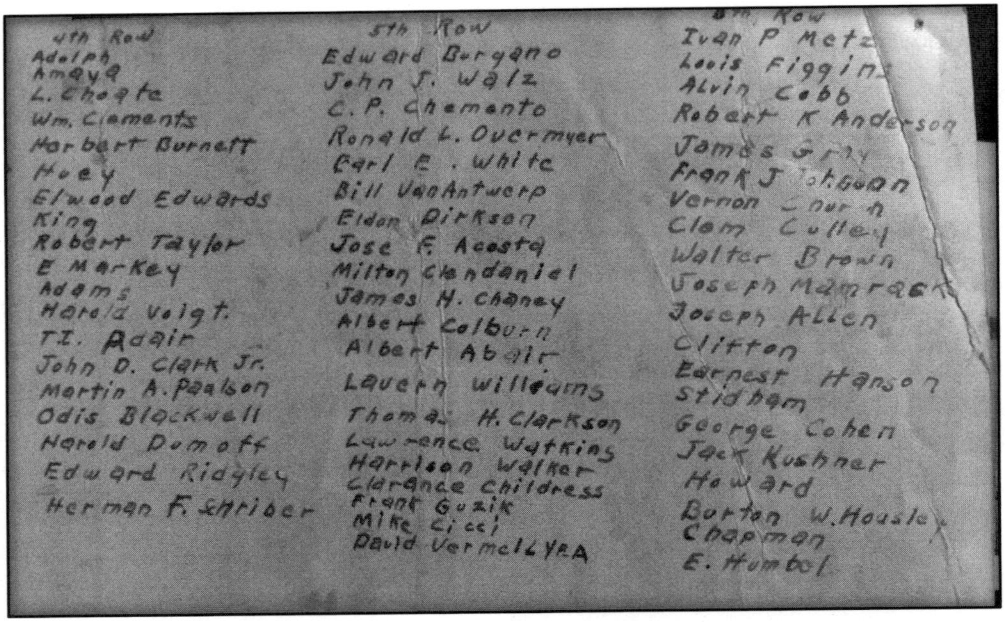

4th Row
Adolph
Amaya
L. Choate
Wm. Clements
Horbert Burnett
Hoey
Elwood Edwards
King
Robert Taylor
E Markey
Adams
Harold Voigt.
T.I. Adair
John D. Clark Jr.
Martin A. Paalson
Odis Blackwell
Harold Domoff
Edward Ridgley
Herman F. Schriber

5th Row
Edward Borgano
John J. Walz
C. P. Chemento
Ronald L. Overmyer
Carl E. White
Bill VanAntwerp
Eldon Dirkson
Jose F. Acosta
Milton Chandaniel
James H. Chaney
Albert Colburn
Albert Abair
Lavern Williams
Thomas H. Clarkson
Lawrence Watkins
Harrison Walker
Clarence Childress
Frank Guzik
Mike Cicci
David Vermelj YEA

6th Row
Ivan P Metz
Louis Figgins
Alvin Cobb
Robert K Anderson
James Gray
Frank J Johnson
Vernon Churh
Clem Culley
Walter Brown
Joseph Mamrack
Joseph Allen
Clifton
Earnest Hanson
Stidham
George Cohen
Jack Kushner
Howard
Burton W. Housley
Chapman
E. Humbol

If you know any of the men in these pictures and/or know their story, the author would love to hear from you. Please contact the author at…

gafurford@gmail.com

EPILOGUE

Martin with his father, Adolf Paulson
Cranberry Bog in background

Martin falls in love with Mabel!

Martin marries single mom, Mabel, with young daughter, Janice (sharing a Christmas together)

Martin holds newborn son (Martin Jr.), with big sister (Janice), and wife (Mabel) 1953

Martin returned home, he was determined to enjoy life with his father, family and friends. The families eventually settled around Westport, North Cove, & Grayland, Washington.

Martin said, "*After being bossed around in the Army, I decided to do something where I could be my own boss. Several men in the area were buying land and putting in cranberry bogs and I felt that would be a good fit for me, so I bought 4 1/2 acres of land* [over25 acres today]. *It takes 2-3 years before cranberries begin to produce so I worked for the Forestry and Commercial Fishing with Curly to supplement money needed while working the cranberry bogs.*"

Over the years the cranberries became a very successful business. Martin eventually passed the business to his son Martin Jr. (Marty). Marty will one day pass the business to his son, Ryan.

Below the news picture at left it says… '*Martin Paulson of Grayland removes a bag of newly-picked cranberries from his harvesting machine. There is a photo-feature on cranberry harvest on page A-10, October 21, 1977*' (Article on next page)

Old Cranberry Scoop (owner of this scoop: Marty Paulson)

The Furford Picker, operated by Martin Paulson, is named for its inventor, Grayland grower Julius Furford.

Bag of freshly picked cranberries

The Furford Picker has replaced the wooden scoops used in cranberry harvests years ago.

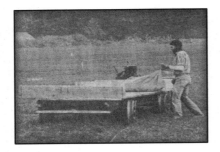

The inventor of the Furford Picker, Julius Furford, is "Curly's" brother.

Grant Castor of Salem, Oregon (harvest worker) fills bins that will be shipped to Ocean Spray, Inc.

Grant Castor loading full bags of cranberries onto cart.

TIME RIPE FOR CRANBERRIES
By Bruce McKenny
World Staff Writer
1977

North Cove – This is the time of year when a cranberry grower feels like it's all worthwhile. He can see the fruit of a year's labor bouncing up the conveyer belt of his picking machine and into a burlap sack.

Every 10 yards or so he has to stop the machine and unload another fat sack of ripe cranberries, varied in hue from pink to purple. At the end of each trip down the bog he looks back and sees the swath his machine has cut, turning the bog from maroon speckled with green, to green speckled with maroon.

He's worked a long time for this. Last winter it was pruning. Then in the spring the bog had to be sanded and weeded by hand. He remembers sprinkling for frost in the spring and for heat in the summer. And now he sees the seasonal help loading sacks of ripe cranberries into carts to take them back to the packing shed.

Soon those berries will be shipped to the Ocean Spray cannery in Markham and from there to Thanksgiving Day tables throughout the western states. Then he'll have to start getting ready for next year's harvest.

"Sure it's a lot of work and everything, but I like it," said Martin Paulson, a North cove grower who has been in the business since 1946. "Yes, it's a good business," his wife, Mabel agreed. "All the growers take off for Arizona and California in the wintertime." But according to Paulson, a little time off in the winter is all cranberry growers – not farmers, they insist – get for their money. Other than that it's full time.

"If you've got quite a few acres you have to sort of babysit them if nothing else," Paulson explained. He knelt on the thick cushion of tangled vines and dug down with his hands to show the composition of the bog. Below the vines was a layer of black sand brought from local beaches. Beneath that was the peat which the vines grow in. Paulson explained that the peat is the rotted vegetation from what was once a lake bed.

"I've heard the old timers say they can remember when the Indians rode their canoes through here, but I don't believe that," he said.

The first cranberry bogs in the area were started by Ed Benn in 1912. Now there are 110 growers cultivating the 650 acres of bogs that stretch along the lowland area between North Cove and Grayland. The business has changed a lot since 1912, when all the berries were harvested by hand with wooden scoops. Now Paulson uses a Furford Picker, a machine invented by Grayland grower Julius Furford. It looks like a cross between a Rototiller and lawnmower with a conveyer belt running up the handles. Its gas motor whines and its rotors make a steady clicking sound as it moves down the bog.

About a mile from Paulson's bog, Ron and Judy Miller were operating a different kind of picker. Ron used a large flexible hose hanging from a boom to suck the berries up off the vines. Judy pushed the cart (on which the large vacuum cleaner like contraption was sitting) down a set of small railroad tracks. The vacuum picker was used exclusively for many years but the faster and more efficient Furford picker has almost put it out of business. Now growers only vacuum between the tracks where the Furford picker won't go. The tracks are necessary for the carts that haul the bags of picked cranberries out of the bogs.

Most bogs in the Grayland-North Cove area are family operated and the bog the Millers were harvesting was no exception. They were helping Judy's father, Al Hebert, harvest his crop. Hebert himself was operating a Furford Picker in another part of the bog.

Herbert stopped the picker for a moment to explain why he was still not finished vacuum picking when most other growers finished a week earlier. He said this was the first time he had found time off from his job at a sawmill to get started on the picking. He said he bought the bog a few years ago to supplement his income and for something to do after retirement.

"This is what you call a sideline," he said, "Like some guys collect beer bottles; I grow cranberries." Herbert has only four acres, and according to Paulson it takes at least 12 to support a full time business. Paulson has 17 acres. About a third of the local growers have four acres or less, and many others are only in the business part time.

This year's crop is better than usual, both in quantity and quality, according to Tom Wagner of the Ocean Spray Cannery in Markham. He estimated that the Grayland-North Cove bogs will produce about 95,000 of the 2.2 million barrels of cranberries produced in the United States this year.

Martin Paulson with Furford Picker

Grandchildren, Ryan & Jeni Paulson when they were younger

Marty talks about his Dad with great respect and honor, and tells of how after the war the community banded together in helping one another. He said his Dad used his welding to make equipment for individuals and businesses free of charge, and when he had a need they reciprocated. What remarkable character and it speaks volumes of who Martin Paulson has been since the war years.

Martin's wife passed away in the 1990's. His daughter, Janice, lives today in California. Marty lives in Grayland and aside from working the cranberry bogs, watches over his Dad's care, not only visiting daily but making coffee and providing breakfast for him in the morning, but also cooking his evening meals. A next-door neighbor, Jane Brook, has voluntarily provided lunch to Martin for years. She says she needs to fix her and her husband lunch so it is easy to fix another for Martin. What wonderful neighbors! At 95 (July 2013), Martin lives in the house his father built.

Martin's daughter, Janice, had no children. Sadly, Marty lost his daughter, Jeni, in a car accident when a teenager, so Ryan is now the only grandchild. Ryan looks forward to continuing the family cranberry business.

Marty's daughter, Jeni

Ryan, Marty, Kris, & Jeni Paulson

Martin,   Marty,   Ryan,   Martin, Marty,   Ryan & Colllete

Cranberry Field & Harvested Cranberries

Marty with son, Ryan, and daughter, Jeni

Martin at time of first interview, Nov. 2012 (age 94)

Your living is determined not so much by what life brings to you as by the attitude you bring to life; not so much by what happens to you as by the way your mind looks at what happens. Circumstances and situations do color life but you have been given the mind to choose what the color shall be.

- By John Homer Mill

BRONZE STAR & OCCUPATION of JAPAN MEDALS AWARD CEREMONY
(Photos by Miriam Espinoza)

When the author applied to the Army for a Purple Heart for the injuries Martin Paulson received during the Battle of Okinawa, the Army was not able to verify through documentation the awarding of a Purple Heart, but did find Martin Paulson was deserving of the Bronze Star and Occupation of Japan medals. On August 29, 2013, 95 year old Martin A. Paulson, was presented the medals at the VFW Hall in Westport, Washington by Colonel Lynda Cranfield with Full Honor Guard from Fort Lewis-McCord, Washington. The following pictures tell the story!

Fort Lewis-McCord Honor Guard - Photo by Barb Aue

Martin's Japanese weapons, picture of the 105th, and Gail's manuscript, soon to be a book. – Photo by Barb Aue

Fort Lewis-McCord Honor Guard - Photo by George

Local Legionnaires - Photo by Barb Aue

Ryan, Marty, Martin – Photo by Mariam Espinoza